Finding Tipperary

A Guide to the Resources of the Tipperary Studies Department,
Tipperary County Library, Thurles, County Tipperary

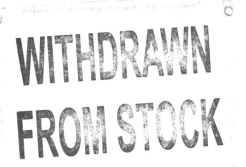

Denis G. Marnane
Mary Guinan Darmody

ISBN-10 0-9553690-0-2
ISBN-13 978-0-9553690-0-1

Published by
County Tipperary Joint Libraries Commitee

Printed by Fitzpatrick Printers, Tipperary.

Front cover art work by Mairead Hayes shows the Mainguard Clonmel and Nenagh Castle.

Back cover photograph by Christian Richters shows The Source, Thurles.

Typeface used ACaslon 12Pt.

This publication has received support from the Heritage Council under the 2006 Publications Grant Scheme.

Dedicated to
all our Tipperary Studies users and benefactors, past, present and future.

Le gach dea-mhéin.

FOREWORD

For anyone contemplating even a cursory investigation of the history and heritage of County Tipperary, this book is essential reading. This comprehensive guide to the veritable treasure that is the Local Studies Department of the County Library in Thurles will make the search for answers to Tipperary's past so much more enjoyable and fruitful. While the evolution of this unique collection has been anything but fluid, its stature as the most respected collection of material relating to the county now in existence, is indicative of the importance given to its development down through the years, and the compilation of this guide is further evidence of the ongoing commitment to further develop this great resource.

Unlike many guides to special collections, this is not merely a list of books, articles and so on; it is virtually a guided tour, with insightful analysis, of the Tipperary Studies Centre. Denis G. Marnane, Mary Guinan Darmody and Donnchadh Ó Duibhir are to be applauded for their dedication and professionalism in the compilation of this guide. Aimed at the seasoned researcher as much as at the first-timer, it presents the material in a logical and interesting way, allowing quite a number of gateways into the study of Tipperary history and heritage.

The study of local history and heritage in Tipperary has become hugely popular, particularly over the last twenty years or so. The 1984 celebrations of the founding of the GAA in Thurles one hundred years previously certainly gave impetus to this popularity. So too did the founding of the County Tipperary Historical Society in 1987 and the alignment of that Society with the County Library and its Local Studies Department. That popularity of Local Studies is set to further increase in future years with the addition of a Local Studies element in the Primary School Curriculum in History and Geography, a long overdue move, and one, which will establish a more structured approach to the way in which public libraries can support education.

Undoubtedly, the publication of this guide, which coincides with the relocation of the Local Studies Centre to The Source, the ultra modern new library and arts centre in Thurles, will take a lot of the mystery and frustration out of the study of local history: it unlocks, for the first time, the 'secrets' of the Tipperary Studies Collection: more than anything else, it provides a starting point in the study of self, family and place.

Martin Maher
Co. Librarian

ABBREVIATIONS

Anal. Hib.	Analecta Hibernica
Archiv. Hib.	Archivium Hibernicum
CLASP	Clare Local Studies Project
CTS	Catholic Truth Society
DHA	Dublin Historical Association
IER	Irish Ecclesiastical Record
IESH	Irish Economic and Social History
IHS	Irish Historical Studies
IMC	Irish Manuscripts Commission
Ir. Geneal	The Irish Genealogist
JCHAS	Journal of the Cork Historical & Archaeological Society
JRSAI	Journal of the Royal Society of Antiquaries of Ireland
MSS	Manuscripts
NA	National Archives
NLI	National Library of Ireland
n.d.	no date
OPW	Office of Public Works
PRIA	Proceedings of the Royal Irish Academy
PRONI	Public Record Office of Northern Ireland
RIA	Royal Irish Academy
THJ	Tipperary Historical Journal
UP	University Press

CONTENTS

INTRODUCTION

The most comprehensive collection of sources for all aspects of County Tipperary, its history, heritage and culture, its very identity, is held in the Tipperary Studies Research Library in Thurles, one of the services operated by County Tipperary Joint Libraries Committee. *Finding Tipperary* both lists and discusses all the sources held by Tipperary Studies up to the end of 2005. In August 2006 Tipperary Studies moved from Castle Avenue to its new home in the aptly named The Source in the centre of Thurles and the publication of *Finding Tipperary* is an important part of the provision of an expanded service to the entire county and beyond.

Tipperary Studies now has accommodation for around twenty readers/researchers and with four microfilm reader-printers and two PCs, together with a greatly expanded microfilm newspaper collection and longer opening hours including Saturdays, a much improved service is now available. A vital part of this service has not changed, namely the local knowledge and personal service offered by the staff. The County Librarian places a high priority on this part of the work of the county's library service and is fully supported by the County Tipperary Joint Libraries Committee, a unique authority representing two county councils.

Tipperary Studies which is a research and not a lending library has a comprehensive and always increasing collection of sources, of interest to every person looking for information about any aspect of the county such as archaeology, history, sport, institutions, genealogy, personalities, literature, Irish language and of course My Own Place. No matter if information is being sought for academic purposes (from primary to post-graduate), for community reasons (a local study or GAA club history) or for personal development (a family history or professional advancement), Tipperary Studies should be your first point of reference. With the importance of Ongoing Learning increasingly recognised and longer retirement, Tipperary Studies is a vital county resource.

Finding Tipperary while not a bibliography of Tipperary sources, is a very useful alternative because of the comprehensive range of sources in the Tipperary Studies Library. Within the pages of *Finding Tipperary* will be found signposts, not only to specific information about the county but perhaps more entertainingly, to byways forgotten by some and unknown by most. For Tipperary people elsewhere in Ireland or abroad, *Finding Tipperary*, not only its text but its wealth of illustrations (all taken from Library sources) will evoke the county in its richness and diversity. With the opening of the new research library in The Source and the publication of *Finding Tipperary*, the county assumes a leading position in the country with respect to preserving and making accessible regional history and heritage. With increasing recognition of the importance of preserving records and in order to make its holdings as comprehensive as possible, it is hoped that *Finding Tipperary* will focus attention on Tipperary Studies as a suitable place to deposit sources of information that frequently come to light, both manuscript and print.

Irish language sources are some of the treasures recovered from the shelves of the old library in Castle Avenue and are displayed in *Finding Tipperary* and available in Tipperary Studies, thanks to Donnchadh Ó Duibhir whose contribution to this book has been *thar na bearta*. One of the more pleasing features of *Finding Tipperary* is the range of illustrations, thanks in no small measure to the skill and enthusiasm of Jess Codd and John O'Gorman of the library staff. Thanks also to Mairead Hayes for her art work. Finally, more personal acknowledgements to John Darmody and Dan Finnan.

Denis G. Marnane
Mary Guinan Darmody

TECHNICAL SCHOOLS THURLES

Tipperary Libraries Hq.

The Source -
Home to Tipperary Studies

COUNTY OF
TIPPERARY
English Miles
Railways —— Sta —— Roads —— Canals
Baronies thus ELIOGARTY
Revised by P. W. JOYCE. LL.D; M.R.I.A.

PART ONE: Secondary Sources

Section One:
County, Towns, Villages and Countryside

Tipperary (Bassett)

County

A search for information on "my own place" brings many people to the Tipperary Studies Department of the County Library in Thurles. Starting with the big picture, the county; there is no published narrative history.[1] The alternative is the first volume in the county *History & Society* series.[2] Most of the nineteen essays discuss aspects of the county's history: prehistoric archaeology, medieval settlement, church history, politics, land ownership and socio-economic history. The comprehensive reference section is of particular value, signposting many avenues of further exploration. A handful of other books provide lightweight surveys of aspects of Tipperary history.[3] There is a narrative history of South Tipperary.[4] Because of the lure of the parish, with two exceptions, historians have avoided taking regions within the county as their areas of study. Eoghan Ó Néill chronicled the region

---

[1] For a history of Tipperary history see Denis G. Marnane, Writing the Past: Tipperary History and Historians in THJ (1997), pp. 1-41. For an earlier Tipperary bibliography, see M. McLoughney, *A Bibliography of Tipperary History and Antiquities* (Typescript, 1970). For North Tipperary see George Cunningham's bibliography in Rev. John Gleeson, *History of the Ely O'Carroll Territory or Ancient Ormond* (Kilkenny, 1982 reprint) volume 1. For Tipperary Studies see M. Maher, The Local Studies Dept. of the County Library in THJ (1989), pp. 119-22. For Tipperary Joint Libraries Committee see M. Guinan Darmody *The establishment of a 'Workers' university': a history of Tipperary Joint Libraries Committee 1927-66* (MA thesis, University of Limerick, 2004).

[2] W. Nolan, T.G. McGrath (eds.), *Tipperary: History & Society* (Dublin, 1985).

[3] Rev. J.H. Cotter, *Tipperary* (New York, 1929); M. Ó Corrbuí, *Tipperary* (Dingle, 1991); M. Hallinan (ed.), *Tipperary County: People and Places* (Dublin, 1993); E. Burke Houlihan (ed.), *Tipperary: A Treasure Chest* (Nenagh, 1995).

[4] P.C. Power, *History of South Tipperary* (Dublin, 1989).

Nenagh

between Clonmel and Carrick-on-Suir, while Tipperary town and its hinterland (the barony of Clanwilliam) is the subject of Des Marnane's two-volume study.[5]

At the heart of any study of the county are geology and place names. A comprehensive if technical account of Tipperary geology is available.[6] The best guide to place-names, especially townlands is the *General Alphabetical Index* published as part of the 1851 Census of Ireland.[7] The current official version of place-names in the county in both Irish and English is available.[8] An account of the meaning of place-names in North Tipperary has also been published.[9] There is also a reference work to seventeenth century places.[10]

Towns

John Betjeman in his poem *The Small Towns of Ireland* responded to the changes brought by Independence: the decline into shabby gentility of the best houses, witnesses to a vanished superiority; the presence of administrative buildings, reminders of past resistance and suppression and the promise of better housing for the poor. All of these aspects of urban history and much more are described, discussed and analysed in the Library's sources on Tipperary towns. An essential starting point is a collection of articles, mainly by geographers, discussing all aspects

Weir at Cahir

5   E. Ó Néill, *The Golden Vale of Ivowen* (Dublin, [2001]); D.G. Marnane, *Land and Settlement: a History of West Tipperary to 1660* (Tipperary, 2003) and *Land and Violence: a History of West Tipperary from 1660* (Tipperary, 1985).

6   J.B. Archer, A.G. Sleeman & D.C. Smith, *Geology of Tipperary* (Geological Survey of Ireland, 1996). See also G.A.J. Cole, *Memoirs of the Geological Survey of Ireland: Mineral Resources* (Dublin, 1922); W.E. Nevill, Sand Volcanoes, Sheet Lumps and Stratigraphy of part of the Slieveardagh Coalfield Co Tipperary in *Jn. RDS Scientific Proceedings*, 27, 14 (1957); A. Farrington, A sketch of the geological history of the Glen of Aherlow and Notes on the glacial geology of the Glen of Aherlow in *Geol. Soc. Ire. Bull. 2* (1945), pp. 39-45.

7   Reprinted by Genealogical Publishing Co. Ltd., (Baltimore, Maryland, 1984).

8   P. Ó Cearbhaill (ed.), *Liostaí Logainmneacha Contae Thiobraid Árann* (Dublin, 2004). Also his Logainmneacha dar críoch – ach i gCo. Thiobraid Árann in *THJ* (2005), pp. 9-23.

9   *Placenames of Townlands in Tipperary North* (North Tipperary Federation ICA, n.d.). The classic account is P.W. Joyce, *The Origin & History of Irish Names of Places* (Dublin, 1995 ed.) 3 volumes. Also P.J. O'Connor, *Atlas of Irish Place-Names* (Author, 2001). See also Eamonn O Duibhir, Folklore and Placenames of Central Tipperary (Published in *Tipperary Star*, 17 Aug 1935 to 18 July 1936 – see relevant file). Fr M. O'Flanagan, O.S. Name Books, Co Tipperary, 9 volumes.

10 Y.M. Goblet, *A Topographical Index of the Parishes & Townlands of Ireland in Sir William Petty's MSS Barony Maps [c.1655-9] & Hiberniae Delineatio [c.1672]* (IMC Dublin, 1932).

of Irish towns, not least how the writing of their history should be approached. As the title indicates, this book is an excellent guide to source material. However it does not deal specifically with towns in Tipperary.[11] The previously mentioned *Tipperary: History & Society* has an important article on the origins of many of these towns.[12] The OPW published heritage surveys of Tipperary towns in the 1990s.[13] These surveys are useful with respect to specific urban features. In the past decade guides have been published for most Tipperary towns.

Each Tipperary town has its own story but few would deny the particular interest of the tales in stone narrated by the county's own "golden triangle" of Cahir-Cashel-Fethard. Where else in the country is there such a concentration of features: castle, cathedral, round tower, walled town? Like much in the county, Cahir is a town that owes everything to the Butlers, making the author of its guidebook particularly appropriate.[14] Between 1986 and 1991, a series of newsletters were produced full of fascinating if disparate information about the town's history and heritage.[15] Guidebooks to the town's two most famous buildings are also available.[16] Aspects of Cahir's history will be found in general studies, especially dealing with the medieval and early modern periods.

Fethard and its abbey (Knowles)

Two narratives cover the entire span of Carrick-on-Suir's history.[17] Two late nineteen-century works reflect the enthusiasm of J.F. Meagher.[18] Of particular interest to genealogists is a publication giving detailed information from *The Primary Valuation of Tenements*, popularly known as *Griffith's Valuation* and the 1901 and 1911 census returns.[19] Rather more specialised are four articles exploring economic life in the

Greystones St., Carrick-on-Suir

11 W. Nolan & A. Simms (eds.), *Irish Towns: A Guide to Sources* (Dublin, 1998).
12 J. Bradley, The medieval towns of Tipperary, pp. 34-59. See also A. Thomas, *The Walled Towns of Ireland* (Dublin, 1992), 2 volumes; J.S. Fleming, *The Town-wall Fortifications of Ireland* (Paisley, 1914). The illustrative sketches in this work are excellent.
13 J. Farrelly & L. Fitzpatrick, *The Urban Archaeological Survey: Tipperary SR, parts i and ii* (Dublin, 1993); J. Farrelly & H. Carey, *The Urban Archaeological Survey: Tipperary NR, parts i and ii* (Dublin, 1994).
14 D.J. Butler, *Cahir: a guide to heritage town and district* (Cahir, 1999). For another important family see M. Ahern, The Fennells of Cahir in *THJ* (2004), pp. 91-100.
15 J. Walsh, *Cahir Heritage Newsletter* (Cahir, 1986-91). See M.T. Keane, *Isteach's Amach Sa Chathair no 'In And Out Of Cahir'* (Cahir, n.d.). Also, M. Luddy, The Lives of the Poor in Cahir in 1821 in *THJ* (1991), pp. 73-79.
16 H.A. Wheeler, *Cahir Castle* (OPW, n.d.); S. O'Reilly, *The Swiss Cottage* (OPW, 1993). Also M. Girouard, The Swiss Cottage Cahir Co. Tipperary in *Country Life*, 26 Oct 1989.
17 P.C. Power, *Carrick-on-Suir and its People* (Dun Laoghaire, 1976); P.C. Power, *Carrick-on-Suir Town & District 1800-2000* (Carrick-on-Suir, 2003). Also his Carrick-on-Suir: its origin and growth in *THJ* (1992), pp. 187-96 and The Lower Suir- boats and boatmen long ago in *THJ* (1991), pp. 149-58.
18 J.F. Meagher, *Annals, Antiquities and Records of Carrick-on-Suir* (Dublin, 1881) and *The Story of Carrick* (Dublin, 1892).
19 N. Farrell (ed.), *Exploring Family Origins in Carrick-on-Suir* (Longford, 2001).

town in the late eighteenth-century, using unique sources.[20] The town's most important building, Ormond Castle is the subject of an excellent OPW booklet.[21] Economic life in the town in the 19th century is the subject of an unpublished study.[22] The parish church celebrated its centenary in 1980.[23]

RYAN'S CENTRAL HOTEL & DR. CROKE JUBILEE CROSS.

Given the fame and spectacular impact of St Patrick's Rock, it is not surprising that much has been written about Cashel. It is disappointing that the general tourist guide is inadequate.[24] Tadhg O'Keefe's "Thomas Davis Lecture" is a useful introduction to the growth of the town.[25] Aspects of cultural and religious life in Cashel are discussed in a parish history.[26] Unfortunately most of the articles are not sourced. Urban archaeology is dealt with comprehensively in a recent major study, which includes a useful account of the town's historical background.[27] A detailed bibliography is included. Cashel Palace is discussed in a work co-authored by T.U. Sadleir.[28] Aspects of local government: the old corporation and workhouse, are described in two monographs.[29]

THE ROCK OF CASHEL, CO. TIPP.

Two Cashel residents left us fascinating accounts of everyday life in the town during the nineteenth and early twentieth centuries, unique sources for a Tipperary town. John Davis White's perspective was protestant and unionist, while that of Francis Phillips was catholic and nationalist.[30] Cashel has always been a diocesan centre and much of protestant Cashel in the late eighteenth and early nineteenth centuries is revealed in a monumental biography of one of its Church of Ireland archbishops.[31]

Cashel

20 L.M. Clarkson, The demography of Carrick-on-Suir, 1799 in *PRIA*, 87, C, 2 (1987), pp. 2-36; L.M. Clarkson, The Carrick-on-Suir woollen industry in the eighteenth-century in *IESH*, 16, (1989), pp. 23-41; L.A. Clarkson & E.M. Crawford, Life after death: widows in Carrick-on-Suir, 1799 in M. Mac Curtain & M. O'Dowd (eds.), *Women in early modern Ireland* (Edinburgh, 1991), pp. 236-51; L.A. Clarkson, Love, labour and life: women in Carrick-on-Suir in the late eighteenth-century in *IESH*, 20, (1993), pp. 18-34.

21 J. Fenlon, *Ormond Castle* (OPW, 1996). See also J. Maher (ed.), *Ormond Castle Carrick-on-Suir an anthology* (Clonmel, 1970).

22 M. Glascott, *The changing functional structure of Carrick-on-Suir during the 19th century* (Unpublished BA thesis, Dept of Geog. UCD, 1983.).

23 *1880-1980: St Nicholas (Parish Church Centenary Pageant)*, Carrick-on-Suir, 1980.

24 T. O'Reilly, Cashel Tourist Trail (Cashel, n.d.); (A. Finn), *Cashel Co Tipperary Official Guide* (ITA, n.d.).

25 T. O'Keeffe, Cashel in A. Simms & J.H. Andrews (eds.), *More Irish Country Towns* (Dublin, 1995), pp. 156-67.

26 B. Moloney (ed.), *Times to Cherish: Cashel and Rosegreen Parish History 1795-1995* (Cashel, 1994).

27 E. O'Donovan et al. Excavations at Friar Street, Cashel: a story of urban settlement AD 1200-1800 in *THJ* (2004), pp. 3-90.

28 T.U. Sadleir & P.L. Dickinson, *Georgian Mansions in Ireland* (Authors, 1915).

29 A. Finn, *Cashel and its ancient Corporation* (Dublin, 1930); Also *Appendix to the 1st report, Municipal Corporations* (Ireland), (London, 1835) and T. Laffan, Abstracts from the ancient records of the corporation of Cashel in *JRSAI*, (1904). E. Lonergan, *A Workhouse Story: a history of St Patrick's Hospital, Cashel 1842-1992* (Cashel, 1992).

30 D.G. Marnane, John Davis White's Sixty Years in Cashel in *THJ*, (2001), pp. 57-82; (2002), pp. 199-226; (2003), pp. 121-140; (2004), pp. 169-206. Martin O'Dwyer (Bob) (ed.), *Cashel Memories by Francis Phillips* (Cashel, n.d.).

31 A.P.W. Malcomson, *Archbishop Charles Agar Churchmanship and Politics in Ireland*, 1760-1810 (Dublin, 2002).

St Patrick's Rock has always attracted attention. In the early nineteenth-century, Sir Aubrey de Vere declared in a sonnet about the Rock: "I would gaze upon the wreck of thy departed powers … at the close of dim autumnal days", a melancholy disposition also found in the earliest guide in the Collection, dating from 1873 and which has curiosity rather than scholarly value.[32] Two guides from around 1920 are illustrated with drawings and photographs and apart from information about Cashel, reveal something about prevailing attitudes when they were written.[33] It is of interest that one was printed by the *Nationalist* (Clonmel) and the other by the *Chronicle* (Clonmel). Far more substantial is *Cashel of the Kings*, a compendium of material spanning nearly two thousand years.[34] More recent publications include various editions of the "official handbook"[35], and several other short accounts.[36] Of genealogical interest are gravestone inscriptions, including burials on the Rock.[37] Of special interest (and probably value) is the volume of photographs, drawings and elevations of Cormac's Chapel, from the 1870s.[38] Two articles discuss Inchiquin's attack in 1647.[39]

Any study of Clonmel's history must start with Canon Burke's magnum opus, especially strong on the medieval and early modern periods, not least because it is based on sources now destroyed.[40] Burke is weak on the nineteenth-century but this

32 M. St. John Neville, *Historical and Legendary Recollections of the Rock of Cashel* (Dublin, 1873, 2nd ed.). Also J. Davis White, *Cashel of the Kings* (2nd ed. Cashel, 1876) and *A Guide to the Rock of Cashel* (3rd ed., Cashel, 1888).

33 A. Finn, *Illustrated Guide to Rock and Ruins of Cashel* (Clonmel, 1920); A. Finn, *Royal and Saintly Cashel* (CTS, 1929); L. M. McCraith, *Cashel of the Kings* (Clonmel, 1920).

34 Rev. John Gleeson, *Cashel of the Kings* (Dublin, 1927).

35 H.G. Leask, *St Patrick's Rock Cashel Co. Tipperary* (OPW, n.d.).

36 St. L. Hunt, *Cashel and its Abbeys* (Dublin, 1952); Rev. A. O'Donnell, *St Patrick's Rock* (Cashel, 1961, 1974); K. MacGowan, *The Rock of Cashel* (Dublin, 1973); T. Wood, *Historical & Pictorial Cashel* (Cashel, n.d.).

37 T. Wood & C. Huftier (eds.), *Our People are on the Rock* (Cashel, n.d.).

38 A. Hill, *Monograph of Cormac's Chapel Cashel* (Cork, 1874). A similar volume deals with Holy Cross: S.P. Close, *Medieval Architecture of Ireland Holy Cross Abbey* (Belfast, 1868).

39 Rev. St John D. Seymour, The storming of the Rock of Cashel by Lord Inchiquin in 1647 in *English Historical Review*, (1917), pp. 373-81 and J.A. Murphy, The Sack of Cashel, 1647 in *JCHAS*, lxx (1965), pp. 55-62.

40 Rev. W.P. Burke, *History of Clonmel* (Waterford, 1907, reprint Kilkenny, 1983).

topic is covered in Sean O'Donnell's fine study.[41] Something of the history of Clonmel Corporation is in a report of 1835.[42] In 1909, Clonmel was among the places discussed in a Tipperary feature in a learned journal.[43] The most accessible guide is well

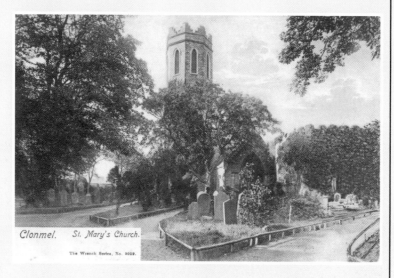

St. Mary's Church, Clonmel

illustrated and by the title obviously focused on the town's buildings.[44] Two publications deal with Old St Mary's Church, that by Colonel Watson much more than the history of a building but giving a generous Church of Ireland perspective on much of Clonmel's history.[45] The catholic parish of St Mary's was the subject of a compilation of basic information.[46] Accounts have been compiled about two of the town's hospitals, St Luke's and St Joseph's. These are of interest because the author

made use of primary sources.[47] A report on the town's Mechanic's Institute lists the contents of its library.[48]

Perhaps the best-known book about Clonmel is in the nature of a journalist's scrapbook and has been reprinted several times.[49] Of particular interest are Charlie Boland's contributions. "The Three Pilgrims" from Cashel, Carrick-on-Suir and Ballymacarbery, meeting on the Coleville Road, still amuses. Boland tells the story of the ill-fated Lt. Frederick Close and Anna Grubb.[50] In 1950 and 1966, the town noted its role in seminal historic events, the 1650 siege being perhaps the town's key scene

The Fanciscan Friary, Clonmel

---

[41] S. O'Donnell, *Clonmel 1840-1900: Anatomy of an Irish Town* (Dublin, n.d. [1999]).

[42] *Appendix to the 1st report, Municipal Corporations (Ireland) Commission* (London, 1835).

[43] *JRSAI* (1909), H.S. Crawford on Loughmoe and Carrick castles, Kilkieran & Ahenny, Donaghmore church; J.F. Morrissey on Clonmel and T.J. Morrissey on St Patrick's Well. Also P. Lyons, Norman Antiquities of Clonmel Burgh in *JRSAI*, (1936), pp. 285-94.

[44] E. Shee & S.J. Watson, *Clonmel an architectural guide* (Dublin, n.d.).

[45] S.J. Watson, *A Dinner of Herbs: a history of Old Saint Mary's Church, Clonmel* (Clonmel, 1988); *Old St Marys Memories and Images* (Clonmel, n.d.).

[46] D. Pyke, *Parish Priests and Churches of St Mary's 1320-1984* (Clonmel, 1984).

[47] E. Lonergan, *St Luke's Hospital Clonmel 1834-1984* (Clonmel, n.d.) and *St Joseph's Hospital Clonmel* (Clonmel, 2000).

[48] *Report of the committee of the Clonmel Mechanic's Institute* (Clonmel, 1845).

[49] J. White, *My Clonmel Scrap Book* (Waterford, 1907). Note that Tipperary Studies has its own "Clonmel Scrap Book": a folder with seventeen misc. items.

[50] For another source see: J.P. Entract, "The Clonmel Mystery" in *Jn. Of the Royal Ulster Rifles*, 40 (1968).

[51] P. O'Connell & W.C. Darmody (eds.), *Tercentenary of the Siege of Clonmel Souvenir Record* (Clonmel, 1950); *Easter Monday 1966 Commemoration* (Clonmel, 1966).

in the national drama.[51] One of the editors of the Siege book also compiled a record of St Patrick's Well.[52] Of great interest is an unpublished survey of Clonmel's architectural heritage.[53] Finally, two celebrations decades apart, of moments in time captured and frozen in light: the photographs of William Despard Hemphill and Justin Nelson.[54] An early "official" guide is of interest.[55]

Minella, Clonmel

Since the early 1980s the RIA has been publishing the *Irish Historic Towns Atlas*. To date the only Tipperary town to be included is Fethard.[56] This means that wonderfully detailed information is available about the development of that town: maps, photographs, drawings and text. A small-scale more popular guide to Fethard by the same author has also been published.[57] Michael O'Donnell has produced a deal of work (apart from his contributions to *Tipperary Historical Journal*.)[58] Fethard Historical Society has also produced a booklet on their local Sheela na Gig (medieval sexually explicit carving of a female figure).[59] The parish of Fethard and Killusty publishes an annual newsletter, a substantial booklet with a good deal of local history.[60] The records of the old Fethard Corporation are a treasure trove of information relating to the eighteenth-century.[61] One of the writers who used this information has also described other aspects of life in Fethard.[62] Two families, Everard and Barton, impacted greatly on Fethard. Thanks to a member of the former family, a deal of information about family and place is accessible.[63]

Information about Nenagh is most easily accessed in two guides to that town written by Donal and Nancy Murphy respectively.[64] The latter booklet has an index and is well illustrated. An older guide to Nenagh is that by E.H. Sheehan, first

The Mall, Thurles

52 P. O'Connell, *St Patrick's Well, Clonmel* (Clonmel, 1956).
53 *Clonmel Architectural Heritage Inventory Study* (Duchas, 1997) 2 volumes.
54 P. Holland, *Tipperary Images: The Photography of Dr W. D. Hemphill* (Cahir, 2003); J. Nelson, *Faces and Places Clonmel 1955-1960* (The Author, 1996).
55 Clonmel: *The Official Guide* (London, n.d.).
56 Tadhg O'Keeffe, *Irish Historic Towns Atlas No. 13 Fethard* (RIA, 2003).
57 T. O'Keeffe, *Fethard Co. Tipperary a guide to the medieval town* (Fethard, 1997). Also his *Fethard Co. Tipperary - an archaeological and historical survey* (The National Heritage Council, 1995) and also Townscape as Text: the topography of social interaction in Fethard, Co Tipperary, AD 1300-1700 in *Irish Geography*, 32 (1999), pp. 9-25. An older guide is Canon Lee PP, *A short history of the parish of Fethard & Killusty* (1960s?).
58 M. O'Donnell, *Fethard Householders, 1850- an alphabetical list from Griffith's Valuation* (Unpublished typescript); M. O'Donnell, *An Outline History of Fethard* (Unpublished typescript, 1977).
59 J. O'Connor, *Sheela na Gig* (Fethard, 1991).
60 *Fethard & Killusty Newsletter* (Fethard, 1966 - to date).
61 Rev. W.G. Skehan, Extracts from the minutes of the Corporation of Fethard Co. Tipperary in *The Irish Genealogist*, iv, 2 (1969) pp. 81-92; iv, 3 (1970), pp. 183-93; iv, 4 (1971), pp. 308-22; iv, 6 (1973), pp. 616-24; v, 1(1974), pp. 72-86; v, 2 (1975), pp. 201-15; v, 3 (1976), pp. 370-82. M. O'Donnell, Life in Fethard in the 1700s in *THJ* (1988), pp. 22-38.
62 M. O'Donnell, The Great Famine in Fethard 1845-50 in *THJ* (1996), pp. 49-70; Lighting the streets of Fethard 1870-1914 in *THJ* (1998), pp. 128-32. See also M. Luddy, The Lives of the Poor in Fethard in 1821 in *THJ* (1990), pp. 121-27.
63 R.H. Everard, Family of Everard in *Ir. Geneal.* vii (1988), pp. 328-48; vii (1989), pp. 505-42; viii (1990), pp. 175-206; viii (1993), pp. 575-601. For a view of the Barton family see M. Healy, *For the Poor & For the Gentry* (Dublin, 1989).
64 D.A. Murphy, *Rian Cuarda Aonach Urmhumhan* (Shannonside, 1977); N. Murphy, *Walkabout Nenagh* (Nenagh, 1994).

published in 1948 and 1949 and reprinted with an index by Relay in 1976 and again in 1988.[65] The town's recent past is captured in two books of photographs.[66] For Nenagh Castle there is a classic article from the 1930s and a recent short pamphlet.[67] As a county town, Nenagh was the centre of a poor law union and Danny Grace who also wrote about an episode from 1849 details the story of its workhouse during the Famine.[68] Nenagh was also the centre of a famous incident related to the Crimean War.[69] There is a history of one of the schools.[70] An "official" guide from the 1920s is of interest.[71]

Templemore is an example of a Tipperary settlement owing everything to a particular family, the Cardens.[72] There is a short narrative history of the town.[73] For genealogists, local gravestone inscriptions are of interest.[74]

Seal from Nenagh Gaol

PETER STREET AND COURT HOUSE, NENAGH

Peter St. and Court House, Nenagh

---

65 E.H. Sheehan, *Nenagh and its Neighbourhood* (Nenagh, 1988).
66 B. Treacy (ed.), *Nenagh Yesterday* (Nenagh, 1993); N. Murphy & F. O'Brien (eds.), *More of Nenagh's Yesterdays* (Nenagh, 1997).
67 D.F. Gleeson & H.G. Leask, The Castle and Manor of Nenagh in *JRSAI*, lxvi (1936); N. Murphy (ed.), *Nenagh castle chronology and architecture* (Nenagh, 1993). See also D.F. Gleeson, The priory of St John at Nenagh in *JRSAI*, lxviii (1938), pp. 201-18.
68 D. Grace, *The Great Famine in Nenagh Poor Law Union Co. Tipperary* (Nenagh, 2000); The Barricading of Nenagh Chapel in 1849 in *THJ* (1990), pp. 103-108.
69 D. Murphy, "The Battle of the Breeches": the Nenagh Mutiny, July 1856 in *THJ* (2001), pp. 139-46.
70 *The Story of St Mary's Secondary School, Nenagh* (Committee, 2000).
71 *Official Guide to Nenagh Co Tipperary* (Dublin, 1927).
72 See articles by A. Carden, "Woodcock" Carden - a balanced account in *THJ* (2000), pp. 120-31; Templemore Houses and Castles - drawings by Robert Smith in *THJ* (2002), pp. 115-30. Also his *Carden of Barnane* (Author, 2004).
73 P. Walsh, *A History of Templemore and its Environs* (The Author, 1991). N. Kevin, *I Remember Karrigeen* (Dublin, 1944) is a series of essays based on life in Templemore. Rev. H. Johnstone, *A History of the Parish of Templemore, Cashel Diocese* (Author, n.d.); Rev. H. Johnstone, *Some Information about Richmond, now McCan Barracks, Templemore* (Typescript, n.d.); J. Reynolds, *History of the Garda College, Templemore* (www.garda.ie).
74 W.J. Hayes, *The Old Church and Graveyard Templemore* (Templemore, 1995). The Library also holds a copy of Templemore UDC burial register.

George Cunningham is the modern historian of Roscrea.[75] Two modern surveys of the town are of value.[76] For an older history see Dermot Gleeson's parish history.[77] Roscrea Castle has been written about in detail.[78] Shopfronts in country towns are always of interest and those of Roscrea were surveyed in the 1980s.[79] Mount St. Joseph Abbey is the subject of a devotional work from the 1920s and of a modern history.[80] A resident of the town gives an affectionate portrait in two publications.[81] There are monographs on three of the town's schools.[82] A collection of photographs provokes memories.[83]

There are two separate well-illustrated popular guides to Thurles.[84] A chronology was an unusual format for an urban history and J.M. Kennedy's work on the town from the 1940s was expanded and reprinted in the late 1970s.[85] The most substantial work on Thurles history is a collection of essays in honour of Archbishop Thomas Morris (1914-1997) who led the diocese from 1960 and was an enthusiastic supporter and promoter of all aspects of history and heritage in both county and diocese. This collection of twenty essays covers a wide spread of interests: personalities, power, poverty and Pallottines.[86] The cathedral has received scholarly notice from the perspective of the arts.[87] The Church of Ireland has

Presentation Convent and Cathedral Street, Thurles

The Waterfall Mount St. Joseph, Roscrea

75 G. Cunningham, *Illustrated Guide Roscrea and District Monuments and Antiquities* (Roscrea, 1976); *Roscrea Rian Cuarda* (Roscrea, 1977); *100 Years of Roscrea* (Roscrea, 1979); Roscrea in Simms & Andrews, *More Irish Country Towns* (Dublin, 1995 Thomas Davis Lectures), pp. 144-55. *Éile Journal of the Roscrea Heritage Society 1* (1982), 2 (1983); *Monastic Roscrea* (foldout).

76 *Roscrea Architectural Heritage Study* (Duchas, 2000), 2 volumes; W.J. Hayes (ed.), *Heritage Atlas of the Civil Parish of Roscrea* (FAS, n.d.).

77 D.F. Gleeson, *Roscrea Town & Parish* (Dublin, 1947).

78 C. Manning (ed.), *Excavations at Roscrea Castle* (Dublin, 2003).

79 *Shopfronts of Roscrea* (Roscrea Heritage Society/ An Co., 1984).

80 A Cistercian, *An Epitome of Cistercian History from Citeaux to Roscrea* (Roscrea, 1925); L.S. Maher & C. Brady (eds.), *Céad Bliain Faoi Rath the story of Cistercian College Roscrea, 1905-2005* (Roscrea, 2005). See also *Mount St Joseph's Abbey Roscrea* (Roscrea, 1971).

81 K. Moloughny, *Roscrea Me Darling* (Roscrea, 1987); *Roscrea My Heart's Home* (Roscrea, 1992).

82 T. Prior & G. Cunningham (eds.), *The Convent of the Sacred Heart Roscrea 1842-1992* (Roscrea, 1992); A. Hewson, *No Ivory Tower: a century of vocational education in Roscrea* (Roscrea, n.d.); L.S. Maher & C. Brady, *Céad Bliain Faoi Rath: the story of Cistercian College Roscrea 1905-2005*, (Roscrea, 2005).

83 C. MacNiocláis, *Muintir Ros Cré 1918-2005* (Roscrea, 2005).

84 D. O'Gorman, *Historic Thurles Co. Tipperary A Walking Tour* (Shannonside, 1984); W.J. Hayes, *Thurles: a guide to the Cathedral Town* (The Author, n.d.). See also *An Droichead* (Nov 1981-April 1986). The *Tipperary Star* published a series of articles on the town, "Thurles: Pages From Its Past" between 25 Feb 1933 and 7 April 1934. These are available in a file.

85 D. O'Gorman, L. Long, M. Dundon (eds.), *A Chronology of Thurles 580-1978* (Thurles, n.d.). A 1935 typescript of Kennedy's work is in Tipperary Studies.

86 W. Corbett & W. Nolan (eds.), *Thurles: The Cathedral Town essays in honour of Archbishop Thomas Morris* (Dublin, 1989).

87 J. O'Toole, *The Cathedral of the Assumption, Thurles Co Tipperary* (Typescript, n.d.). Also *Cathedral of the Assumption Thurles: an historical outline* (Thurles, 2005).

received attention.[88] For over two hundred years the Ursulines have been a feature of Thurles life and that history has been written.[89] Older works are available with respect to the Christian Brothers and Presentation Sisters.[90] However, a substantial work on Thurles parish remains unpublished, the work of the late Canon Fogarty.[91] There is also an unpublished study of the sugar factory.[92] The Croke memorial has received scholarly attention.[93]

St. Patrick's Cathedral, Thurles

A good deal has been written about Tipperary town, most accessible being a walking guide concentrating on the history of its buildings.[94] A much more detailed historical survey of the town and its hinterland, by the same writer, is also available.[95] A number of local institutions have been examined in some detail.[96] Some volumes of memoirs cast light on the day-to-day life in times both routine and exceptional also a number of biographical studies are of interest.[97] Two articles by Des Marnane examine aspects of social and political life in the town in the early 20th century.[98] Much information and pleasure may be derived from two collections of photographs.[99] An "official" guide, probably from the 1920s is of interest.[100]

Villages and Countryside

In *Elegy for a Countryman* Padraic Fallon celebrated the quiet anonymity of ordinary rural life: "He made no history, even at home in one quiet townland … He was never a speaker at meetings … never broke walls and scattered a landlord's herd … nor … was he one with the Gunfighters." Virtually all parish history has been written

[88] Rev. M. Johnstone, *St Mary's Parish Thurles, Diocese of Cashel* (Author, 1972).

[89] Sr M. Lillis, *Two Hundred Years Agrowing the story of the Ursulines in Thurles 1787-1987* (Thurles, 1987).

[90] *Souvenir of the Centenary of the Monastery and Schools Christian Brothers, Thurles* (Thurles, 1916); *Records and Memories of One Hundred Years 1817-1917 - Presentation Convent, Thurles* (Thurles, 1917).

[91] Canon Fogarty, *The Parish of Thurles: its civil and ecclesiastical history* (typescript, 4 volumes). See booklet on blessing and solemn opening of the Church of St Joseph & St Brigid, Oct 1971. Also P. Conlon OFM, The Franciscan House in Thurles in *N. Munster Antiq. Jn.*, xix (1977), 43-9. Rev. F. Ryan, St Patrick's College Thurles in *Capuchin Annual* (1960).

[92] É. de Stafort, *Thurles Sugar Factory, 1933-1989* (UL, M.A. Local Studies, 1998). See also M. Foy, *The Sugar Industry in Ireland* (Irish Sugar Company, 1974).

[93] M. Ó Drisceoil, Commemorating Croke: ethnic nationalism as spectacle in *THJ* (2004), pp. 161-68. Tipperary Studies also has a file of relevant material.

[94] D.G. Marnane, *The Excel Guide to the Heritage of Tipperary Town* (Tipperary, 2002).

[95] D.G. Marnane, *Land & Violence: a history of West Tipperary from 1660* (Tipperary, 1985); *Land & Settlement: a history of West Tipperary to 1660* (Tipperary, 2003).

[96] W. Jenkins, *Tipp Co-Op: Origins and development of Tipperary Co-operative Creamery Ltd* (Dublin, 1999); D.G. Marnane, *"To Do and To Teach": a history of the Christian Brothers in Tipperary Town 1868-1994* (Tipperary, 1994); D.G. Marnane, The Coming of the Railway to Tipperary in 1848 in *THJ* (1998), pp. 138-49; D.G. Marnane, *A History of St Michael's parish Church Tipperary* (Tipperary, 1999); D.G. Marnane, *"A Lamp Kindled": The Sisters of Mercy and Tipperary Town* (Tipperary, 2000); W.S. O'Shea, *A Short History of Tipperary Military barracks 1874-1922* (Tipperary, n.d.); M. Bourke, Erasmus Smith and Tipperary Grammar School in *THJ* (1989), pp. 82-99; M. Tierney, *The Story of Muintir na Tire 1931-2001 - the First Seventy Years* (Tipperary, 2004).

[97] S. Fitzpatrick, *Recollections of the fight for Irish Freedom* (Tipperary, n.d.); D. Breen, *My Fight for Irish Freedom* (Tralee, 1964); J. Dowling, *An Irish Doctor Remembers* (Dublin, 1955); P. Cranley, *Just Standing Idly By* (Tipperary, 1993) and *Moving On* (Tipperary, 1995); M. Bourke, *John O'Leary: a study in Irish separatism* (Tralee, 1967); D. Ryan, *Sean Treacy and the 3rd Tipperary Brigade IRA* (Tralee, 1945); S. Rynne, *Father John Hayes* (Dublin, 1960).

[98] D.G. Marnane, Tipperary Town One Hundred Years Ago: the evidence of the 1901 census in Tipperary in *THJ* (2001), pp. 1-26 and Tipperary Town One Hundred Years Ago: issues of identity in *THJ* (2002), pp. 173-98.

[99] G. Riordan (ed.), *Tipperary Town & District: a photographic record* (Cullen, 1995), E. Fitzpatrick (ed.), *Tipperary People – over a century of familiar face*s (Tipperary, 2005).

[100] *A Concise Guide to Tipperary with notes on the surrounding district* (Derby, n.d.).

Paddy Mealy, Cloughjordan

R.I.C. Barrack Mullinahone

during the past twenty years and it is not surprising that this initial encounter with the past concentrates on the "broken walls" and less on ordinary lives. While this kind of local study has generally been undertaken with great enthusiasm, the result is often poor and is invariably weak with respect to medieval and early modern history. Different problems are confronted but not overcome when making sense of the nineteenth and twentieth centuries. Writers are overwhelmed by the quantity and variety of sources and often do little more than reproduce the relevant records of local and central government. Surprisingly, oral history has had little impact.[101]

The Tipperary Studies Library holds a large collection of this type of material, ranging from the ordinary to the extraordinary, but all having some interest. An example of the extraordinary is the monumental three-volume history of the parish of Moyne-Templetuohy.[102] The story of one parish told in over fifteen hundred pages is likely to stand alone in Tipperary historiography. Not all of the items listed below are historical surveys based on the unit of the catholic parish. Some publications deal with an aspect of parish history, perhaps an institution or incident. The most important of these institutions appears to be the GAA, regarding which a great deal has been written at a local level. This material is covered separately in **Section Two** of *Finding Tipperary*. A small number of parishes produce annual serial publications, in which various writers exploit their curiosity about their own places and produce some interesting work.

R.C. Church Ballyneale

Listed below is material of this nature held in the Library and published up to 2005.[103]

As information about date of publication indicates, very little of local historical interest was published before the 1970s. Lee on Newport (1934) or Kenny on Glankeen (1944) were very much exceptions. When material was published, the absence of information about date or place of publication makes its own statement about the gap between enthusiasm and professionalism. The catholic parish is the

101 A rare example: *Talking with Denis O'Brien*, [Life in Aherlow in the early 20th century] (CD recorded in 1984, with transcript). This situation has changed dramatically (2005) with the forty-five recordings *Irish Life and Lore Series Tipperary Collection* compiled by M. O'Keeffe (See catalogue for information).

102 W.J. Hayes (ed.), *Moyne-Templetuohy A Life of its own The story of a Tipperary parish* (Moyne, 2002) 3 volumes.

103 E. Carew et al., *Anacarty/Donohill History* (Anacarty, 1997); K.M. & K.A. Griffin, *Ballina/Boher Parish: Our History and Traditions* (Ballina, n.d.); D. O'Donoghue, *Ballyporeen* (The Author, n.d.); P. Meskell, *History of Boherlahan-Dualla* (The Author, n.d.); E. Dwyer et al (eds.), *Millennium Memories: Boherlahan & Dualla* (Boherlahan, n.d.); J. Meskell (ed.), *A Pictorial View of Boherlahan-Dualla* (The Author, 1996); P. Meskell & M. Ryan (eds.), *Boherlahan-Dualla Historical Journal* (Boherlahan, 1998 -ongoing); E. Slevin (ed.), *A Parish History of Borrisokane* (Borrisokane Historical Society, 1994); *Borrisokane Parish Video* (FAS, n.d.); File of misc. notes on Borrisokane; B. Conway, *God Be With the Chimneys of Cappawhite* (Bray, n.d.); A. Ryan, *Toemverig Toom, Toem or Toemverig (now the modern parishes of Cappagh White/ Hollyford)* (The Author, n.d.); S. Fitzgerald, *Cappawhite and Doon* (The Author, n.d.); E. O'Riordan, *Historical Guide to Clogheen* (The Author, 1996); A. Hewson, *Clonakenny & Bourney: a local history* (Roscrea, 1982); D. Glynn & H. Heffernan, *The Story of Clonoulty* (Committee, 1979); R. Williams, *In and Out of School - In the Home of the MacDonaghs* (Nenagh, 1999); Fr E. Burke et al, *The Church of SS Michael & John Cloughjordan* (The Authors, n.d. [1999]); The Contributors, *Cloughjordan: Presenting the Past* (Cloughjordan, n.d.); D. Grace (ed.), Cloughjordan Heritage (Cloughjordan, 1985- ongoing); Rev. R.W. Jackson, *Corbally & Mona Hincha* (Author, n.d.); E. & M. Hall, *Drangan Co-Operative Creamery Society Ltd., A Century of Success 1897-1997* (Drangan, n.d.); Ó Grada et al., *Souvenir of Re-dedication of Church of The Immaculate Conception Drangan 5 December 1993* (Drangan, 1993); B. Dunne & B. Murphy (eds.), *Drombane 1914-1989* (Drombane, 1989); S. O Riain, *Dunkerrin:*

territorial unit attracting most attention from local historians. However what might be termed the standard parish history has been published for very few parishes in the county. Tipperary has about 64 parishes: Cashel & Emly 35, Waterford & Lismore 17 and Killaloe 12 (O'Shea, *Priest, Politics and Society*, p.10). However, standard histories have been published for less than a quarter of these parishes.

The first item listed in footnote 103, the parish history of Anacarty/Donohill, north of Tipperary town, is a good example. Published as a collaborative effort by the community, there is no narrative voice and no thematic thread. Separate topics from "The Medieval Parishes" to "Local Organizations" are covered, each with a large amount of interesting information, some useful tables and many fascinating photographs. The final chapter outlined the process. "Items of local history and folklore had to be collected: people were delegated to visit the County Library, the National Library, Heritage Centres, the Land Registry Office, the National Archives

Moyne-Templetuohy parish history

A Parish in Ely O Carroll (Dunkerrin, 1988); *Emly: Its founder and his successors* (Cork, 1914); M. & L. O'Dwyer, *The Parish of Emly: its History and Heritage* (Emly, [1987]); M. O'Dwyer, *The Gravestone Inscriptions of Emly* (New Orleans, 1993); T. Duhig, *St Ailbe's Church Emly Centenary 1882-1982* (The Author, 1982); [Galbally] M. Lynch, *Behold Aherlow: The Glen from Bansha to Galbally* (Portlaw, 2002); T. Whyte, *The Religious Heritage of Clonbeg* (The Author, 1986); M. Kenny, *Glankeen of Borrisoleigh* (Dublin, 1944); The Contributors, *Glengoole- New Birmingham Memories* (Glengoole, n.d.); *Gortnahoe-Glengoole: A Guide* (Glengoole, n.d.); J. Hogan, *History of houses and their occupiers in some townlands in Gortnahoe-Glengoole* (Typescript, 1984); Senator W. Ryan, *Golden-Kilfeacle: The Parish and its People* (Golden-Kilfeacle, 1997); Senator W. Ryan, *A Short History and Reference Guide to Kilfeacle Cemetery* (The Author, 1985); *A Short Ecclesiastical Survey of Golden/Kilfeacle - The Re-opening of the Church of the Blessed Sacrament Golden* (Golden, 1991); *Grangemockler Church and People 1897-1997* (Grangemockler, 1997); M. McHugh (ed.), *The History of Hollyford Parish* (Hollyford, 1989); G. Carville, *The Heritage of Holy Cross* (Belfast, 1973); M. Callanan, *The Abbey of Holy Cross* (The Author, n.d.); J.B. Cullen, *The "Santa Croce" of Ireland* (CTSI, n.d.); W.J. Hayes, *Holy Cross Abbey an illustrated history and guide* (Holy Cross, n.d.); C.A. Lewis, *The Bells of Holy Cross* (Dublin, 1976); W.J. Hayes, *Souvenir of the Solemn Mass of the Restoration of Holy Cross Abbey* (Holy Cross, n.d.); [Archbishop] T. Morris, *Holy Cross Abbey* (Dublin, 1986); B. O'Brien, *How We Were in the Parish of Kilbarron-Terryglass Co Tipperary* (Nenagh, 1999); W.G. Neely, *Kilcooley: Land and People in Tipperary* (The Author, 1983); Rev. W. Healy, The Cistercian Abbey of Kilcooley Co Tipperary in *JRSAI* (1890); Rev. M. Moloney, Kilcooley: Foundation and Restoration in *JRSAI*, (1944), pp. 219-23; Fr Columbkille, Kilcooley Abbey in *Old Kilkenny Review* (1984), pp. 55-63 and (1985), pp. 177-82; J. & P. Flood, *Kilcash: A History 1190-1801* (Dublin, 1999); J.J. Hassett (ed.), *The History & Folklore of Killenaule-Moyglass* (Killenaule, n.d.); J. Ryan, *History & Traditions of Knock & Timoney* (The Author, 1980); M. Mac Carthaigh, *A Tipperary Parish: a history of Knockavilla-Donaskeigh* ([The Author, 1986]); P. Buckley & G. Riordan, *History of a Tipperary Parish: Lattin & Cullen* (The Authors, n.d.); G. Riordan (ed.), *The Lattin- Cullen Journal* (Cullen, 1988 - Occasional); Mount Bruis: *Remembrance of Things Past* (ICA, 1984); J. Tobin (ed.), *Loughmore Parish* (Loughmore, n.d.); S. Ryan, *History of Loughmore* (Typescript, n.d.); Rev. W. Skehan, *History of the Parish of Loughmore* (Typescript, n.d.); M. Power, *Dear Land- Native Place: Monsea & Dromineer* (The Author, 1998); D. Grace, *Portrait of a Parish: Monsea & Killodiernan* (Nenagh, 1996); E. Gorman, *Records of Moycarkey & Two-Mile-Borris with some fireside stories* (Galway, 1935); W.J. Hayes (ed.), *Moyne-Templetuohy A Life of its own The Story of a Tipperary parish* (Moyne, 2002) 3 volumes; M. Larkin, *Mullinahone: Its Heritage and History* (The Author, 2002); D. Foley, *Mullinahone Co Op The First One Hundred Years* (Mullinahone, 1993); *Notes on New Inn & Knockgraffon* (Manuscript – no provinance); E. Bell (ed.), *Around New Inn & Knockgraffon* (The Author, 2003); M. Hallinan, *Tales from the Deisi* [Newcastle] (Dublin, 1996); *Church of St John, Newport, 1795-1934* (Newport, 1996); Rev. P.J. Lee, *History of the Parish of Newport* (Newport, 1934); W.J. Hayes, *Newport Co Tipperary: The Town, Its Courts and Gaols* (The Author, n.d.); J. Duggan (ed.), *In the Shade of the Comeraghs: a profile of Rathgormack/Clonea* (Rathgormack, n.d.); N. MacMahon, *In the Shadow of the Fairy Hill Shinrone & Ballingarry: A History* (The Author, 1998); N. MacMahon, *Shinrone & Ballingarry in Focus* (The Author, 2003); G.E. Russell, *The Story of Silvermines: the mine and the company* (Silvermines, 1990); *The Parish of the Silvermines* (Silvermines, n.d.); P. Burke, *Sliabh Felim's Slopes* (typescript, n.d.); *Templederry My Home* (Templederry, 1980); T. Shanahan et al, *Toomevara; the Unbroken Chain* (Toomevara, 1981); *Toomevara: Life, Song, Sport and Story* (BVP Productions, 180 mins, n.d.); H. Maher (ed.), *2000 Toomevara: Thanks for the Memories* (Toomevara, 2000).

Directory of the market towns (Leet)

14

and local folklorists. Every book, pamphlet, map, newspaper article, parochial record and diary that might be of any possible use was procured - and read again and again." The perspective of this kind of local history is indeed local. The notion that someone outside the parish might be interested is absent. Specific sources are not cited allowing for a train of inquiry to compare what happened in one parish with another part of the county or the country; a process also hampered by the lack of an index. Taking a sociological approach is an interesting comparative study of "three Tipperary parishes" (Moyne, Newport & Kilcommon).[104]

Illustrating a different approach is Danny Grace's study of Monsea & Killodiernan, a parish near Nenagh. In this instance the voices of the parish, many long since silent, are interpreted and articulated by a single author. All too common in such detailed local studies is the impression given to the reader that the parish in question is an island. However, the only sound of water in this book is Lough Derg, the author having an understanding that local events are best explained by placing them in a wider context. Comprehensive source notes and an index mean that the threads constituting the fabric of this particular place can be traced by readers who are not native but who are searching for answers to perhaps different questions. These three: context, sources and index allow a local study to resonate, telling a story both local and universal.

Hall's Ireland, 1846 (Golden)

In the absence of a full-scale parish history, a deal of interesting local information is found in the many accounts of national schools published in recent years. The collection in Tipperary Studies is listed below but given the intensely local nature of such publications, some may have escaped attention.[105] (Tipperary Studies would be delighted to have any gaps filled.) The scope of these publications varies enormously but all have comprehensive lists of past-pupils, information of obvious interest to those on the trail of ancestors. Some are particularly good with respect to the origin and development of the system of national school education. Much social history is recorded as schooldays are remembered, though given the nature of these celebrations, viewed more fondly than reality might warrant. At their best, there are moments in these accounts when feelings for place are intensely felt and movingly expressed.

---

[104] T. Roseingrave & D. Talbot (eds.), *Parish & Community: a social inventory of three Tipperary parishes* (Muintir na Tire, 1970).

[105] T. Whyte, *Aherlow National School 1911-1971* (Aherlow, 2002); P. Ryan, P. Ryan & P. Meskell (eds.), *Ardmayle National School Reunion 1993* (Ardmayle, [1993]); J. Kelly (ed.), *Ayle National Schools 1876-1990* (Committee, 1990); *Ayle National School Cappawhite Co Tipperary 1952-2002* (Committee, [2002]); J. Hannon (ed.), *Ballagh National Schools 1834-1999: 165 Years of Education* (Committee, n.d.); *Ballydrehid National School 1871-1998 past pupils reunion Oct 1998* (Committee, n.d.); M Russell, *Centenary of a Village School Ballylanders National School 1893-1993* (Committee, n.d.) N. Ó Duinnín, *An Scoil agus a raibh ann: Ballyporeen Boys National School* (BOM, 1999); *Cappawhite National School Ceiliúradh Céad Bliain 1897-1997* (Committee, 1997); P.C. Power, *St Mary's Parochial School Clonmel* (BOM, 1993); K.M. & K.A. Griffin, *The story of Derrycastle Model Farm School* (Authors, 1997); D. Ó Duibhir, *Donaskeigh/Curraghpoor National School Céad Bliain 1891-1991* (Committee, n.d.); *Scoil Bhride Fantane Celebrates 50 Years 1949-1999* (Committee, n.d.); M. Guinan-Darmody (ed.), *Gaile Days a century recalled 1900-2000* (Committee, 2000); G. Riordan (ed.), *Glenbane National School Reunion 8 Aug 1997* (Committee, 1997); *Glengoole-New Birmingham Memories* (Committee, n.d.); M. Ryan (ed.), *Hollyford National School 1891-1991* (Committee, n.d.); *Killurney: The School, its people and its neighbourhood Centenary 1889-1989* (Committee, 1989); D. Ó Muirgheasa, *Education in the parish of Knockavilla* (Knockavilla, 1995); M. Carr (ed.), *Knockgraffon School 1871-1992 From its dawn to its dusk* (Committee, n.d.); *Latteragh National School [1884-1974]*,(Committee, n.d.); [Lisnamrock] *The Acres Re-visited* (Committee, 1992?); P. Bracken (ed.), *Littleton National School 1847-1997 History & Memories* (Committee, n.d.); E. Ryan, *Mohera National School A History 1847-1996* (Committee, 1996); *Poulacapple 1891-1991 Centenary of a Rural School* (Committee, n.d.); *Memories of Scoil Ailbhe 1949-99 Fifty Years of Scoil Ailbhe CBS Primary Thurles* (Committee, 1999).

15

PLAYER'S CIGARETTES

OSPREY HAWK

OSPREY HAWK. Black dog by *Hillcourt–Prairie Hawk*, whelped March, 1915. Breeder: Mr. F. Peet, Rathanny House, Tralee. Owner: Mr. Martin O'Halloran, The Mall, Tralee. "The Flying Hawk" was one of the greatest greyhounds ever bred in Ireland. He divided and afterwards won the Irish Cup, and won the Cork Cup, the Greenall Cup, the Tipperary Cup and other important events. Although his stud career was brief he has been a valuable acquisition to Irish breeding. (No. 43.)

QUEEN OF THE SUIR. Brindled bitch by *Mutton Cutlet–Burette*, whelped June, 1930. Breeder and owner: Mr. J. A. Byrne, Outrath, Cahir, Co. Tipperary. *Queen of the Suir* has established a unique record by winning the Oaks at White City two years in succession (1932 and 1933) and the Coronation Stakes at Wembley, also in two successive years (1933 and 1934). She won the Orient Cup and the London Cup (Clapton), 1933, in the latter establishing a new record for 550 yards. Before crossing to race on English tracks, *Queen of the Suir* won the Irish Oaks. (No. 44.)

PLAYER'S CIGARETTES

QUEEN OF THE SUIR

PLAYER'S CIGARETTES

SAIRSHEA

SAIRSHEA. Brindled bitch by *Dick the Liar–Leaves of Memory*, whelped June, 1921. Breeder: P. J. O'Reilly, Clonmel. Owner: Miss Kitty O'Reilly, Clonmel. This fast daughter of *Dick the Liar* won the Castleyard Stakes at Tinvane-sheelan, divided the Ballycohan Stakes, Waterford, and the Dunbrody Stakes (Kilmannock), and ran up for the Bessborough Stakes (Piltown). She divided the North Tipperary Cup with her litter brother and won the Gurteen Stakes Kilsheelan and the Mayfield Stakes, Tuam. *Sairshea* crowned

Section Two: Sports

TIPPERARY'S
G.A.A.
STORY

CANON PHILIP FOGARTY

GAA

In his memoir of growing up in Tipperary in the 1930s and '40s, Laurence Power wonderfully conveys the almost religious intensity of travelling to Thurles in 1945 to see Tipperary v. Cork in a Munster Final (*Half the Battle*, p.117). Over the past decades, certainly since the Centenary Year 1984, dozens of worshippers have spent countless hours pouring over the newspaper holdings in Tipperary Studies, intent on paying homage to the achievements of the clubs to which their loyalty is pledged. The Library has a large collection of these publications.[106] While each of these monographs is undoubtedly of local interest, they vary enormously with respect to

Famous Irish Greyhounds
(Player & Sons)

---

[106] J. Ryan, *Playing with the Hill: a GAA history of the parish of Ballinahinch/Killoscully* (Committee, 2005); *Ballingarry: 100 Years of Gaelic Games 1887-1987* (Ballingarry, n.d.); *Ballingarry Parish Sportsfield: Official Opening 1985* (Ballingarry, 1985); P. Moran (ed.), *Ballybacon-Grange Hurling Club 1928-1984* (Committee, n.d.); J.G. Maher & P.F. Ryan, *Boherlahan & Dualla: A Century of Gaelic Games* (Committee, 1987); P. Meskell, *Suir View Rangers 1895-1998: a history* (Author, n.d.); *A Century of GAA in Borris-Ileigh* (Committee, n.d.); *J.K. Bracken's GAA Club Centenary Celebration* (Committee, n.d.); B. Delaney, *The Burgess Story: A GAA History* (Author, 2001); J. Kelly (ed.), *The Cappawhite GAA Story 1886-1989* (Committee, n.d.); S. J. King, *GAA History of Cashel & Rosegreen 1884-1984* (Cashel, 1985); M. Bourke, *GAA History of Clonmore, Killea & Templemore* (Author, 1988); S. O Donnell, *St Mary's Hurling Club Clonmel 1929-89* (Clonmel, n.d.); Rev. E.J. Whyte, *Kilruane Mac Donaghs & Lahora De Wets: The Story of the GAA in Cloughjordan Parish 1884-1984* (Committee, 1985); E. Hall (ed.), *History of the GAA in Drangan & Cloneen 1885-2000* (Committee, n.d.); M. O'Dwyer (ed.), *The Parish of Emly: A History of Gaelic Games & Athletics* (Emly, 2000); M. Ahearne, *Fethard, Coolmoyne & Killusty GAA Story* (Committee, n.d.); D.J. Treacy, *The History of Glengar GAA Club* (Committee, n.d.); Senator W. Ryan, *Golden-Kilfeacle: The Parish and its People* (Committee, 1997); *The History of Gortnahoe-Glengoole GAA 100 Years* (Committee, n.d.); B. Stakelum, *Gaelic Games in Holycross, Ballycahill 1884-1990* (Committee, n.d.); *Horse & Jockey: All Ireland Hurling Champions 1899* (Committee, 1999); C. McNiocláis, *Inane Rovers Gaelic Football Club 1950-2000* (Committee, n.d.); *100 Years and More of GAA in the Parish of Kilsheelan & Kilcash 1884-1988* (Committee, n.d.); J.J. Kennedy, *Kickhams: Gaelic Games in Knockavilla & Donaskeigh* (Committee, 2003); J. Hannon, *A History of Gaelic Games in Lattin & Cullen 1886-2000* (Committee, 2001); S.J. King, *The Lorrha & Dorrha GAA Club History* (Committee, 1984); C. O'Keeffe (ed.), *Marlfield Hurling Club 1946-1996* (Committee, 1996); *A Century of Gaelic Games in Mid-Tipperary* (Committee, n.d.); *Moycarkey-Borris GAA Story* (Committee, 1984); M. Collins & D. Floyd, *By the Mulcaire Banks 1886-1986: The Story of the GAA in the Parish of Newport* (Committee, n.d.); *Roscrea Hurling Club: Commemorative Programme, St Cronan's Park 1980* (Committee, 1980); T. O'Donoghue, *The Arravale Rovers Story: The GAA in the Parish of Tipperary* (Committee, 1995); D. Shanahan, *The Green and Golden Years of Toomevara GAA 1885-1985* (Committee, 1985); P.F. Ryan, *The Tubberadora-Boherlahan Hurling Story* (Committee, n.d.); *Two Mile Borris 1900 All Ireland Hurling Winners: A Souvenir History* (Committee, n.d.); J.J. Kennedy, *West Tipperary GAA* (Committee, 2001).

Foxhounds at Cloughjordan

scope and quality. Tom O'Donoghue's account of the GAA in the parish of Tipperary is a massive compilation (564 pp.), especially good on the various post-foundation clubs in the parish. The work of the late Senator Willie Ryan, the passion of his final years, brought to publication by Seamus King, is an excellent example of the integration of GAA and socio-political history, making the point all too often ignored that GAA clubs do not function in isolation from everyday life.

The Dan Breen Cup is presented to Thurles Sarsfields captain, Mickey Byrne, after the 1955 county final. Included in the photograph are Dan Breen and Archbishop J. Kinane.

Photo from Seamus King's Tipperary G.A.A. Story

With respect to the GAA in Tipperary, the doyen of chroniclers is Seamus King, the focus of his research being both narrow and wide. One of his first works was a history of his local club.[107] Since then his publications encompass all aspects of the association's history, especially hurling.[108] He also co-authored an account of camogie in the county.[109]

Along with Liam Ó Donnchú and Jimmy Smyth, Seamus King performed a great service by compiling a mammoth collection of ballads, the lines of which continue to echo with the sounds of distant matches.[110] Marcus Bourke, a Dubliner with close ties to Tipperary, is the official historian of the GAA and his history of that organization has been published in different editions.[111] Prior to the huge amount of publications produced since 1984, the standard reference was the work of Canon Philip Fogarty (1889-1976), PP of Templemore from 1948 to 1974.[112]

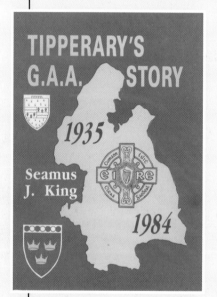
TIPPERARY'S G.A.A. STORY
1935
Seamus J. King
1984

Two key figures in the early history of the GAA, Davin and Cusack, have been the subjects of biographies.[113] Cusack's short-lived periodical *The Celtic Times*, a vital source for historians has been made available with an introduction by Marcus Bourke.[114] A handful of players have been the subjects of monographs.[115] If only because he was always a

107 S.J. King, *GAA History of Cashel & Rosegreen 1884-1984* (Cashel, 1985).
108 S.J. King, *Tipperary's Bord-na-nOg Story* (Committee, 1991); S.J. King, *Tipperary's GAA Story 1935-1984* (Committee, 1988); S.J. King, *Tipperary's GAA Story 1985-2004* (Committee, 2005); S.J. King, *A History of the GAA in the North Tipperary Division* (Committee, 2001); S.J. King, *A History of Hurling* (Dublin, 1996); S.J. King, *The Clash of the Ash in Foreign Fields: Hurling Abroad* (Author, 1998).
109 M. Bourke & S.J. King, *The History of Camogie in Tipperary 1904-2003* (Authors, 2003). See also G. Slevin, *Years of Plenty 1999-2005* (Nenagh, 2005).
110 S.J. King, L. Ó Donnchú & J. Smyth (eds.), *Tipperary's GAA Ballads* (Co Tipperary GAA, 2000).
111 M. de Búrca, *The Story of the GAA to 1900* (Irish Life, 1990); M. de Búrca, *The GAA: A History* (Dublin, 1999 2nd ed.); M. de Búrca, *Céad Bliain ag Fás: GAA 1884-1984* (Dublin, 1984). Also M. de Búrca, The GAA and Organised Sport in Ireland in G. Jarvie (ed.), *Sport in the making of Celtic Cultures* (Leicester UP, 1999), pp. 100-111.
112 Canon P. Fogarty, *Tipperary's GAA Story* (Thurles, 1960).
113 M. de Búrca, *Michael Cusack & the GAA* (Dublin, 1989); S. O Riain, *Maurice Davin 1842-1927* (Author, n.d.).
114 *The Celtic Times Feb-Dec 1887* (CLASP, 2003).
115 T. Doyle (R. Smith), *A Lifetime in Hurling* (London, 1955); V. Hogan (ed.), *Beyond the Tunnel: The Nicky English Story* (Dublin, 1996); D. Keenan, *Babs: The Michael Keating Story* (Dublin, 1996).

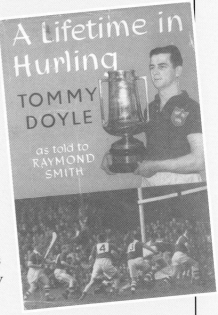

presence in Tipperary hurling, a spectre at the feast, another work should be mentioned.[116] Eddie Keher's compilation includes a treatment of Jimmy Doyle.[117] A variety of more general works, especially on hurling, are of Tipperary interest.[118]

Of particular interest is the collection of early printed material relating to the GAA and Tipperary. In 1934, the 50th anniversary of the Association, the rival newspapers *Irish Independent* and *Irish Press* each published supplements of around one hundred pages.[119] An official guide from 1919–20; an account of a Tipperary team in the United States in the 1920s and a retrospective from the 1930s are especially rare.[120]

Tipperary Studies also holds various books of general GAA interest.[121] These include works by the prolific journalist Raymond Smith.[122] Also two other works written by Marcus Bourke.[123] Finally, two works of an academic nature, one historical, and the other philosophical.[124]

Of inestimable value to researchers is the Tipperary GAA Yearbook, edited by Liam Ó Donnchú.[125] Of considerable interest is this same writer's article on hurling in the county prior to 1884.[126] Tipperary Studies holds a collection of miscellaneous match programmes.

---

[116] V. Dargan, *Christy Ring* (Dublin, 1980).

[117] E. Keher, *Hurling Heroes* (Dublin, 2000).

[118] S. Leahy, *The Tipperary Revival: Return to Glory 1987-94* (Dublin, 1995); A. Ó Maolfabhail, *Camán: 2000 years of hurling in Ireland* (Dundalk, 1973); R. Smith, *The Greatest Hurlers of Our Time* (Dublin, 1990); R. Smith, *The Clash of the Ash 1884-1972* (Dublin, 1972); R. Smith, *The Hurling Immortals 1884-1984* (Dublin, 1984); T. Wall, *Hurling* (?, 1965).

[119] *Irish Independent Supplement 1884-1934 GAA Golden Jubilee* (Easter, 1934); *Irish Press Supplement 1884-1934 GAA Jubilee* (1934). Each is 96 pp. The Library's copy of the latter is a photocopy.

[120] *GAA Official Guide 1919-20*; T.J. Kenny, *Tour of the Tipperary Hurling Team in America 1926* (London, 1928); An tAthair S. Ó Meachair S.O., *Conventions or A Dozen Years with the Gaels of Tipperary* (?, [1938]). Also, T.F. Sullivan, *The Story of the GAA* (?, n.d.).

[121] J. Cronin, *Munster's GAA Story*, 2 vols. (Author, n.d.); M. O'Hehir, *The GAA: 100 Years* (Dublin, 1984); S. Ó Ceallaigh, *Story of the GAA* (Author, 1977); M. O'Meara, *Bloody Sunday 1920-1995* (GAA, 1995); P. O'Neill, *History of the GAA 1910-1930* (?, n.d.); P. Puirséal, *The GAA in its Time* (Author, 1982).

[122] R. Smith (ed.), *Complete Handbook of Gaelic Games 1887-1999* (Dublin, 1999); R. Smith, *Decades of Glory* (In very bad condition); R. Smith, *The Football Immortals* (Dublin, 1968).

[123] M. de Búrca (ed.), *Gaelic Games in Leinster 1900-1984* (Committee, 1984); M. Bourke, *The Early GAA in South Ulster* (Committee, n.d.).

[124] W.F. Mandle, *The Gaelic Athletic Association & Irish Nationalist Politics 1884-1924* (Dublin, 1987); J. Lennon, *The Playing Rules of Football & Hurling 1884-1995*; *A Comparative Analysis of the Playing Rules of Football & Hurling 1884-1999*; *Towards a philosophy for legislation in Gaelic Games* (Ph.D, 2000).

[125] Published annually since 1970.

[126] L. Ó Donnchú, Hurling in Mid Tipperary pre-1884 in *THJ* (2001), pp. 43-52.

Other Sports

On the evidence of what is on the shelves in Tipperary Studies, sport in Tipperary means hurling. However, the printed records of a few other sports can be found in the Collection: Athletics,[127] Handball,[128] Rugby,[129] Soccer,[130] Hill Walking,[131] Golf,[132] Tennis,[133] Racing,[134] and Hunting.[135] Clearly, a great deal remains to be written about the history of sport in the county. The recognition of sports history as an academic interest can only promote more publications. An example of what can be done is Pat Bracken's recovery of part of the county's forgotten sporting heritage, his history of cricket in Tipperary.[136]

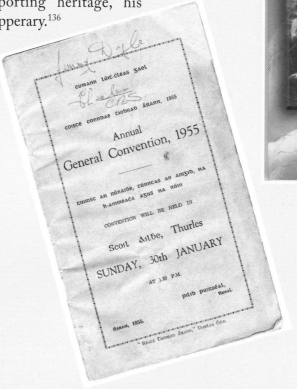

---

[127] P. Doyle, *Moyne Athletics Club 1948-1998* (Moyne, 1998); J. Healy, *Proceed to Banteer* (Author, 1997); P. Davin, *Recollections of a Veteran Irish Athlete* (?, n.d.); J.J. Barry, *The Ballincurry Hare: the Life and Times of a Champion* (Author, 1986); P. Holland (ed.), *Tom Kiely 'For Tipperary & Ireland'* (Clonmel Museum, 1997); R.M.N. Tisdall, *The Young Athlete* (London, 1934).

[128] S. Murphy (ed.), *A History of Handball in Munster 1884-1984* (?, n.d.); D. O'Donoghue, *A History of Handball in Bally[poreen]*, (?, n.d.).

[129] *Thurles Rugby Club 1924-1974: Fifty Years of Rugby Football* (Thurles, n.d.); D.A. Murphy, *Nenagh Ormond's Century 1884-1984: A Rugby History* (Nenagh, 1984); D.G. Marnane, *Clanwilliam Football Club 1879-1979 Centenary History* (Committee, 1979).

[130] P. Bracken (ed.), *St Kevin's Schoolboys AFC 1988-1998* (Committee, 1998); *The Carrick United Campaigns 1968-1993* (Committee, n.d.).

[131] F. Martindale, *Irish Walk Guides The South East Tipperary/Waterford* (Dublin, 1979); T. O'Brien, *Paths and Tracks around Clonmel and The Nire* (1990, also typescript of this book).

[132] M. Lynch, *Tipperary Golf Club 1896-1996: A History* (Tipperary, 1996); G. Cunningham (ed.), *Roscrea Golf Club 1892-1992* (Roscrea, 1992).

[133] P. Daly, *Lattin Lawn Tennis Club: reviewing a half-century 1952-2002* (Committee, 2002).

[134] T. Fitzgeorge-Parker, *Vincent O'Brien: A Long Way from Tipperary* (London, 1974); M. Clower, *Michael Kinane Race King* (Edinburgh, 1996); R. Smith, *Better One Day as a Lion* (Dublin, 1996); B. Barich, *A Fine Place to Daydream: racehorses, romance and the Irish* (London, 2005).

[135] *British Hunts & Huntsmen* (London, 1911) 4 volumes (copies of "The Tipperary Hounds", pp. 516-27 and "The Templemore Staghounds" pp. 528-29; J. Lalor, *To Hunt, Shoot and Stalk* (Cahir, 2000); M. MacEwan, *The Ryan Family and the Scarteen Hounds* (Lambourne Press, 1990); M. MacEwan, *Ten Great Irish Hunts* (New Inn, 1996); M. MacEwan, *Tipperary: The People, The Horses, The Hounds* (Tipperary Hunt, 2003).

[136] P. Bracken, *'Foreign and Fantastic Field Sports' Cricket in County Tipperary* (Thurles, 2004).

CASHEL AND GOLDEN ANGLERS' ASSOCIATION

MEMBERSHIP CARD

1940

O'Leary. Printer. Cashel.

I.T.A. Topographical Survey (1943)

Section Three: Genealogy

Most of the foreign and not a few of the Irish visitors to Tipperary Studies are in search of information about their ancestry. Researching roots is a growth industry, providing both intellectual and emotional satisfaction. Irish people of course traditionally had a strong sense of themselves as blossoms on a flourishing tree. More than a century and a half ago, the comic writer Charles Lever poked fun at the belief cherished by Irish people that their ancestry is distinguished.

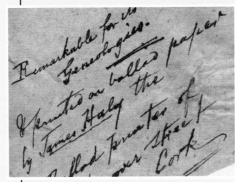

Inscription from History of Ireland (Comeford)

Oh! once we were illigint people
Though we now live in cabins of mud;
And the land that ye see from the steeple
Belonged to us all from the Flood.
My father was then King of Connaught,
My grand-aunt Viceroy of Tralee;
But the Sassenach came, and, signs on it!
The devil an acre have we.

Tipperary Studies has a large collection of general works on family history; monographs on specific families; emigration studies; genealogical periodicals and sources of information relating to Tipperary ancestors. For a person beginning a search for their roots, the journey should start with general guidebooks, what might be termed searchers' manuals.[137] A few more specialised guides are also of interest: Fr Wallace Clare's work because it is an example of such a book before the search for ancestors became a mass-participation sport.[138] Robert E. Matheson, secretary

---

[137] D.F. Begley, *The Ancestor Trail in Ireland: a companion guide* (Dublin, 1982); D.F. Begley, *Handbook on Irish Genealogy: how to trace your ancestors and relations in Ireland* (6th ed. Dublin, 1984); M. Yurdan, *Irish Family History* (London, 1990); S.E. Quinn, *An Introduction to Irish Ancestry* (3rd ed. Author, 2002); J. Grenham, *Tracing your Irish Ancestors: The Complete Guide* (2nd ed. Dublin, 1999); J. Grenham (ed.), *Grenham's Irish Surnames* (CD-ROM); T. McCarthy, *The Irish Roots Guide* (Dublin, 1991); J.G. Ryan, *Irish Records: Sources for Family and Local History* (Dublin, 1997); I. Grehan, *Irish Family Names* (Belfast, 1985); J. Grenham, *The Little Book of Irish Clans* (Dublin, 1994); I. Grehan, *Irish Family Histories* (Cork, 1993); W. Nolan, *Tracing the Past: Sources for Local Studies in the Republic of Ireland* (Dublin, 1982); M. Dickson Falley, *Irish & Scotch-Irish Ancestral Research: A guide to the genealogical records, methods and sources in Ireland* (Baltimore, 1988).

[138] Rev. Wallace Clare, *A Simple Guide to Irish Genealogy* (Originally published in 1937 and revised by R. ffolliott, London 1966). Also his *The Testamentary Records of the Butler Families in Ireland* (Author, 1932).

of the General Register Office a century or so ago issued an official report on the nature and distribution of Irish surnames[139] and guides to the records of specific denominations have also been published.[140] Some indices to wills may be of interest.[141] There is a genealogical guide to Cashel & Emly diocese.[142]

Two names at the centre of family history are Burke and MacLysaght. John Burke (1787–1848), a native of North Tipperary, began the series of genealogical works that continue to bear his name. These volumes are only useful with respect to landed families and the Library has some editions.[143] Perhaps the most interesting of these volumes is *Burke's Irish Family Records*, which has genealogies of dozens of Tipperary families from Armitage of Noan to White of Cappawhite. The books of Edward MacLysaght provide the best information on the historical background of Irish family names.[144] Older sources of information on family pedigrees are the works of John Lodge and John O'Hart.[145] The Library has one edition of the *Walford County Families* series.[146] While these works are of great value to historians, signposting the lives of the great and the often not so good, it is a case of people who having status in life, continuing to have attention in death.

Contagh		Hths.	s.
Illegible	,,	2	4
Thomas McGrath	,,	1	2
Illegible	,,	1	2
John Murphy	,,	1	2
Francis Thomas	,,	1	2
Darby Murphy	,,	1	2
Edmund Bourke	,,	1	2
William Kennoe	,,	1	2
Three wast howses	,,	3	6
Ballythomas			
Mortagh Dorane	,,	1	2
Edmund Tobin	,,	1	2
3 illegible	,,	1	2
Thomas Davin	,,	1	2
Morrish Shulalan	,,	1	2
Thomas M'Edmond	,,	1	2
three wast houses	,,	3	6
John Bourke	,,	1	2
PARISHES OF CAHIR AND MORTLES-TOWNE.			
Edmund Daniell	//	3 & a kiln	8
Thomas White	//	2	4
Richard Goulding	//	1	2
Mathew Evans	//	1	2
Walter Poore	//	1	2
Leonard Creagh	//	2	4
Thomas Carrell	//	1	2
Thomas Cooke	//	1	2
Constance Daniell	//	1	2
Walter Nory	//	1	2
William Murphy	//	1	2
James Murphy	//	1	2
Patrick Shurshall	//	1	2
Thomas Meagher	//	1	2
Nicholas Butler	//	1	2
Nciholas Morony	//	1	2
Thomas Kearney	//	1	2
Daniell Hiskey	//	1 & a forge	4
Edmund Tobin	//	1	2
Thomas Cohane	//	1	2

Tipperary Families (Laffan)

---

[139] Sir R.E. Matheson, *Special Report on Surnames in Ireland* (Dublin, 1909) and *Varieties & Synonymes of Surnames & Christian Names in Ireland* (Dublin, 1901).

[140] S.C. ffeary-Smyrl, *Exploring Irish Genealogy I: Irish Methodists- where do I start?* (Dublin, 2000); O.C. Goodbody, *Guide to Irish Quaker Records 1654-1860* (IMC Dublin, 1967); R. Refaussé, *Church of Ireland records* (Dublin, 2000); P.J. Corish & D. Sheehy, *Records of the Irish Catholic Church* (Dublin, 2001).

[141] Sir A. Vicars, *Index to the Prerogative Wills of Ireland 1536-1810* (Dublin, 1897); *Index to Irish Wills 1484-1858* [in NAI] (CD-ROM).

[142] *St Ailbe's Heritage: a guide to the history, genealogy and towns of the archdiocese of Cashel & Emly* (Tipperary, 1999). See also N. Higgins, Genealogical Sources for Co. Tipperary in *THJ* (1991), pp. 181-89.

[143] *Burke's Landed Gentry of Great Britain & Ireland, 10th ed. (1904); Burke's Peerage, 71st ed., 2 vols. (1909); Burke's Peerage, Baronetage & Knightage, 99th ed., (1949); Burke's Landed Gentry of Ireland, 4th ed., (1958); Burke's Irish Family Records* (London, 1976).

[144] E. MacLysaght, *Bibliography of Irish Family History* (Dublin, 1981); *Guide to Irish Surnames* (Dublin, 1964); *Irish Families: Their Names, Arms and Origins*, (Dublin, 1978 and revised ed. Dublin, 1991); *More Irish Families* (Dublin, 1982); *The Surnames of Ireland* (Dublin, 1980). Also, Rev. P. Woulfe, *Irish Names and Surnames* (Dublin, 1923).

[145] J. Lodge, *The Peerage of Ireland*, (Dublin, 1789) 7 volumes; J. O'Hart, *Irish Landed Gentry when Cromwell came to Ireland* (Dublin, 1887); *Irish Pedigrees or the origin and stem of the Irish Nation*, 2 vols., (New York, 1923).

[146] E. Walford, *The County Families of the United Kingdom* (London, 1860).

Over the past decades, researchers, both sentimental and academic, have produced a significant number of studies of individual families; monographs and articles anatomising generations and individuals. Particularly with American and Australian researchers in family history, what begins as casual interest often ends with the private publication of a family history. By their nature many of these publications have limited circulation but thanks mainly to donations, Tipperary Studies has a substantial collection of family histories.[147]

---

[147] [Note that the relevant family name is highlighted]

Sir A.F. Baker, The **Bakers** of Lismacue in *THJ* (1994), pp. 115-28; J.S. **Bermingham**, *True Stories from Irish History* (Author, 1992); F.A. **Corcoran**, *From Unlikely Beginnings: a history of Roger Corcoran, Pioneer settler of Boorowa, NSW and his family* (Author, Canberra, 1992); M. **Cummins**, *It's a long way from Tipperary* (Author, 1993); A.E. **Carden**, *Carden of Barnane* (Author, 2004); R. Austin-Cooper, *Butterhill & Beyond: an illustrated history of the* **Cooper** *family of Byfleet, Killenure Castle, Co Tipperary & Abbeville House Co Dublin* (Author, 1991); E.A. Lahey, **Cosgrove** *from Borrisnoe Co Tipperary Ireland to Morgan Co Illinois* (Author, n.d.); G.E. Horrigan, *The* **Damer** *Family 1662-1825* (Unpublished BA thesis, TCD, 1983); O. Miller, *The* **Donnellys** *Must Die* (Toronto, 1962); R. Fazakas, *The* **Donnelly** *Album* (Toronto, 1977); T.P. Keeley, *The Black* **Donnellys** (Ontario, 1993); R.H.A.J. Everard, The Family of **Everard** in *The Irish Genealogist*, vii, 3 (1988), vii, 4 (1989), viii, 2 (1991), viii, 4 (1993); F.B. Falkiner, *A pedigree with personal sketches of the* **Falkiners** *of Mount Falcon* (Dublin, 1894); M. Ahern, The **Fennells** of Cahir in *THJ*, (2004), pp. 91-100; M.J. Fennessy & A.C. Ni Fhiannusa (eds.), *Fiangus to* **Fennessy** (Authors, 1999); R.J. Fennessy, **Fennessy** *of the County Tipperary: chronicle of an Irish family* (Baltimore, 1999); Rev. C.C. Ellison, **Going** of Munster in *The Irish Ancestor*, 1 (1977), pp. 21-43; A.P. Grant, The **Grant** Family of Co Tipperary in *JCHAS*, lxxii (1972), pp. 65-75; J. Grant, *Providence: The Life and Times of John* **Grant** *1792-1866* (Author, 1994); Lt-Col J. Greene, *Pedigree of the Family of* **Greene** (Author, 1899); G.W. Grubb, *The* **Grubbs** *of Tipperary* (Cork, 1972); T. Hayden, The **Haydens** of Tipperary in *THJ* (1994), pp. 142-54; P.C. Hayes, *From the Minehouse: a* **Hayes** *family history 1819-1994* (Author, 1995); P. Heffernan, *The* **Heffernans** *and their Times* (London, 1940); Fr P. Bateman, **Heffernans** *of Clonbonane* (Author, 1990); E. Cregan Anderton, *The* **Howes** *who Left: the long journey of Martin and Michael* **Hough** *of Co Tipperary Ireland* (Author, 2000); Typescript file on the **Keays** family of Abington & Bilboa (n.d.); W.J. Hayes, *The* **Keeffes** *of The Jockey* (Lisheen Publication, 2001); M. Aggeler, *Dear Richard [**Kennedy**]:Letters to an Irish Emigrant 1865-1925* (X libris Corporation, 2001); R. **Kennedy**, *From Bun Ciamálta to New South Wales* (Relay Nenagh, 1999); A. Spenser, *Thomas Patrick* **Levins** *of Thurles c.1865-1896* (Typescript, Author, 1985); *Long of* **Longfield** (Typescript); *Genealogy of the Earls of Landaff [**Mathew**] of Thomastown Co Tipperary Ireland* (Private, 1898?) and also M. Bence Jones, Thomastown Castle in *Country Life*, 2 Oct 1969; S. Trant McCarthy, *The* **Mac Carthys** *of Munster* (Dundalk, 1922); W. & T. Morrissey, *The* **Morrissey** *Family, Toor, Kilcash, Clonmel* (Authors, 1975); E.D. Murnane, *It's Not Such a Long Way to Tipperary: the story of the* **Murnane** *family of Cappauniac, County Tipperary* (Author, 1991); J. O'Carroll Robertson, *A Long Way from Tipperary* (Author, 1994); Sir M. O'Dwyer, *The* **O'Dwyers** *of Kilnamanagh* (London, 1933, 2nd ed. Limerick, 2000); M. Healy, *Railways & Pastures: the Australian* **O'Keeffes** (Author, 1988); M. Callanan, *Records of Four Tipperary Septs: the* **O'Kennedys**, O'Dwyers, O'Mulryans, O'Meaghers (Galway, 1938); B.P. Kennedy, *The Irish Kennedys: the story of the 'Rebellious* **O'Kennedys**' (Author, 1998); J.C. O'Meagher, *Some Historical Notices of the* **O'Meaghers** *of Ikerrin* (New York, 1890); D.H. Pennefather, **Pennefathers** (Typescript, Author, 1998); *History of the* **Prittie** *Family* (Typescript); M. MacEwan, *The* **Ryan** *Family and the Scarteen Hounds* (Salisbury, 1989); L.F. Ryan, **Ryan** *Family 1841-1972* (Author, 1972); M. Barrett CSSR, *A Riot of* **Ryans**: *the 19th century Ryans of Boorowa* (Author, 1994); M. Barrett CSSR, *King of Galong Castle: the story of Ned* **Ryan** *1786-1871* (Author, 1978); M. Barrett CSSR, *Because of These [**Ryan**, **Corcoran**, **Murphy**]* (Church Archivists' Press, 1992); M. Barrett, *Galong Cemetery New South Wales* (Author, 1995); **Sadleir** of Sopwell Hall (file of misc. material); P. MacCotter, History of the **Sall(e)** Family of Cashel in *The Irish Genealogist*, x, 2 (1999); B.C. MacDermot, Letters of John **Scully** to James Duff Coghlan in *The Irish Genealogist*, vi, 1 (1980), vi, 2 (1981), vi, 3 (1982), vi, 4 (1983); A. McCan, **Scully** Tombstones on the Rock of Cashel in *The Irish Genealogist*, x, 2 (1999); M. R. Smeltzer, *The* **Smeltzers** *of Kilcooly and their Irish-Palatine Kissing Cousins* (Author, 1981); C. Smith-Barry, *Notes on the* **Smith-Barry** *Family* (Author, 1933); G.N. Nuttall-Smith, *The Chronicles of a Puritan Family in Ireland [**Smith**]* (Oxford, 1923); R.C. Ryan-Hackett, *The* **Stapletons** *of Drom, alias Font-Forte*, Co Tipperary (Author, 1995); Major Stoney RA, *Some Old Annals of the* **Stoney** *Family* (Privately published, n.d.); H. Gallwey, *The* **Wall** *Family in Ireland 1170-1970* (Author, 1970).

These works vary enormously. Some are acts of family piety; others are sustained labours whereby the history of a family is recovered from records and memory. All are of interest. Many are linked with the enforced emigration of the nineteenth century, especially to Australia.[148] The numerous publications of Max Barrett are of particular interest, detailing the fates of individuals transported to Australia in the early nineteenth century because of agrarian crime in Clonoulty.[149] The most famous link between Tipperary and Australia is Ned Kelly, about whom a great deal has been written.[150] Bruce Elliott has investigated the fortunes of over seven hundred Tipperary families who emigrated to Canada between 1815 and 1855.[151] The Irish-American connection is explored in a collection of articles from *The Journal of the American Irish Historical Society*, which was published, between 1898 and 1941.[152] *Returning Home* is a record of incoming passengers to all the major ports in Britain and Ireland between 1858 and 1870, compiled on police orders because of fear of Fenians.[153] American writers discuss their Irish roots in two books, the first of which is by a black American whose grandmother was from Tipperary.[154]

The number of periodicals dealing with Irish genealogy reflects both the worldwide search for 'roots' and the extent of the flight from Ireland in the nineteenth and twentieth centuries. Tipperary Studies holds issues of The *Irish Ancestor* between 1969 and 1986 and includes Tipperary topics such as a census of protestants in Shanrahan in the 1860s and in Clogheen in the 1870s.[155] *Irish Family History* is the journal of the Irish Family History Society and the Library holds issues between 1987 and to date.[156] *The Irish Genealogist* is the primary journal but the Library only holds two index volumes.[157] The *Journal of the Butler Society* began publication in 1968 and has articles dealing with this premier

---

[148] See D. Fitzpatrick, *Oceans of Consolation: Personal Accounts of Irish Migration to Australia* (Cornell UP, 1994). This includes material relating to the **Dalton** family of Athassel.

[149] See his article *THJ* (1991), pp. 63-72.

[150] C. Osborne, *Ned **Kelly*** (London, 1970); B. Carroll, *Ned Kelly Bushranger* (Lansdowne Press, Australia, 1976); J. McQuilton, *The Kelly Outbreak 1878-1880: the geographical dimension of social banditry* (Melbourne UP, 1979); B. Reece, Ned Kelly and the Irish Connection: a Re-Appraisal in *THJ* (1990), pp. 47-62.

[151] B.S. Elliott, *Irish Migrants in the Canadas: a new approach* (McGill-Queen's UP, 1988).

[152] M.J. O'Brien (ed.), *Irish Settlers in America* (Baltimore, 1979). Also, M. Glazier (ed.), *The Encyclopaedia of the Irish in America* (Notre Dame UP, 1999); W. Mulligan Jr., 'The Merchant Prince of the Copper Country' one emigrant's American success story in *THJ* (2004), pp. 151-60.

[153] J.P. Maher (ed.), *Returning Home: transatlantic migration from North America to Britain & Ireland*, 1858-70 (CD-ROM).

[154] S.T. Haizlip, *The Sweeter the Juice: a family memoir in black and white* (New York, 1994); J. Mathieu, *Zulu: an Irish-American's quest to discover her roots* (Edinburgh, 1998).

[155] *The Irish Ancestor*, iii, 1 (1971), iii, 2 (1971), viii, 1 (1976), viii, 2 (1976), ix, 2 (1977), x, 1 (1978), x, 2 (1978), xi, 1 (1979), xi, 2 (1979), xii, 1&2 (1980), xiii, 1 (1981), xiii, 2 (1981), xiv, 1 (1982) xiv, 2 (1982), xv, 1&2 (1983), xvi, 1 (1984), Shanrahan Census, xvi, 2 (1984); S. O'Mahony, Emigration from the Workhouse of Nenagh Union 1849-60. Also Clogheen Union Census, xvii, 1 (1985); xvii, 2 (1985); J. Condon, **Ryan of Inch**, xviii, 1 (1986). Since this was written, the Library has a full run (CD-ROM).

[156] *Irish Family History*, iii, (1987) to ixx, (2003). See also their Directory of Parish Registers, indexed in Ireland (1997).

[157] *The Irish Genealogist*, iii Index of Persons 1956-67; iv Index of Persons 1968-1973.

Tipperary family.[158] Due to the immense work undertaken by the Mormon community, Salt Lake City has become hugely important for genealogists. Tipperary Studies has six volumes of a genealogical newsletter issued from this American city.[159]

With regard to genealogical sources for County Tipperary, the reader is referred to the collections of civil and religious records held in Tipperary, Cashel and Nenagh.[160] Some general guides to Tipperary sources are available.[161] Of interest to genealogists is the collection of commercial directories held in Tipperary Studies. The earliest of these is Richard Lucas, *Irish Provincial Directories, 1788* covering Borrisoleigh, Carrick-on-Suir, Cashel, Clonmel, Thurles and Tipperary.[162] By the later nineteenth century, these directories are especially comprehensive with respect to urban centres.[163] Of special interest is Kinder's 1839 directory for Carrick-on-Suir and Clonmel.[164] This has contemporary annotations for Clonmel indicating individuals who "left" or "died". There is also a modern listing of surnames for both towns.[165] Of value is a listing of officers who served with the county militia.[166] Two parliamentary returns of the 1840s are of genealogical value.[167]

Tipperary Studies holds other major national genealogical sources: data on some sixty thousand flax growers from 1796,[168] information on some thirty thousand individuals who defaulted on tithe payments in 1831,[169] the William Smith O'Brien petition of 1848 with around eighty thousand names,

---

158 *Journal of the* **Butler** *Society*, Number 1(1968) to Number 8 (1978-79) and second series vol. 2, 3 issues (1980-1984), vol. 3, one issue (1986-87), vol 4, Number 1 (1997) & Number 2 (2000).

159 *The Irish at Home and Abroad*, I, 1-4 (1993-4), 2, 1-4 (1994-5), 3, 1-4 (1995-6), 4, 1-4 (1997), 5, 1-3 (1998), 6, 1-4 (1999). See G.K.J. Betit, County Focus: County Tipperary in 3, 4 (1995-6).

160 Excel Centre in Tipperary for baptism and marriage records of Cashel & Emly archdiocese; Bru Boru in Cashel for civil records for south Tipperary and church records for Tipperary parishes in Waterford and Lismore diocese and also North Tipperary Genealogical & Heritage Services, Governor's House, Kickham St., Nenagh for civil records for north Tipperary and church records for Tipperary parishes in Killaloe diocese. (Also for Killaloe, R.T.D. Fitzgerald, Killaloe Marriage Licence Bonds, 1680-1720 & 1760-1762 in *Irish Genealogist*.)

161 N. Murphy, *Tracing North West Tipperary Roots: genealogical sources for Upper & Lower Ormond, Owney & Arra* (Typescript, Nenagh, 1982); N. Higgins, Genealogical Sources for Co. Tipperary in *THJ* (1991), pp. 181-189.

162 *The Irish Genealogist*, iii, 11 (1966).

163 Pigot (1824); Shearman (1839); Thom (1844, 1845, 1849); Pettigrew & Oulton (1845); Slater (1846, 1856, 1870); Henry & Coughlin (1867); Bassett (1880-81, 1889); Guy (1886, 1893); *Cork & Munster Trades Directory* (1915, 1920, 1924, 1925, 1927, 1930, 1933, 1938, 1969); *Macdonald's Irish Directory and Gazetteer* (1957-8).

164 F. Kinder & Sons Limerick, *The New Triennial & Commercial Directory*, 1839 and also 1842 ed.

165 T. Veale, *An Extract of Surnames for Clonmel and Carrick* (Dublin, 1993).

166 Major A.C. Ryan, *Records of the Tipperary Artillery with a list of officers*, 1793-1889 (Clonmel, 1890).

167 *Abstract returns of persons qualified to serve as Jurors in Tipperary SR, 1843–49 and the juror's panel from which jurors were selected at each assizes held in the same period* (226), 1849. Also *A list of the names of persons returned by the several collectors of barony cess in the county of Tipperary to serve as petty jurors* (393), 1846. A similar list of jurors for North Tipperary, 1839-44.

168 *Irish Flax Growers*, 1796 (CD-ROM).

169 S. McCormack (ed.), *The 1831 Tithe Defaulters* (CD-ROM).

addresses and occupations,[170] a register of students and academic staff in Trinity College Dublin from 1637 to 1846,[171] the first volume (1836) of the annual Catholic Almanack, listing parishes and clergy[172] and especially moving, details of some forty nine thousand Irishmen who died fighting in the First World War.[173]

There is also a listing of all those who served in the Irish Constabulary.[174]

Gravestone Inscriptions

While scrambling about ancient and overgrown Tipperary graveyards perhaps has an appeal, sitting in a comfortable library might be preferred. Gravestone inscriptions are a vital source of genealogical information. Unfortunately only the north and extreme south of the county have received the systematic attention of enthusiasts willing to devote time to copying inscriptions. In North Tipperary members of the Ormond Historical Society transcribed inscriptions from graveyards in the baronies of Owney & Arra, Upper and Lower Ormond.[175] The list here is by civil parish arranged alphabetically. Within some parishes there is more than one graveyard.

---

[170] R. Lawler (ed.), *The 1848 Petition* (CD-ROM).

[171] *Alumni Dublinenses*, 1924 ed (CD-ROM).

[172] *A Complete Catholic Registry, Directory and Almanack (1836)* (CD-ROM).

[173] *Ireland's Memorial Records: World War 1, 1914-1918* (CD-ROM). Tipperary Studies also has general listings of the hundreds of thousands who died in the British forces, information that was originally published in 81 volumes in 1921: *Soldiers Died in the Great War 1914-19* (CD-ROM).

[174] J. Herlihy, *The Royal Irish Constabulary: a complete alphabetical listing of officers and men. 1816-1922* (Dublin, 1999).

[175] This work was done in the 1980s and organised on the basis of civil parishes. Historically each civil or medieval parish (smaller than the modern catholic parish) had its church and graveyard. This structure was associated with the Church of Ireland. Note that the heritage centres in Cashel and Nenagh hold more complete gravestone inscriptions.

Barony of Owney & Arra

Abington Parish:	(Partly in this barony but the graveyard is in County Limerick).
Burgessbeg Parish:	Burgessbeg graveyard
Castletown Arra Parish:	Castletown Arra graveyard
	Castletown Arra Church of Ireland graveyard
	Portroe RC Church graveyard
Kilcomenty Parish:	Cragg graveyard
	Kyle graveyard
Killoscully Parish:	Killoscully RC Church graveyard
Kilmastulla Parish:	Kilmastulla graveyard
Kilnarath Parish:	Kilnarath graveyard
	Ballinahinch graveyard
Kilvellane Parish:	Ballymackeogh graveyard
	Newport St John's graveyard
	Newport RC Church graveyard
Templeachally Parish:	Templeachally graveyard
	Ballina RC Church graveyard
Youghalarra Parish:	Youghalarra graveyard
	Youghalarra Church graveyard

Barony of Lower Ormond

Aglishclochane Parish:	Aglishclochane Church of Ireland graveyard
Ardcroney Parish:	Ardcroney graveyard
	Congor Church of Ireland graveyard
Ballingarry Parish:	Ballingarry Church of Ireland graveyard
Borrisokane Parish:	Borrisokane Church of Ireland graveyard
Cloughprior Parish:	Cloughprior graveyard
Dorrha Parish:	Dorrha Church of Ireland graveyard
	Bonahum graveyard (Derry townland)
	Rathcabbin RC Church graveyard
Dromineer Parish:	Dromineer graveyard
Finnoe Parish:	Finnoe Church of Ireland graveyard
Kilbarron Parish:	Kilbarron Church of Ireland graveyard
	Kilbarron graveyard
Killodiernan Parish:	Killodiernan graveyard
	Killodiernan Church of Ireland graveyard
	Puckane RC Church graveyard
Kilruane Parish:	Kilruane graveyard
Knigh Parish:	Knigh graveyard
Lorrha Parish:	Dominican Priory graveyard
	Lorrha Church of Ireland graveyard
Loughkeen Parish:	Loughkeen Church of Ireland graveyard
Modreeny Parish:	St Kieran's Church of Ireland graveyard
	Grawn graveyard
Monsea Parish:	Monsea graveyard
Nenagh Parish:	Franciscan Friary graveyard
	St Mary's of the Rosary
	Convent of Mercy
Rathurles Parish:	Rathurles graveyard

27

| Terryglass Parish: | Terryglass Church of Ireland graveyard |
| Uskane Parish: | Uskane graveyard |

Barony of Upper Ormond

Aghnameadle Parish:	Aghnameadle graveyard
	Augustinian Priory
	Church of Ireland graveyard
	Gortagarry RC graveyard
Ballinaclough Parish:	Ballinaclough graveyard
Ballygibbon Parish:	Ballygibbon graveyard
Ballymackey Parish:	Ballymackey graveyard
Dolla Parish:	Kilboy graveyard
Kilkeary Parish:	Kilkeary graveyard
Kilnaneave Parish:	Kilnaneave graveyard
Kilmore Parish:	Kilmore graveyard
Latteragh Parish:	Latteragh graveyard
Lisbunny Parish:	Lisbunny graveyard
Nenagh Parish:	Tyone graveyard
	Workhouse graveyard
	St John the Baptist graveyard
	Kenyon Street graveyard
	St Mary's Church of Ireland graveyard
Templederry Parish:	Templederry Church of Ireland graveyard
	Templederry RC Church graveyard
	Curreeny graveyard

This collection of gravestone inscriptions also includes Glenkeen and Kilcommon in the barony of Kilnamanagh.

In the early 1990s, gravestone inscriptions were collected from the following parishes in the Clonmel region:

Ballyclerihan	Marlfield	Rochestown
Derrygrath	Newchapel	St Mary's
Donoughmore	Old Ardfinnan	St Necklos
Kilronan	Powerstown	St Stephen's
Kiltegan	Quakers	Tullameelin

There is an index.[176]

Tipperary Studies Library holds a small number of miscellaneous sets of inscriptions for the following graveyards: St Patrick's Rock Cashel,[177] Fennor,[178] Kilcash,[179] St Mary's Thurles,[180] Churchtown (Dysert),[181] Kilfeacle,[182]

[176] *Clonmel Gravestone Inscriptions Index (1994)* (Co Tipperary Joint Libraries Committee & FAS, 1994).

[177] T. Wood & C. Huftier (eds.), *Our People are on the Rock* (Authors, n.d.).

[178] *Fennor Graveyard: Inscriptions and Register of Interments.*

[179] J. & P. Flood, *Kilcash 1190-1801* (Dublin, 1999).

[180] *Irish Family History*, x, (1994), pp. 78-119.

[181] E. Connolly, Survey of gravestone inscriptions at Churchtown graveyard Dysert [between Carrick and Kilsheelan] in *Decies*, xxv (1984).

[182] W. Ryan, *A Short History and Reference Guide to Kilfeacle Cemetery* (Author, 1985).

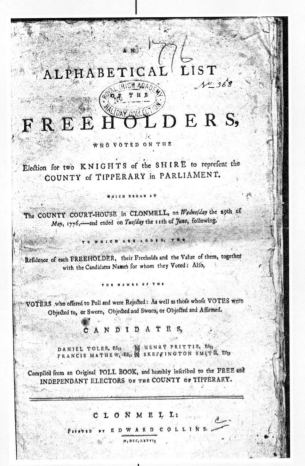

List of Clonmel Freeholders

Loughmore,[183] Mount Bruis,[184] Templemore,[185] Thurles,[186] Emly,[187] Toem,[188] British military graves in Tipperary town,[189] Mullinahone,[190] Dovea and Drom,[191] Ardmayle.[192]

Other Sources

The British conducted a census at the beginning of each decade but the returns prior to 1901 were destroyed. The original returns from 1901 and 1911 are in the National Archives. However, Tipperary Studies has microfilm copies for County Tipperary.[193] Organised by district electoral division and townland for those in a given household on the nights of 31 March 1901 and 1 April 1911 respectively, information is given with regard to name, age, religion, occupation, marital status, literacy, knowledge of Irish, relationship to householder, county of birth (or country if born outside Ireland). If an individual was absent from his home on the night in question, he will not be listed but will have to be sought in some other return. Information about the quality of housing is also given: number of rooms, building material, number of windows and number of out-buildings. The 1911 census obliged married women to state the duration of their present marriage, the number of children born and how many were still living. There was no census in 1921 for obvious reasons (civil unrest). Information from 1901 and 1911 returns have been abstracted for the parish of Loughmore-Castleiney.[194] The 1901 census returns for Tipperary town have been used as the basis for a comprehensive discussion.[195]

For the mid-nineteenth century, the great genealogical source is the primary valuation of tenements carried out under the direction of Richard Griffith. For taxation purposes, land and houses were valued and occupiers of property were all listed, as were the individuals from whom these occupiers held. (Not necessarily the 'landlord' as sometimes several layers of tenancy intervened between the occupier on the ground and the ultimate owner of the property). The county was divided into baronies and each barony into civil parishes and each parish into townlands. Heads of households are named in both town and country and extents of land held.

---

183 *Index to burials in Loughmore and Templeree Graveyards* [No actual inscriptions].

184 D. Leahy, *Survey of Mount Bruis Graveyard* (Author, 1990).

185 W.J. Hayes, *The Old Church and Graveyard Templemore* (Templemore, 1995); *Templemore Burial Register* (Templemore UDC, 1993).

186 St Mary's Churchyard, Thurles in *Irish Family History*, x (1994), pp. 78-119.

187 M. O'Dwyer, *The Gravestone Inscriptions of Emly* (New Orleans, 1993).

188 A. Ryan, *Toemverig* (Author, 1992).

189 W.S. O'Shea, *Record of British military graves Tipperary Town, 1880-1922* (Typescript, n.d.).

190 M. Larkin, *Mullinahone parish burial grounds: a record* (Author, 2005).

191 Incomplete typescript.

192 P. Maher, *Ardmayle: a resting place full of memories* (Ardmayle, n.d.).

193 Consult the printed index first.

194 List of houses and occupants in each townland.

195 D.G. Marnane, Tipperary town one hundred years ago: the evidence of the 1901 Census in *THJ* (2001), pp. 1-26.

Relative valuations allow an idea of individual prosperity. The valuation for County Tipperary was carried out around 1850, at a time when the impact of the Great Famine was still being felt. Tipperary Studies has these records for each barony in the county.[196] Information with respect to each occupier includes a map reference and these maps offer a wealth of information.[197] Information is available with respect to landholders in the parish of Modreeny.[198]

Modreeny Protestant Church, Cloughjordan

Tipperary Studies holds scant genealogical sources for the eighteenth-century. Two sources of interest are records of those who became members of the Church of Ireland, motivated more by economics than faith and the Religious Census of 1766 which was carried out by Church of Ireland parochial clergy and lists heads of households.[199] The search for catholic ancestors is difficult but there are some pre-nineteenth century sources. However, they are not easy to use and require some background reading on the part of the researcher. Taxation records for the 1660s were destroyed during the Civil War (1922) but a Cashel MD Thomas Laffan copied and published such records for County Tipperary.[200] Householders are listed for various parishes, together with the tax paid on hearths. Another seventeenth-century source is the *Civil Survey*, a Cromwellian undertaking of the mid 1650s listing proprietors of land in 1640. As with other sources, information is given by barony and civil parish. Townlands are mentioned but can be quite different to modern townlands. This source is less useful with respect to specific family ancestors but shows where particular families were clustered in the county. This source has been published for Tipperary.[201] A related source is the *Book of Survey and Distribution*, which traces changes in land ownership in the decades after 1640. This has not been published for Tipperary.[202]

A very important sixteenth-century genealogical source but difficult to use is the Tudor Fiants. These were government documents and especially for the reign of Elizabeth (1557-1603) include land grants and pardons naming many individuals and their townlands. The originals were destroyed in 1922 but were published in a series of reports issued by the Deputy Keeper of the Public Records in Ireland between 1875 and 1890.[203] The modern edition includes an index.

---

[196] Some are original documents, others are microfilms. There is a national index to this source, 1848-1864 (CD-ROM).

[197] The Library holds copies of these maps for the county (originals are in the Valuation Office in Dublin).

[198] *Modreeny Land Holders, c.1850-1930* (Typescript, n.d.).

[199] E. O'Byrne (ed.), *The Convert Rolls* (IMC Dublin, 1981). 1766 Census: Photocopies of originals in N.A. Also J. D'Alton, *King James Irish Army List* [1689], (Reprinted Limerick, 1997).

[200] T. Laffan, *Tipperary's Families: being the Hearth Money Records for 1665-6-7* (Dublin, 1911).

[201] R.C. Simington (ed.), *The Civil Survey A.D. 1654-1656 County of Tipperary: vol. 1 Eastern and Southern Baronies* (IMC Dublin, 1931) and *vol. 2 Western and Northern Baronies* (IMC Dublin, 1934).

[202] Tipperary Studies has a MSS copy, once the property of the Limerick historian Maurice Lenihan.

[203] *The Irish Fiants of the Tudor Sovereigns during the reigns of Henry VIII, Edward VI, Philip & Mary and Elizabeth I*, 4 volumes (Edmund Burke Dublin, 1994).

Finally, if a search for Irish ancestry is all consuming, a study of the work of the seventeenth-century scholar Dubhaltach Mac Fhirbhisigh may be of interest. His *Great Book of Irish Genealogies* explores the mixture of myth and history out of which Gaelic families emerged.[204] Francis John Byrne's classic study may be of interest.[205]

History of Ireland
(Comerford)

TIPPERARY'S FAMILIES:

BEING THE

HEARTH MONEY RECORDS

FOR 1665-6-7

REFERENCE

BY

THOMAS LAFFAN

ERRATUM

For "ineligible" *read* "illegible" throughout.

JAMES DUFFY & CO., LTD., PUBLISHERS,
38, WESTMORELAND STREET, DUBLIN.
1911.

PRESS I

PARISH OF THURLES—Continued.

		Hths.	s.
Over the Bridge			
John Donoghow	"	1	2
Edmond Kelly	"	1	2
John Lahey	"	1	2
Connor Lahey	"	1	2
Daniell Cahill	"	1	2
Teige Rian	"	1	2
Without-Gates			
John Hackett	"	1	2
Thomas Stapleton	"	1	2
Marcus Lehane	"	1	2
Conor McMuragh	"	1	2
James Reyan	"	1	2
Phillipp Holickan	"	1	2
Teige McKey	"	1	2
Darby McOwen	"	1	2
William Shea moer	"	1	2
George Palinor	"	1	2
Connor Bryen	"	1	2
John Power	"	1	2
Maurice Nugent	"	1	2
Thomas Dodd	"	1	2
William Parratts	"	1	2
Morgan Williams	"	1	2
Darby Meagher	"	1	2
Teige Meagher	"	1	2
Edmund Fitz Gerald	"	1	2
William Lahey	"	1	2
Teige Sulevane	"	1	2
William Britt	"	1	2
Thomas Williams	"	4	8
William Hickey	"	1	2
William Reyan	"	1	2
Thomas McDaniell	"	1	2
John Scully	"	1	2
Bernard Saul	"	2	4

		Hths.	s.
Without-Gates			
Darby Reyan	"	1	2
Richard Headen	"	1	2
Phillipp McDaniell	"	1	2
Richard Butler	"	1	2
John Rafter	"	1	2
John McRory	"	1	2
John Hackett	"	1	2
John McTeige	"	1	2
William Purcell	"	1	2
John Dwire	"	1	2
Thomas Doughane	"	1	2
Walter Shea	"	1	2
Paul Shea	"	1	2
Thomas Power	"	1	2
Daniell McOwen	"	1	2
Donnogh Meagher	"	1	2
John Meagher	"	1	2
John Headin	"	1	2
Casiestowne			
Teige Cahell	"	1	2
Thomas Kissin	"	1	2
Thomas Lowroe	"	1	2
Donogh Cahill	"	1	2
Keneday Brian	"	1	2
James Davies	"	1	2
John Meagh	"	1	2
Daniell Ternan	"	1	2
Patrick Kenedy	"	1 & a forge	4
David Power	"		
Six-Bridges			
Daniell Hearen	"	1	2
William Thompson	"	1	2
Donnogh Kennedy	"	1	2

extract from Tipperary's Families Hearth Money Records

---

204 N. Ó Muraíle (ed.), *Leabhar Mor na nGenealach The Great Book of Irish Genealogies compiled (1645-66) by Dubhaltach Mac Fhirbhisigh 5 volumes* (Edmund Burke Dublin, 2003).
205 F.J. Byrne, *Irish Kings and High-Kings* (London, 1973).

Charles Bianconi a biography
(O'Connell)

32

Section Four: Remarkable Individuals

faithfully yours
John O'Leary

Recollections of Fenians and Fenianism

Remarkable individuals cast long shadows. How daunting that shadow can be is summed up in the remark attributed to the 2nd Duke of Wellington: "Think of it, the Duke of Wellington is announced and I walk into the room". Tipperary Studies has a large collection of remarkable lives, stories of individuals who in some way impacted on the county and indeed in many instances, on the country. The scale of these works varies enormously, from magisterial monographs to short sketches. Perspectives also differ: ranging between biography both critical and hagiographical and autobiography both analytical and self-serving. The biographer Richard Holmes strikingly described his role as standing at the end of a broken bridge and looking across, carefully, objectively, into the unattainable past on the other side. For the autobiographer it is a matter of memory augmented by record and shaped by design. The stages on which the dramas of these many individual lives were performed include politics, a great deal of politics and often with no happy endings, religious life, commerce, culture and sport.

Published lives of individuals who impacted on the political life of the county very much reflect the fact that the future was shaped by the victory of Sinn Fein in the early 20th century. Doheny, Kickham, O'Leary, MacDonagh, Treacy and Breen, iconic figures in the context of the republican tradition in Tipperary, all have their places in the list below. Studies of much less well-known individuals such as Michael Flannery are of interest. He was an unrepentant hard-line republican from Knockshegowna in North Tipperary. It is of interest that the only figure in the constitutional tradition to receive serious scholarly attention is John Sadleir and of course his claim to fame is peculation rather than politics. Outside nationalist politics, the only sustained biographical treatment is of some members of the Butler family, particularly the 10th earl and 1st duke, each of whom had a national profile. The most unlikely political career was that of Brendan Bracken who soared from

Statue of Charles Kickham, Tipperary Town

Templemore to Westminster and Whitehall by way of Australia.[206]

One of the finest biographies of recent years, that of Charles Agar, Church of Ireland archbishop of Cashel in the late 18th century, serves to illustrate the paucity of clerical lives in print.[207] Together with Agar (an unlikely couple), only Thomas Croke also of Cashel has received anything like due scholarly and published recognition. Thanks to the work of Fr Walter Skehan and Dr James O'Shea a great deal of biographical information is available with respect to catholic clergy in the county. The O'Carroll diaries are especially interesting, giving an insight to the 19th century clerical mind. Lives of a few priests in modern times have been published; perhaps the most unusual career being that of Fr Robert Bradshaw whose missionary work reached from Iceland to Russia.[208]

Joseph Benedict Chifley
Australian Prime Minister
1945 - 1949
The Tipperary Connection

Tipperary man who became Prime Minister of Australia

---

[206] Note: entries are arranged by subject, not author.
M. O'Donnell, Thomas Francis Bourke (1840-1889) in THJ (1990), pp. 27-38 and *THJ* (1991), pp. 109-120; A. Boyle, *Poor Dear Brendan: the quest for Brendan Bracken* (London, 1974); C.E. Lysaght, *Brendan Bracken* (London, 1979); D. Breen, *My Fight for Irish Freedom* (Dublin, 1924 and subsequent eds.); J.G. Ambrose, *The Dan Breen Story* (Dublin, 1981); T. Carte, *An History of the Life of James Duke of Ormonde* 2 vols. (London, 1736); Lady Burghclere, *The Life of James First Duke of Ormonde 1610-1688*, 2 vols. (London, 1912); T. Barnard & J. Fenlon (eds.), *The Dukes of Ormonde 1610-1745* (The Boydell Press, 2000); C. Brady, *Thomas Butler earl of Ormond* (1531-1614) in C. Brady (ed.), *Worsted in the Game: Losers in Irish History* (Dublin, 1989); M. Doheny, *The Felon's Track* (various eds.); S. Fitzpatrick, *Recollections of the fight for Irish Freedom* (Tipperary, n.d.); D. O'Reilly (ed.), *The Memoirs of Michael Flannery* (Dublin, 2001); E. Gaynor, *Memoirs of a Tipperary Family: The Gaynors of Tyone 1887-2000* (Dublin, [2003]); W. Murphy, *C.J. Kickham, Patriot, Novelist, Poet* (Dublin, 1903 reprint Blackrock, 1976); R. Kelly, *C.J. Kickham* (Dublin, 1914); J.J. Healy, *Life and Times of C.J. Kickham* (Dublin, 1915); R.V. Comerford, *C.J. Kickham: a study in Irish nationalism and literature* (Dublin, 1979); K. Amos, James Kiely – Clonmel's Forgotten Fenian in *THJ* (1989), pp. 35-37; L. Fogarty, *Fr John Kenyon a patriot priest of '48* (Dublin, n.d.); W.J. Fitzpatrick, *Irish Wits and Worthies including Dr Lanigan, his life and times* (Dublin, 1873); M. Loft, *Lt Harry Loft of Louth & the 64th Reg. of Foot* (Churnet Valley Books, 2003); D. O Bric, Pierce McCan MP in *THJ* (1988), pp. 121-32 and *THJ* (1989), pp. 105-17. See also newscuttings file on McCan; N. Murphy, A Profile of Thomas MacDonagh in T. MacDonagh, *Literature in Ireland* (Relay Nenagh 1996 reprint of 1916 original); E.W. & A.W. Parks, *Thomas MacDonagh: The Man, the Patriot, the Writer* (Georgia UP, 1967); J. A. Norstedt, *Thomas MacDonagh: a critical biography* (U.P. of Virginia, 1980); K. Rafter, *Martin Mansergh: A Biography* (Dublin, 2002); M. Mansergh, *The Legacy of History* (Dublin, 2003); P. Buckley (ed.), *The Memoirs of Maurice Meade a forgotten freedom fighter* (Cullen, 2003); R. Mulcahy, *Richard Mulcahy 1886-1971: a family memoir* (Dublin, 1999); M. Lysaght, Norbury "The Hanging Judge" (1745-1831) in *Dublin Historical Record*, xxx, 2 (1977), pp. 58-66; J. O'Leary, *Recollections of Fenians and Fenianism*, 2 vols. (London, 1896); D.J. O'Donoghue, *John O'Leary and his friends* (news cuttings, Sunday Independent 1913); M. Bourke, *John O'Leary a study in Irish separatism* (Tralee, 1967); B. Ryan, *A full private remembers the Troubled Times* (Author, 1969) and *Rambling Down the Ould Bog Road* (Author, 1973); J. O'Shea, *Prince of Swindlers: John Sadleir MP 1813-1856* (Dublin, 1999); D. Ryan, *Sean Treacy and the 3rd Tipperary Brigade* (Tralee, 1945).

[207] A.P.W. Malcomson, *Archbishop Charles Agar Churchmanship and Politics in Ireland, 1760-1810* (Dublin, 2002). Also of interest: K. Homfray, The Rev. Henry Woodward, Rector of Fethard, 1812-63 in *THJ* (2005), pp. 87-96.

[208] W.G. Skehan, *Cashel & Emly Heritage* (Abbey Books, 1993). This book only deals with priests who became parish priests. Tipperary Studies however have typescripts of Skehan's work on other diocesan priests. J. O'Shea, *Priest, Politics and Society in Post-famine Ireland – a study of County Tipperary 1850-1891* (Dublin, 1983). Tipperary Studies holds a copy of the Ph.D thesis on which this book was based. Anon., *Three Apostolic Lives, Tipperary's Gift to China 1863-98* (CTS, 1919); Rev. M. Maher, *The Archbishops of Cashel* (Catholic Truth Society, 1927); J. O'Flynn, *Two Centuries of Catholic Bishops of Waterford & Lismore (1629-1829)* (Waterford, 1917); D. Forristal, *Seventeen Martyrs* [includes Dermot O'Hurley, Terence Albert O'Brien and William Tirry] (Dublin, 1990); A.P.W. Malcomson, *Archbishop Charles Agar: Churchmanship and Politics in*

James Butler 12th Earl
afterwards 1st Duke of Ormond
from a painting by Egmont at Clayton House

James Duke of Ormonde (Burghclere)

34

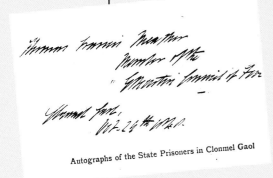

Autographs of the State Prisoners in Clonmel Gaol

signature of
Thomas Francis Meagher

MICHAEL DOHENY

The Felons Track (Doheny)

Up to fairly recently, land was the basis of wealth in Ireland. However, there are very few studies of individual landlords. Given that writers are naturally attracted to extremes, the 'good' and the 'bad', Arthur Moore and Charles Bianconi on the one hand and William Scully and 'Woodcock' Carden have attracted attention. General business life has received little attention. Bianconi of course is centre stage but in her own way, Agnes Ryan (Harding from near Tipperary town) of the Monument Creameries in Dublin was just as revolutionary.[209]

Ireland, 1760-1810 (Dublin, 2002); Canon P. Power (ed.), *A Bishop of the penal Times being letters and reports of John Brenan* (Cork, 1932); C. Breathnach, Archbishop John Brenan (1625-1693) in *THJ* (1993), pp. 148-159; Fr M. Kennedy, *Fr Robert Bradshaw: Priest and Legionary* (Tipperary, 2003); M. Tierney, *Croke of Cashel* (Dublin, 1976); T.B. Allen, Dr Everard Archbishop of Cashel (1752-1821) in *IER*, 2 (1897), pp. 56-75; J.A. Feehan, *An Hourglass on the Run: the story of a preacher* (Dublin, 2000); I. Murphy , Denis Harty – Vicar Apostolic of Killaloe 1657-1667 in *THJ* (1989), pp. 100-104; S. Rynne, *Father John Hayes* (Dublin, 1960); W.J. Hayes, (Fr) Paul Higgins, a man of legend in Killea in *THJ* (1995), pp. 140-144; D.G. Marnane, Fr David Humphreys and New Tipperary in W. Nolan (ed.), *Tipperary: History & Society* (Dublin, 1985); L. Maher, *I Remember Neil Kevin (1903-1953): an assessment of his life and writings* (Roscrea, 1990); Rev. J. Feehan, Forgotten by History: the life and times of John Lanigan, Priest, Professor and Historian in *THJ* (2005), pp. 43-60; Ó Ó Duáin OFM, *Rógaire Easpaig* (Dublin, 1975); R. Wyse Jackson, *Archbishop Magrath the scoundrel of Cashel* (Dublin, 1974); J.F. Maguire, *Fr Mathew: a biography* (London, 1863); K. Tynan, *Father Mathew* (London, 1908); P. Rogers, *Fr Theobald Mathew, apostle of temperance* (London, 1945); Rev. Fr Augustine, *Footprints of Father Theobald Mathew Apostle of Temperance* (Dublin, 1947); C. Corrigan, *Fr Mathew and the Irish Temperance Movement 1838-49* (Cork, 1992); P.A. Townsend, *Father Mathew, Temperance and Irish Identity* (Dublin, 2002); J.A. Feehan, *A Fool for Christ: the priest with the trailer [Fr James Meehan]* (Dublin, 1993); Rev. J. Feehan (ed.), *The O'Carroll Diaries [1846 & 1862-64]* (Typescript, Editor, 1997); P.F. Moran (ed.), *The Analecta of David Rothe Bishop of Ossory [Dermot O'Hurley, pp. xiii-xlvi]* (Dublin, 1884); M. O'Halloran, *Dermot of Cashel* (CTS, 1910); T. Gavin, *Dr Dermot O'Hurley* (CTS, 1963); W.J. Hayes, Dermot O'Hurley: heroic archbishop of Cashel in W.J. Hayes (ed.), *Tipperary Remembers* (Thurles, 1976); W. Hayes, Dermot O'Hurley's Last Visit to Tipperary in *THJ* (1992), pp. 163-73; A.M. Chadwick, Alice O'Sullivan, Clonmel missionary and martyr (1836-70) in *THJ* (2001), pp. 83-88; C. McHale, *Patron of Partition: Bishop Thomas Quinlan 1896-1970* (Dublin, 1995); J. Holohan, *They will remember him forever: great miracles performed by Fr James Russell of Kilcommon* (Author, 1994); *The dead priest who speaks to the living* (Author, 1995); *The mass rock and saints of Kilcommon* (Author, n.d.); (TFR), *The Pastor of Kilcommon [Fr E.J. Ryan]* (Author, n.d.); J.P. Gordon CSSP, *Bishop Shanahan of Southern Nigeria* (Dublin, 1949); Editor, *Father Ailbe Sadlier (1879-1949): 33 Years President of Mount St Josephs* (Roscrea, n.d.); T. Power, Father Nicholas Sheehy (c.1728-1766) in G. Moran (ed.), *Radical Irish Priests 1660-1970* (Dublin, 1998), also R.R. Madden, *The United Irishmen, their lives and times* (Dublin, 1857), volume 1, pp. 21-89 and in Burke, *Clonmel* (Clonmel 1907); J. O'Connor OSA, *A Ballad of William Tirry* (Author, 1976); *A Priest on the Run: William Tirry OSA 1608-1654* (Dublin, 1992); K.K. O'Donoghue, *P.A. Treacy and the Christian Brothers in Australia and New Zealand* (Melbourne, 1983).

[209] D. G. Marnane, The Diary of Frederick Armitage of Noan for 1906 in *THJ* (1994), pp. 48-65; Mrs Morgan John O'Connell, *The Life of Charles Bianconi* (London, 1878); M. O'Connell Bianconi & S.J. Watson, *Bianconi King of the Irish Roads* (Dublin, 1962); I. Herring, The "Bians" in *Ulster Journal of Archaeology* (1939), pp. 130-37 and (1940), pp. 118-22; T.P. O'Neill, Bianconi and his Cars in K.B. Nowlan (ed.), *Travel and Transport in Ireland* (Dublin, 1965), pp. 82-95. See also file of newscuttings and articles on Bianconi; M. Neenan, Martin Burke of the Shelbourne Hotel in *THJ* (1994), pp. 113-14; A. Carden, 'Woodcock' Carden – a balanced account in *THJ* (2000), pp. 120-31; D.G. Marnane, Samuel Cooper of Killenure (1750-1831) - a Tipperary land agent and his diaries in *THJ* (1993), pp. 102-27; Editor, *General Michael Joseph Costello (1904-1986)* (Dublin? N.d.); M. Gleeson [Borrisoleigh], *A Tipperary Story: memoirs from a Life* (Author, 1991); W.A. Maguire, The murder of Constantine Maguire, 1834 in *THJ* (2003), pp. 103-120; D.G. Marnane, A Tipperary Landlord's [Massy Dawson] Diary of the 1860s in *THJ* (1991), pp. 121-28; A. Barry CSSR, *The Life of Count Arthur Moore* (Dublin, 1905); I.M. Ní Riain, *The Life and Times of Mrs A.V. Ryan* (Author, n.d.); T.U. Sadleir, *An Irish Peer [Lord Mountcashell] on the Continent 1801-1803* (London, 1920); H.E. Socolofsky, *Landlord William Scully* (Kansas, 1979); G. Moran, William Scully and Ballycohey – a fresh look in *THJ* (1992), pp. 63-74;

British military figures associated with the county have received scant attention.[210] David Beatty of the Battle of Jutland fame was a grandson of Nicholas Sadlier of Tipperary town. Perhaps the most unusual career was that of Marty Maher from Roscrea whose long career at West Point was the subject of a 1955 John Ford film *The Long Grey Line* starring Tyrone Power and Maureen O'Hara. The memoir of Clonmel native David Power describes his experiences in the British army during the Second World War. Most unusual perhaps was Thomas Carew, born in Mobarnan around 1590 who wrote a classic account of the Thirty Years War (in Latin).[211]

Individuals with Tipperary connections who devoted themselves to the arts are more numerous (not perhaps in reality but on the library shelf). (See **Section Sixteen**) Clonmel is linked with two of the most distinctive writers in English, one eighteenth century and the other nineteenth: Laurence Sterne born in Clonmel in 1713 and George Borrow resident in the town 1815–16 when his father was in the military. More conventional writers, novelists and poets, are also part of the county's cultural heritage.[212] This list also includes architects, two pioneering photographers, an opera singer, the Italianate 'Signor Foli'- from Cahir and Jack Judge, a man with no Tipperary connection except a song with a global resonance. Published lives of Tipperary men who made an impact on the world of science fit in a very narrow space.[213]

Birth place of Sean Treacy, ITA Survey (I.T.A.)

[210] P. Anderton, *Before I Forget* (Author, 1995); S. Roskill, *Admiral of the Fleet Earl Beatty* (London, 1980); Sir W. Butler, *An Autobiography* (London, 1911); E. McCourt, *Remember Butler* (London, 1967); M. Ryan, *William Francis Butler: A Life 1838-1910* (Dublin, 2003); A. Chadwick, 'Tipperary Joe': Field Marshal Viscount Gough in *THJ* (1994), pp. 91-95; General Sir H. Gough, *Soldiering On* (London, 1954); M. Maher, *Bringing Up the Brass – My 55 Years at West Point* (New York, 1951); D. Power, *Long Way from Tipperary* (Author, 1994); M. Hennessy, *The Rajah from Tipperary [George Thomas from Roscrea]* (London, 1971); F. Glenn Thompson, Assistant Surgeon William Bradshaw VC [Thurles] in *Irish Sword*, xiv, (1981), pp. 237-39.

[211] T. Carve, *Itinerarium* (London, 1859 ed.).

[212] C.K. Shorter, *The Life of George Borrow* (London, 1919); see also *Lavengro* (London, 1851) for Clonmel references; M. Sadleir, *Blessington-D'Orsay, a Masquerade* (London, 1933); Elizabeth Butler [Battle Artist], *Autobiography* (London, 1922); M. Fitzgerald, David Power Cunningham (1825-1883) in *THJ* (1988), pp. 192-200; L. Price (ed.), *An Eighteenth Century Antiquary: the sketches, notes and diaries of Austin Cooper (1759-1830)* (Dublin, 1942); D. Grace, Larry Dillon- Song-writer and wit of Lower Ormond in *THJ* (1992), pp. 153-58; D. Reynolds, *A Neighbour's Child: the life and times of the Irishman Signor Foli (1835-1899)* (Dublin, 1994); C. Mavor, *Becoming: the photographs of Clementina, Viscountess Hawarden* (Duke UP, 1999); P. Holland, *Tipperary Images: the photographs of Dr William Despard Hemphill* (Cahir, 2003); V.H. Gibbons, *Jack Judge The Tipperary Man* (Sandwell, 1998); N. Higgins, Julia Kavanagh (1824-1877) – a novelist from Thurles in *THJ* (1992), pp. 81-83; RJC, *Geoffrey Keating: priest, poet & patriot* (CTS, 1913); B. Cunningham, *The World of Geoffrey Keating* (Dublin, 2000); Rev. W.P. Burke, Geoffrey Keating in *JWSEI* Arch. Soc.,(1894-95), pp. 173-82; L. Maher, *I Remember Neil Kevin* (Author, 1990); R.V. Comerford, *Charles J. Kickham: a study in Irish nationalism and literature* (Dublin, 1979); N. Higgins, John Mullaney – a Cahir Architect in America in *THJ* (1990), pp. 95-96; G. Smith, *Tommy O'Brien: Good Evening Listeners* (Dublin, 1987); M. Fitzgerald, Margaret Ryan, Poet of Garrynoe in *THJ* (1991), pp. 129-31; I. Campbell Ross, *Laurence Sterne: A Life* (Oxford UP, 2001); J.D. Forbes, *Victorian Architect: the life and work of William Tinsley* (Indiana UP, 1953) and J.D. Forbes, The Tinsley Portrait Sketches of the W. Smith O'Brien Trial in *JRSAI* (1953), pp. 86-92.

[213] M. Goldsmith, *Sage: a life of J.D. Bernal* (London, 1980); B. Swann & F. Aprahamian (eds.), *J.D. Bernal: a life in science and politics* (London, 1999); A. Brown, *J.D. Bernal: the sage of science* (Oxford UP, 2005); E.S. Whitehead, *A Short Account of the Life and Work of John Joseph Fahie* (Liverpool UP, 1939); L. Walsh O Cist, *Richard Heaton of Ballyskenagh 1601-1666* (Roscrea, 1978); R.C. Cox, *Bindon Blood Stoney: biography of an engineer* (1828-1909).

To the Irishman in America said — "I'd rather be a lamp-post in Dublin, than President of the United States".

Michael MacDonagh.

Signature Michael MacDonagh Author of The Irish at the Front

Fr Theobald Mathew

One of the most interesting research areas in recent years is the role of women. (See **Section Nine**) Tipperary Studies has a collection of lives, biographies and autobiographies, of remarkable women. In some instances, women who made their marks in areas as diverse as veterinary medicine, anthropology or women's rights but also memoirs and diaries allowing insights to everyday life.[214]

Surprisingly perhaps, lives of Tipperary sportsmen and women in print are more scarce than might be expected. A comprehensive biography of such a key figure in the history of the GAA as Maurice Davin was published over seventy years after his death. Some of the more interesting material looks at some of the few gathered in Hayes' Hotel on the fateful day in 1884.[215] Rather different is a monograph about how an individual coped with a dreadful accident during a rugby match.[216]

[214] I. White (ed.), *Daisy Bates – the native tribes of Western Australia* (Canberra, 1985); J. Blackburn, *Daisy Bates in the Desert* (London, 1997); E. Gormanston [Butler], *A Little Kept* (London, 1953); E. Mavor, *The Ladies of Llangollen [Lady Eleanor Butler & Miss Sarah Ponsonby]* (London, 1971); C.M. Ford, *Aleen Cust Veterinary Surgeon: Britain's First Woman Vet* (Author, 1990); H. Cooke, *Rectory Days* (Portlaw, 2002); D. Dooley, Anna Doyle Wheeler in M. Cullen & M. Luddy (eds.), *Women, Power and Consciousness in Nineteenth Century Ireland* (Dublin, 1995); D. Dooley, *Equality in Community: sexual equality in the writings of William Thompson and Anna Doyle Wheeler* (Cork, 1996); M. Healy, *For the Poor and for the Gentry* (Dublin, 1989); D. Herbert, *Retrospections of Dorothea Herbert 1770-1806* (Dublin, 1988 – 1st ed. two vols. 1929-30); S. Chuinneagáin, *Catherine Mahon: first woman president of the INTO* (INTO, 1998); M. Luddy (ed.), *The Diary of Mary Mathew* (Thurles, 1991); M. Quarton, *Breakfast the Night Before: recollections of an Irish Horse Dealer* (Dublin, 2000); I.M. Ní Riain, *The Life and Times of Mrs A.V. Ryan* (Author, n.d.); J.M. Feehan, *Tomorrow to be Brave* (Mercier, 1972).

[215] N. Murphy, Joseph K. Bracken, GAA Founder, fenian and politician in W. Nolan (ed.), *Tipperary: History & Society* (Dublin, 1985), also a centenary commemoration (Typescript, 2004); S. Ó Riain, *Maurice Davin (1842-1927): First President of the GAA* (Dublin, n.d.); M. de Búrca the curious career of Sub-Inspector Thomas McCarthy in *THJ* (1988), pp. 201-204; N. Murphy, Frank R. Moloney: Nenagh's GAA Pioneer in *THJ* (1997), pp. 74-83; E. Bell, Lena Rice of New Inn in *THJ* (1988), pp. 13-14; A. MacLochlainn, From Tipperary to Joseph's Prairie: the story of Joe Ryan, the seventh man in Hayes' Hotel in *THJ* (2002), pp. 149-172; T. Ryan MFH, *My Privileged Life: with the Scarteen Black and Tans* (Derrydale Press, 2002).

[216] Anon, *Man of Courage Tom Fahey* (Clonmel? 1976?).

It is a reasonable proposition that any accounting of a life, even a life devoid of obvious significance, will be of interest if only as a witness statement to vanished times. This final list of Tipperary lives, mostly 20th century and mainly first-hand appear increasingly a matter of 'long ago and far away'; evidence of ways of life, attitudes and habits becoming as remote and strange to us as images in sepia-tinted photographs. To adapt Hartley's famous phrase: yes, they did things differently there.[217]

Henry O'Brien
Author of "The Round Towers of Ireland."

Thomas McDonagh

---

[217] Note: a brief reference to context is included between square brackets.
P. Burke, *The Ring of the Anvil* (Author, n.d.) [Slieve Phelim 1940s and '50s]; S. de Buitléir, *Meitheals & Meanderings: a Tipperary childhood of the 1920s* (Relay Nenagh, 1999); P. Cranley, *Just Standing Idly By* (Tipperary, 1993) and *Moving On* (Tipperary, 1995) [Life in Tipperary town from the 1920s]; K. Dalton, *That Could Never Be: a Memoir* (Columba Press, 2003) [Holidays with the Kemmis family of Moyaliffe]; P. Daly, *A View from Bay Lough* (Author, 2000) [1950s Clogheen from Australia]; D. Devitt, *Never Bet: a garda remembers and reflects* (Author, 1997) [Born Thurles 1916]; K.H. Donlon CSSR, *And Ink be on their Hands* (Dublin, 1999) [Born Roscrea, 1925]; M. Doorley, *Stella Days 1957-1967* (Author, n.d.) [Cinema Borrisokane]; J. Dowling, *An Irish Doctor Remembers* (Dublin, 1955) and D.G. Marnane, A Nineteenth Century Tipperary Diary in *THJ* (1990), pp. 39-46 [This latter a diary by the uncle of Jeremiah Dowling]; K. Fitzgerald, *With O'Leary in the Grave* (Oxford UP, 1986) [Farming near Cashel, 1920s]; I. Grubb, *J. Ernest Grubb of Carrick-on-Suir* (Dublin, 1928); M. Hayes, *I Slept with Dan* (Lisheen Publications, 2001) [Rathcoole childhood, 1920s & '30s]; W.J. Heaney, *House of Courage – Life in a Sanatorium* (Dublin, 1952) [Nenagh author's experience of T.B.]; P. Heffernan MD, *An Irish Doctor's Memories* (Dublin, 1958) [From near Cahir, work in Clonmel and India]; H. Howard, *'And the Harvest is Done' life on the land in Offaly and Tipperary* (Dublin, 1990) [Born 1911]; A. Maher, *Signalman's Memories: railway life in rural Ireland* (Thurles, 1998) [CIE in Thurles]; M. Ó Lachtnáin, *My Life and Memories of Rince agus Ceol* (Lisheen Publications, 2002); L. Power, *Half the Battle: Memoirs of a Tipperary Boyhood* (Naas, 2000) [Around Tipperary town, 1930s & '40s]; T. Prittie, *Through Irish Eyes: a journalist's memoirs* (London, 1977) [Son of Lord Dunally of Kilboy]; P. Slattery, *Growing Up in Carefree Days: life in rural Ireland as it was* (Author, 1998); P. Slattery, *God Save Ireland* (Author, n.d.) [Ballylooby]; P.J. Slattery, *The Life and Times of a Railwayman* (Author, n.d.) [Born 1931, career in Limerick Junction]; I. Trant, *Just Across the Water* (Author, 1996) [Life in Dovea]; D.G. Marnane, John Davis White's Sixty Years in Cashel in *THJ* (2001), pp. 57-82; (2002), pp. 199-226; (2003), pp. 121-140 and (2004), pp. 169-206 [Life in Cashel in the 19th century].

Section Five: Institutions

Anniversaries prompt recollection. This is true for institutions as much as for individuals. Survival for one hundred years is an especially important milestone and various institutions in the county such as creameries, churches, sports clubs and schools, have celebrated this and other anniversaries by commissioning institutional histories. Tipperary Studies has a collection of this material. (Of course, the publication of this guide *Finding Tipperary* is itself a means of marking a significant milestone in the county's library service, the building of a new library and home for Tipperary Studies.) Two kinds of institutional histories have already been detailed in this guide: primary schools in **Section One** and sports organizations in **Section Two**. A number of hospitals, religious organisations, parish churches, schools and voluntary groups are listed below.[218]

---

[218] Note: entries are arranged by place.
Anon., *Ballypatrick Co-operative Dairy Society Ltd. 1893-1993* (Committee, 1993); Anon., *From Workhouse to College: Borrisokane Vocational School 1942-1992* (Committee, 1992); Anon., *Sacred Heart Church Borrisoleigh 1893-1993* (Committee, 1993); Anon., *St Mary's Church Cahir 1833-1983* (Committee, 1983); E. Lonergan, *A Workhouse Story: a history of St Patrick's Hospital Cashel 1842-1992* (Cashel, 1992); E. Carew & S. King, *Cashel Lions Club: Silver Jubilee 1961-1986* (Committee, 1986); R. Smith, *A Century of Co-operative Endeavour: Centenary Co-operative Creamery Society Ltd.* (Dublin, 1998); B. Long (ed.), *A Centenary Record of Clonmel High School 1900-2000* (BÓM, 2000); Anon., *Clonmel Theatre Guild: Silver Jubilee 1969-1994* (Committee, 1994); E. Lonergan, *St Joseph's Hospital Clonmel* (Author, 2000); S.J. Watson, *A Dinner of Herbs: the history of Old St Mary's Church Clonmel* (Author, 1988); M. Ahern, The Quaker Schools in Clonmel in *THJ* (1990), pp. 128-32; M. Ahern, Clonmel Mechanics Institute in *THJ* (1991), pp. 159-62; M. Ahern, Clonmel Charter School in *THJ* (1992), pp. 148-52; M. Ahern, Clonmel Grammar School in *THJ* (1993), pp. 128-34; M. Ahern, Clonmel's pay schools – 'urban hedge schools' in *THJ* (2000), pp. 132-35; M. Quane, The Free School of Clonmel in *JCHAS*, lxix, 209 (1964), pp. 1-28 and M. Quane, The Lands of the Free School of Clonmel: a chapter of Famine history in *JCHAS* lxx, 210 (1965), pp. 36-53; Committee, *The Church of SS Michael & John Cloughjordan Co Tipperary: A Centenary History 1899-1999* (Committee, 1999); Anon., *Coolmoyne & Fethard Co-operative Creamery Ltd.: Coolmoyne 1894-1994* (Committee, 1994); Anon., *Drangan Co-operative Creamery Society Ltd.: A Century of Success 1897-1997* (Committee, 1997); W. Corbett (ed.), *Drombane Co-operative Agriculture & Dairy Society Ltd. 1897-1997* (Committee, 1997); Anon., *The Patrician Brothers in Fethard 1873-1993* (Fethard Historical Society, 1997); J. W. McKinney & W. Salters Sterling, *Gurteen College: A Venture of Faith* (Omagh, 1972); E. Lonergan, *The History of the South-Eastern Health Board, 1871-2004* (Health Board, 2005); C. Logue, Kyle Park Agricultural School (1843-1875) in *THJ* (1997), pp. 86-91; D. Foley, *Mullinahone Co-Op - the first one hundred years: the history of Ireland's oldest co-op 1893-*

REGISTER OF *Tipperary Workhouse Male* NATIONAL SCHOOL.

PUPILS' NAMES IN FULL.	Age of Pupil last Birth Day.	Religious Denomination.	RESIDENCE.	Occupation or Means of Living of Parents.	State the Name and School at which the Class in wh[...] School.
Corbett John	12	R.C.	Workhouse	Widow	
Costello Patrick	9	R.C.	do.	Labourer	
Ryan Michael	11	R.C.	do.	Widow	
Callaghan Michael	10	R.C.	do.	Orphan	

In the history of the county, no institution has mattered more than the diocese, exercising influence since the twelfth century. Three dioceses cover the county: Cashel & Emly, Killaloe and Waterford. Only Killaloe has been well served by historians.[219] The Rev. St John D. Seymour contributed to the Church of Ireland history of Cashel & Emly.[220] With reference to the catholic diocese of Cashel & Emly, a great deal of information is available in the calendars of papers of archbishops between 1712 and 1902. These typescript calendars compiled in the 1960s provide a chronological listing and summary of episcopal correspondence and are the main material out of which some day perhaps a history of the diocese will be

TIPPERARY,	.	56. Clonmel Industrial School for R. C. boys. Certified 12th January, 1885. C.M.—Rev. J. Harrington	150
"	.	57. St. Augustine's Industrial School for R. C. girls, Templemore. Certified 20th August, 1870. C.M.—Mrs. M. A. M'Donnell.	60
"	.	58. St. Francis' Industrial School for R. C. girls, Cashel. Certified 8th December, 1869. C.M.—Mrs. M. Catherine Ryan.	110
"	.	59. St. Louis' Industrial School for R. C. girls, Thurles. Certified 11th December, 1869. C.M.—Mrs. M. B. Hogan.	45
"	.	60. Tipperary Industrial School for R. C. girls. Certified 1st May, 1872. C.M.—Mrs. Mary Frances Cantwell.	64

Reformatory and Industrial Schools Report (1905)

CLARKE AND WALSH, Wholesale and Retail Drapers and General Warehousemen CASTLE STREET, CAHIR

Book of Tipperary (Bassett)

1993 (Committee, 1993); G. Lewis, *Loosening the Chains: Nenagh Branch ITGWU-SIPTU, 1918-1997* (Relay Nenagh, 2003); Anon, *Life and Times of Nenagh CBS Concert Band 1985-1995* (Committee, 1995); Anon, *An Fórsa Cosanta Áitiúil Nenagh 1946-1996: 50th anniversary* (Committee, 1996); Sr Pius O'Brien, *The Sisters of Mercy of Birr & Nenagh* (Ennis, 1994); Anon, *St Mary's of the Rosary Nenagh 1895-1990* (Nenagh, n.d.); Anon, *The Story of St Mary's Secondary School Nenagh* (Nenagh n.d.); D.A. Levistone Cooney, *The Ormond Methodists* (Author, 1975); M. O'Shea, *One Hundred Years of Piltown Co-operative and its branches* (Committee, 2001); D. Levistone Cooney, *100 Years of Methodism in Roscrea 1903-2003* (Author, 2003); T. Prior & G. Cunningham (eds.), *The Convent of the Sacred Heart Roscrea 1842-1992* (Roscrea, 1992); G. Cunningham, *The Modern Story of St Cronan's Roscrea, Co. Tipperary - its clergy, people and parochial buildings* (Roscrea, 2001); A. Hewson, *No Ivory Tower: A Century of Vocational Education in Roscrea* (North Tipperary VEC/FAS, 2001); F. Hannon (ed.), *Twenty-one Years of Loyal and Dedicated Service: 3rd Field Artillery Regiment 1959-1980 [Templemore]* (Committee, 1980); Anon, *Sacred Heart Church Templemore 1883-1983* (Committee, 1983); Anon, *Forty Years Serving the Community: Thurles Credit Union 1961-2001* (Thurles, 2001); Anon, *Souvenir of the Centenary of the Monastery and Schools – Christian Brothers Thurles 1816-1916* (Thurles, 1916); W. Jenkins, *Tipp Co-Op: Origin & Development* (Dublin, 1999). The Library also holds a copy of the thesis on which this book was based (Jenkins, M.A. NUI, UCD 1995); W.S. Doyle, *More Fragments: centenary souvenir of St Michael's Church, 1859-1969* (Tipperary, 1959); D.G. Marnane, 'To Do & To Teach' A History of the Christian Brothers in Tipperary Town 1868-1994* (Tipperary, 1994); M. Bourke, Erasmus Smith and Tipperary Grammar School in *THJ* (1989), pp. 82-99; D.G. Marnane, *A History of St Michael's Parish Church Tipperary* (Tipperary, 1999); D.G. Marnane, 'A Lamp Kindled' The Sisters of Mercy and Tipperary Town* (Tipperary, 2000); W.S. O'Shea, *A Short History of Tipperary Military Barracks 1874-1922* (Tipperary, n.d.); D.A. Murphy, *Blazing Tar Barrels & Standing Orders: North Tipperary's First County & District Councils 1899-1902* (Relay Nenagh, 1999); B. Long, *Tipperary S.R. County Council 1899-1999: A Century of Local Democracy* (Clonmel, 1999); Anon, *South Tipperary Beekeepers Association: Golden Jubilee 1945-1995* (Committee, 1995); Anon, *Connradh na Gaeilge 1893-1943: A Garland from Tipperary* (Committee, n.d.); J. R. Shelly, *A Short History of the 3rd Tipperary Brigade [IRA]* (Author, 1996).

[219] Rev. A. Gwynn S.J. & D.F. Gleeson, *A History of the Diocese of Killaloe* (Dublin, 1962); I. Murphy, *The Diocese of Killaloe in the Eighteenth Century* (Dublin, 1991), *The Diocese of Killaloe 1800-1850* (Dublin, 1992), *The Diocese of Killaloe 1850-1904* (Dublin, 1995). See also *Molua* published annually by the diocese 1934-1959. For the Church of Ireland: Rev. P. Dwyer, *The Diocese of Killaloe from the Reformation to the close of the Eighteenth Century* (Dublin, 1878); E.A. Cooke, *The Diocesan History of Killaloe, Kilfenora, Clonfert and Kilmacduagh* (Dublin, 1886); A. Hewson (ed.), *Inspiring Stones: a history of the Church of Ireland Dioceses of Limerick, Ardfert, Aghadoe, Killaloe, Kilfenora, Clonfert, Kilmacduagh and Emly* (FAS, 1995). W. Neely, The Protestant Community of South Tipperary (1660-1815) in *THJ* (1991), pp. 132-40 and *THJ* (1992), pp. 132-39.

[220] Rev. St John D. Seymour, *The Succession of parochial clergy in the united diocese of Cashel & Emly* (Dublin, 1908); *The Diocese of Emly* (Dublin, 1913); *Church Plate and Parish Records – Diocese of Cashel & Emly* (Clonmel, 1930).

written.[221] There is an article about St Patrick's College, Thurles.[222] For Waterford diocese, which stretches into South Tipperary and includes for example Clonmel, Cahir and Carrick-on-Suir, see Power's work.[223] Religious orders have impacted greatly on the county and two works about the Franciscans are of interest, together with Fr Colmcille's study of the Cistercians in Tipperary.[224] Presbyterianism is less rigidly organized, for example not having a diocesan structure. Information on that religion in Tipperary is available in both a general account and a series of place-specific articles by David Butler.[225] This same writer's study of competing religious denominations in South Tipperary is the most important account of this topic.[226]

An unusual source on the administration of workhouses is the writings of a maverick Tipperary priest who had personal experience of several in the county.[227]

Triumphalia Chronologia … (Murphy)

John Gallanan, Miller — Book of Tipperary (Bassett)

CENSUS OF IRELAND, 1901.

(Two Examples of the mode of filling up this Table are given on the other side.)

FORM A.

No. on Form B.

RETURN of the MEMBERS of this FAMILY and their VISITORS, BOARDERS, SERVANTS, &c., who slept or abode in this House on the night of SUNDAY, the 31st of MARCH

NAME and SURNAME		RELATION to Head of Family	RELIGIOUS PROFESSION	EDUCATION	AGE	SEX	RANK, PROFESSION, OR OCCUPATION	MARRIAGE	WHERE BORN	IRISH LANGUAGE
James	Wheeler	Head of Family	R C	Read write	44	Male	General Dealer	Married	Limerick	
Mary	Wheeler	Wife	R C	Read	38	Female	House Keeper	Married	Cork	Irish & English
Lizzie	Wheeler	Daughter	R C	Read write	10	Female	Scholar	Single	Tipperary	
Bridget	Wheeler	Daughter	R C	Read write	7	Female	Scholar	Single	Tipperary	
Kate	Wheeler	Daughter	R C	Cant Read	3	Female	Scholar	Single	Tipperary	
John	Hogan	Boarder	R C	Read write	50	Male	Labourer	Single	Tipperary	
William	Whelan	Boarder	R C	Read write	55	Male	Labourer	Single	Waterford	
Dan	Hogan	Boarder	R C	Cant Read	60	Male	Pensioner	Single	Clair	

221 Sr M. Imelda, *Calendar of Papers of the Butler Archbishops of Cashel & Emly, 1712-1791* (1970); Sr M. Claude, *Calendar of Papers of Dr Thomas Bray Archbishop of Cashel & Emly, 1792-1820* (1966); Dom. M. Tierney, *Calendar of Papers of Dr Michael Slattery Archbishop of Cashel & Emly, 1834-1857* (1965); Dom. M. Tierney, *Calendar of Papers of Dr Patrick Leahy Archbishop of Cashel & Emly, 1857-1875* (1966); Dom. M. Tierney, *Calendar of Papers of Dr Thomas Croke Archbishop of Cashel & Emly, 1875-1902* (1965). See also: Mark Tierney, Cashel Diocesan Archives in W. Corbett & W. Nolan (eds.), *Thurles: The Cathedral Town - Essays in honour of Archbishop Thomas Morris* (Dublin, 1989). Fr C. O'Dwyer, Archbishop Butler's Visitation Book in *Arch. Hib.*, 33 (1975) and 34 (1977); C. Ó Laoí, How Cashel & Emly were United in *THJ* (1990), pp. 149-52. *Cashel & Emly Atlas* (Typescript, Thurles, 1970) and *Pobal Ailbe: Cashel & Emly Census of Population 1841-1971* (Typescript, Thurles, 1975).

222 Fr C. O'Dwyer, 'The Beleaguered Fortress' St Patrick's College Thurles, 1837-1987 in *Luceat* (1987).

223 P. Power, *Waterford and Lismore: a compendious history of the united dioceses* (Cork UP, 1937).

224 C.P. Meehan, *The rise and fall of the Irish Franciscan monasteries* (5th ed. Dublin, n.d.); J.F. O'Donnell, *Memories of the Irish Franciscans* (Dublin, 1871); F. Donovan (ed.), C. Ó Conbhuidhe OCSO, *The Cistercian Abbeys of Tipperary* (Dublin, 1999). See also M. Browne OSB & C Ó Clabaigh OSB (eds.), *The Irish Benedictines* (Dublin, 2005).

225 A.S. Cromie, *Controversy among Southern Presbyterians* (Typescript, Belfast, n.d.); D. Butler, Presbyterianism in the Fethard Area (1690-1919) in *THJ* (2000), pp. 64-72 and *THJ* (2001), pp. 129-38; Presbyterianism in Clonmel (1650-1977) in *THJ* (2003), pp. 81-102.

226 D.J. Butler, *South Tipperary 1570-1841 Religion, Land and Rivalry* (Dublin, 2006) [This book was launched in 2005].

227 Rev. J. Barry, *Life in an Irish Workhouse* (n.d.), *Personal Experiences in Clonmel Workhouse* (1887) and *Workhouse Iniquities Unveiled* (1888). For Barry see M. O'Dwyer, Fr John Barry – the Pauper Priest, 1841-1920 in *Boherlahan-Dualla Historical Journal* (2000), pp. 67-72.

THE ANNALS of the FOUR MASTERS

42

Section Six: Antiquarian Sources

Sketches (Cooper)

Writing to his friend and colleague George Petrie in 1834, twenty-eight year old John O'Donovan declared: "I can never open a book on Irish topography or history in which I do not find innumerable mistakes and unpardonable blunders". He went on to hope that their work would be different – a promise fulfilled by O'Donovan. Subsequent generations of researchers have made use of two great works associated with O'Donovan's name: the material generated during his work with the Ordnance Survey and his edition of the *Annals of the Four Masters*.

Working for the Ordnance Survey during the 1830s, O'Donovan travelled all over Ireland reporting to George Petrie in Dublin on antiquities and folklore.[228] These letters were not intended for publication but were part of an ambitious plan to publish comprehensive memoirs covering antiquities, topography and history, which would accompany and complement the relevant maps. For political and economic reasons, with the exception of Derry (1837), publication was suspended. O'Donovan's wide-ranging observations are all the more valuable and indeed poignant because he described a countryside soon to be ravaged and changed for ever by the Great Famine. The hundreds of letters sent by him from all over Ireland to the Ordnance Survey in Phoenix Park are now in the Royal Irish Academy. Fr Michael O'Flanagan made typescripts and while O.S. Letters have been published for some counties, those for Tipperary have not but are available in Tipperary Studies.[229] Place-names were an essential part of mapping the island and in this, O'Donovan's work was vital, investigating thousands of names. The results with respect to Tipperary are available in Tipperary Studies.[230]

---

[228] Petrie's best-known work: *The ecclesiastical architecture of Ireland Round Towers of Ireland* (2nd ed. Dublin, 1845). See P. Murray (ed.), *George Petrie (1790-1866): the rediscovery of Ireland's Past* (Cork, 2004).

[229] [Fr M. O' Flanagan], *Ordnance Survey Letters, County Tipperary*, 3 volumes. The county is discussed by barony and civil parish. See P. Boyne, *John O'Donovan (1806-1861): a biography* (Kilkenny, 1987). Note that Tipperary Studies has the Ordnance Survey Letters for some other counties. Also of interest: E. Patten, *Samuel Ferguson and the culture of nineteenth-century Ireland* (Dublin, 2004).

[230] *Ordnance Survey Name Books, County Tipperary*, 9 volumes.

Photo of
Derrynaflan Hoard (Courtesy of
the National Museum of Ireland)

In the early seventeenth-century, a handful of Irish scholars collected manuscript records of Irish history and created a new synthesis of the story of Ireland from earliest times to 1616. Known as the *Annals of the Kingdom of Ireland* but more familiarly as the 'Four Masters', the work was familiar to scholars but was not generally accessible. O'Donovan became familiar with the work during his research for the Ordnance Survey and with the encouragement of some of his colleagues began the task of preparing an edition for publication, with translation and annotation. The first three volumes appeared in 1848 and the remaining four volumes in 1851; some four thousand pages of text, translation, notes and index. Described by his biographer as "one of the most important events in our cultural history," these volumes and especially O'Donovan's scholarly notes on all aspects of Irish (and of course Tipperary) topography and history, are an invaluable resource. A second edition was published in 1856.[231] Covering some of the same ground, especially the sixteenth century but from a very different perspective is *Holinshed's Irish Chronicle*.[232] Holinshed is best remembered as a source much used by Shakespeare.

Around the same time as the 'Four Masters' were doing their work in Donegal, Geoffrey Keating was in Tipperary constructing a narrative of Ireland's past from myth and history.[233] "Although the historical Keating is no longer familiar, his writings have had an influence on Irish language and literature as significant as Shakespeare's role in relation to English. Less recognised, but no less influential, has been his role in shaping Irish people's perceptions of their own identity, their country, their history and their religion."[234]

O'Donovan followed on an earlier and less scholarly antiquarian tradition, for example Edward Ledwich and Charles Vallancey whose works did not impress.[235] Francis Grose in keeping with the spirit of the age succumbed to the romance of ruins, as did William Bartlett and George Petrie.[236] Austin Cooper (1759-1830) of the well-known Killenure (Dundrum) family sketched many of these ruins.[237]

Cormacs Chapel from Towers and Temples (Keane)

[231] J. O'Donovan (ed.), *Annals of the Kingdom of Ireland* (2nd ed. Dublin, 1856), 7 volumes. Of interest perhaps, the subscription list for the original edition and background: Rev. B. Jennings OFM, *Michael O Cleireig chief of the Four Masters and his associates* (Dublin, 1936).

[232] L. Miller & E. Power (eds.), *Holinshed's Irish Chronicle* (Dolmen, Dublin, 1979).

[233] G. Keating, *Foras Feasa ar Eirinn* (Irish Texts Society, 4 volumes, eds. D, Comyn (1902) and P.S. Dineen (1908, 1914). Also D. Comyn, *Vindication of the sources of Irish History by Dr Geoffrey Keating* (Gaelic League, n.d.).

[234] B. Cunningham, *The World of Geoffrey Keating: history, myth and religion in seventeenth-century Ireland* (Dublin, 2000). For someone so influential, Keating has been very inadequately remembered in his native county.

[235] E. Ledwich, *Antiquities of Ireland* (Dublin, 1804); C. Vallancey, *Collectanea de Rebus Hibernicis* (2nd ed. Dublin, 1786) 4 volumes.

[236] F. Grose, *The Antiquities of Ireland* (Dublin, 1794), 2 volumes; R. Stalley (ed.), *Daniel Grose (c.1766-1838) - The Antiquities of Ireland: a supplement to Francis Grose* (Dublin, 1991); W.H. Bartlett, *The Scenery and Antiquities of Ireland* (Dublin, n.d.), 2 volumes; G. Petrie, *Round Towers of Ireland* (2nd ed., Dublin, 1845). Also P. Murray (ed.), *George Petrie 1790-1866: The Rediscovery of Ireland's Past* (Cork, 2004).

[237] L. Price (ed.), *An Eighteenth Century Antiquary, The Sketches, Notes and Diaries of Austin Cooper (1759-1830)* (Dublin, 1942). See also P. Harbison, *Cooper's Ireland: Drawings and Notes from an Eighteenth-Century Gentleman* (Dublin, 2000).

Fethard from Town Wall Fortifications (Fleming)

Tipperary Studies hold a number of antiquarian works on Irish biography.[238] Researchers more often than not ignore these, together with antiquarian books on topography. For example, a book from the close of the seventeenth century has some interesting comments on the county and is a classic source on the relationship between man and landscape.[239] "Ware" is a frequently cited source in older history books and Tipperary Studies has a copy.[240] Also of interest are "Sleator", "Seward" and "Wakefield" and of course the well-known "Lewis".[241] The compilers of these books were great gatherers of facts, for example Ambrose Leet, but perhaps the greatest compendium, the *Parliamentary Gazetteer of Ireland* was published in the mid-1840s.[242]

Tipperary Studies has a number of first-hand accounts of visits to Tipperary, including the most entertaining, that by a German dilettante in the 1820s and the most informative, the 1770s report by an English agriculturalist.[243] For the visitor from Britain, Ireland was a disconcerting mix of the foreign and familiar and these differing accounts chart voyages of discovery that sometimes run aground on rocks of prejudice but all make fascinating reading. With the growth in tourism during

Towers and temples (Keane)

238 E. Lodge, *Portraits of Illustrious Personages of Great Britain* (London, 1835), 12 volumes; J. Wills, *Lives of Illustrious & Distinguished Irishmen from the earliest times to the present period* (Dublin, 1840), 10 volumes; A. Webb, *A Compendium of Irish Biography* (Dublin, 1878); J.S. Crone, *A Concise Dictionary of Irish Biography* (Dublin, 1928); Rev. J. O'Hanlon, *Lives of the Irish Saints* (Dublin, n.d.), 10 volumes; C. Plummer, *Lives of Irish Saints* (Oxford, 1922), 2 volumes.

239 *Camden's Britannia 1695* (Facsimile ed.) Co. Tipperary pp. 983-86.

240 Sir James Ware, *The Antiquities and History of Ireland* (Dublin, 1705). Also W. Harris, *Hibernica* (Dublin, 1770).

241 W.W. Seward, *Topographia Hibernica* (Dublin, 1795); Rev. M. Sleater, *Introductory essay to a new system of civil and ecclesiastical topography and itinerary of counties of Ireland* (Dublin, 1805), Co Tipperary, pp. 117-129; E. Wakefield, *An account of Ireland statistical and political* (London, 1812), 2 volumes; S.A. Lewis, *Topographical Dictionary of Ireland* (Dublin, 1837), 2 volumes and atlas.

242 A. Leet, *A Directory to the market towns, villages, gentlemen's seats and other noted places in Ireland* (Dublin, 1844); *Parliamentary Gazetteer of Ireland 1844-45* (Dublin, 1846), 10 volumes.

243 R. Caulfield (ed.), *Journal of the Very Rev. Rowland Davies LL.D Dean of Ross from 8 March 1688-9 to 29 Sept 1690* (Camden Society, 1857); J. Kelly (ed.), *The Letters of Lord Chief Baron Edward Willes to the Earl of Warwick 1757-1762 – an account of Ireland in the mid 18th century* (Aberystwyth, 1990); R. Twiss, *A Tour in Ireland in 1775* (London, 1776); A. Young, *A Tour in Ireland 1776-1779* (1st ed. 1780, Shannon, 1970), 2 volumes; T. Campbell, *A philosophical survey of the South of Ireland, in a series of letters* (London, 1777); S. Holmes, *Sketches of some of the southern counties of Ireland collected during a tour in the Autumn 1797 in a series of letters* (London, 1801); S. Grimes (ed..), *Ireland in 1804* (Dublin, 1980); Sir R. Colt Hoare, *Journal of a tour in Ireland A.D. 1806* (London, 1807); [M. Gough], *A Tour in Ireland in 1813 and 1814, with an appendix written in 1816 on another visit to that island, By an Englishman* (Dublin, 1817); T. Cromwell, *Excursions through Ireland...... forming a complete guide for the traveller and tourist* (London, 1820); (Prince Puckler-Muskau), *Tour in England, Ireland and France in the years 1828 & 1829 etc.* (Philadelphia, 1833) - See also C. Maxwell, *The Stranger in Ireland* (London, 1954); H.D. Inglis, *A Journey throughout Ireland during the spring, summer and autumn of 1834* (3rd ed., London, 1836), 2 volumes; Lady Chatterton, *Rambles in the South of Ireland during the year 1838* (London, 1859); J.G. Kohl, *Ireland* (London, 1843); T.C. Foster, *Letters on the condition of the people of Ireland* (2nd. Ed. London, n.d.); Mr & Mrs S.C. Hall, *Ireland, It's Scenery, Character etc.* (1st ed. London, 1841-3, new ed. London, n.d.).

the Victorian period, a range of guides were published, the most impressive in the Library being that by John Stokes, a guide to Lough Derg with wonderful panoramic scenes.[244]

In Tipperary the most prolific writer and publisher was the Cashel antiquarian John Davis White.[245] A useful source with respect to writers, giving both samples of their work and biographical information is *The Cabinet of Irish Literature*.[246] The Library holds some works of general antiquarian interest.[247]

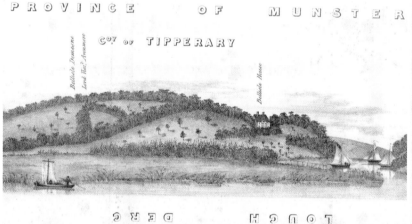

Towers and temples (Keane)

In the nineteenth and early twentieth centuries, gentlemen both clerical and lay, with education and leisure, produced regional histories, which are now eagerly sought by collectors. While they have for the most part been superseded by more modern research, they continue to be of value, not least because their authors made use of material from the old Public Record Office. While not relating to Tipperary, the Library has a collection of these books.[248]

Pictorial Survey and Tourists Guide to Lough Derg (Stokes)

---

244 G. Taylor & A. Skinner, *Maps of the Roads of Ireland* (1st. ed. 1778, Shannon, 1969); W. Stokes C.E., *Pictorial Survey and Tourist Guide to Lough Derg and the River Shannon* (London, 1842); *The Tourist's Illustrated Hand-Book of Ireland* (3rd ed. London, 1854)

245 J. Davis White, *Cashel of the Kings* (2nd. ed. 1876); *A Guide to the Rock of Cashel* (3rd. ed. 1888); *Anthologia Tipperariensis, being some accounts of the abbeys, priories, churches, castles and other objects of interest in the county of Tipperary* (Cashel, 1892); *Sixty Years in Cashel* (Cashel, 1893).

246 (K. Tynan Hinkson), *The Cabinet of Irish Literature* (London, 1902 ed.), 4 volumes.

247 W. Lynch, *A view of the legal institutions, honorary hereditary offices and feudal baronies established in Ireland during the reign of Henry II* (London, 1830); M. Archdall, *Monasticon Hibernicum* (London, 1786); Rev. M.J. Brenan OSF, *An Ecclesiastical History of Ireland from the introduction of Christianity into that country to the year 1829* (Dublin, 1840) 2 volumes; *Edward Earl of Clarendon, The History of the Rebellion and Civil Wars in Ireland* (London, 1720); Rev. J. Lanigan, *An Ecclesiastical History of Ireland* (Dublin, 1822) 4 volumes; G. Story, *An Impartial History of the Wars of Ireland etc.* (London, 1793); *Tracts on Ireland, political & statistical including Mr Scully's celebrated Statement of the Penal Laws* (Dublin, 1824); J.H. Wynne, *A General History of Ireland etc.* (London, 1773) only one volume, to death of William III.

248 Rev. J. Begley, *The Diocese of Limerick Ancient and Medieval* (Dublin, 1906); Rev. W. Carrigan, *The History and Antiquities of the Diocese of Ossory* (Dublin, 1905) 4 volumes – note the Index volume for this, published in 2005; C. Smith, *The Ancient and Present State of the County and City of Waterford* (Dublin, 1746); J. Hansard, *History of Waterford* (1870, reprint n.d.); Rev. P. White, *History of Clare and the Dalcassian Clans of Tipperary, Limerick and Galway* (Dublin, 1893). This volume has the bookplate of Seán T. Ó Ceallaigh; F.E. Ball, *A History of the County Dublin* (Dublin, 1902, 1979 ed.) 6 volumes; V. Rev. J. Canon O'Hanlon et al, *History of The Queens County* (1907 & 1914, Kilkenny, 1981 ed.) 2 volumes; Rev. H. Townsend, *Statistical Survey of the County of Cork* (Dublin, 1810).

Section Seven: Archaeology

The single most important and useful source is the archaeological inventory of County Tipperary, published in two volumes by Duchas The Heritage Service and part of the ongoing archaeological survey of Ireland.[249] This source gives "the monument classification in each case followed by a short description which includes its topographical location and any historical references". All ancient remains on the landscape are listed: different kinds of burials and enclosures, settlement and ecclesiastical sites, castles and tower houses, not excluding mills, weirs, mines, bridges and sweat houses. Illustrations and maps are plentiful. This source should be the first port of call for anyone looking for information about any ancient remains in the county. Due to special circumstances, the region around Moyne has seen comprehensive excavations.[250]

---

[249] J. Farrelly & C. O'Brien (eds.), *Archaeological Inventory of County Tipperary Vol. 1 – North Tipperary* (Dublin, 2002). At the time of writing, the volume for South Tipperary has not yet been published.

[250] M. Gowen, J. O'Neill, M. Phillips (eds.), *The Lisheen Mine Archaeological Project, 1996-98* (Bray, 2005). Also five volumes of unpublished reports.

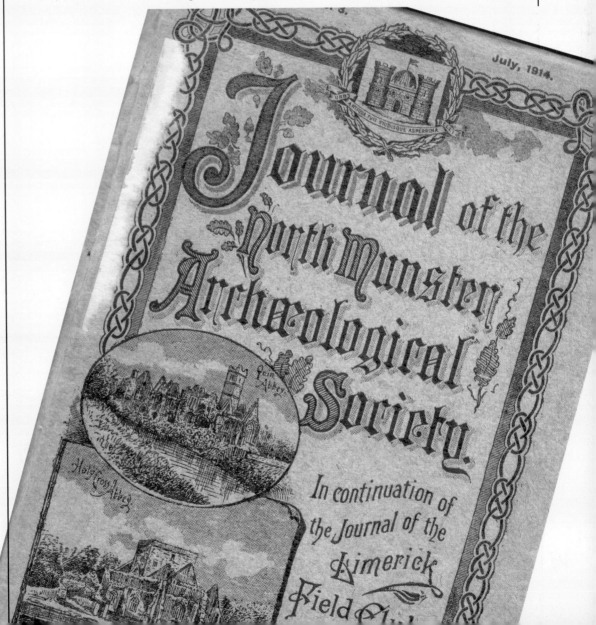

Since 1988, the most importance source for archaeological reports on County Tipperary is *Tipperary Historical Journal*.[251] In some sixty articles, sites throughout the county have been discussed and a great deal of new information made available, from prehistoric burial places to medieval churches and settlements. Of particular note are the comprehensive discussions of aspects of Cashel's settlement history published

Shanbally, Courtesy of the Irish Architectural Archive

[251] M.P. Cahalan & A.M.G. Hyland, Lough Nahinch Crannog in *THJ* (1988), pp. 15-21; E. Rynne, Some Preliminary Notes on the Excavation of Dolla Church Kilboy in *THJ* (1988), pp. 44-52; R.M. Cleary, A Mid-Seventeenth House at Drumlummin, Tubrid in *THJ* (1988), pp. 116-20; M.G. Doody, An Early Bronze Age Burial at Ballyveelish, Co Tipperary in *THJ* (1988), pp. 176-80; L. Wallace, Moorstown Castle – a Neglected Tower House near Clonmel in *THJ* (1989), pp. 17-19; C. Power, Archaeological Excavations at Glenbane in *THJ* (1989), pp. 137-45; M. Cahill, Two Gold Rings from Ardmayle, Co Tipperary in *THJ* (1989), pp. 146-48; M. Ryan & M. Bourke, Derrynaflan Ten Years On in *THJ* (1990), pp. 153-64; J. Waddell & P. Holland, The Pekaun Site: Duignan's 1944 Investigation in *THJ* (1990), pp. 165-86; R. Ó Floinn, The 'Tipperary Brooch' Reprovenanced in *THJ* (1990), pp. 187-92; P. Brennan, Effigial Slab at Athassel Priory in *THJ* (1990), pp. 193-95; G. Cooney, J. Feehan, E. Grogan & C. Stillman, Stone Axes in Co. Tipperary in *THJ* (1990), pp. 197-203; J. Feehan, Fulachta Fiadh in the South Midlands in *THJ* (1991), pp. 202-08; C. Manning, Toureen Peakaun: Three New Inscribed Slabs in *THJ* (1991), pp. 209-14; P. Holland, A Pipeline Trench at Cahir Castle in *THJ* (1991), pp. 215-17; M. Doody, A Bronze Age Ditched Enclosure at Ballyveelish, Co Tipperary in *THJ* (1991), pp. 218-27; D. Maher, Medieval Window Head at Fethard in *THJ* (1991), pp. 228-32; P. Holland, A Carved Stone & Other Late Medieval Fragments in Clonmel in *THJ* (1992), pp. 197-202; D. O'Regan, A Tower House and Ringfort at Pallas Upper, Borrisoleigh in *THJ* (1992), pp. 206-09; J. Sheehan, The Rathmooley Hoard and other Viking Age Silver from Co Tipperary in *THJ* (1992), pp. 210-16; G. Cooney, Irish Prehistoric Mortuary Practice – Baurnadomeeny Reconsidered in *THJ* (1992), pp. 223-29; M. Reilly Counihan, Five Undocumented Stone Figures in *THJ* (1992), pp. 230-31; M.G. Doody, The Bruff Aerial Photographic Survey in *THJ* (1993), pp. 173-80; W.J. Hayes, 'The Prior's Tomb' in Templemore Old Church in *THJ* (1993), pp. 186-88; M. Cahill, Two Gold Ornaments from near Tipperary in *THJ* (1993), pp. 189-93; R.M. Cleary, Medieval Town Walls at Emmet Street, Clonmel in *THJ* (1993), pp. 194-98; K. Daly, The Archaeological Survey of Co. Tipperary in *THJ* (1994), pp. 155-61; D. Maher, Derrynaflan: The Medieval Grave Slabs in *THJ* (1994), pp. 162-66; B. Hodkinson, Excavations at Cormac's Chapel, Cashel, 1992 and 1993 in *THJ* (1994), pp. 167-74; P. Holland, Late Medieval Structures in Clonmel: Further Remarks in *THJ* (1994), pp. 175-77; H. Carey, Borrisoleigh or Two-Mile-Borris? in *THJ* (1995), pp. 145-47; B.J. Hodkinson, The Medieval Priory of St Mary's, Cahir in *THJ* (1995), pp. 148-50; P. Holland et al, Clonmel Excavations since 1990 in *THJ* (1995), pp. 151-74; P. Harbison, A medieval carved wooden altar support (?) from St Patrick's Well, Clonmel in *THJ* (1995), pp. 175-76; D. Pollock, Medieval Midden in Mary Street Clonmel in *THJ* (1995), p 177; J. Farrelly, A recently discovered barrow cemetery in Nenagh in *THJ* (1995), pp. 178-80; P. Holland, A foundation deposit in Drangan? in *THJ* (1995), pp. 181-82; O. Scully, Clonmel Excavation in *THJ* (1996), pp. 175-78; D. Pollock, Excavations at Cahir Abbey in *THJ* (1996), pp. 179-90; M.G. Doody, Bronze Age Settlements in Co Tipperary: Fifteen Years of Research in *THJ* (1997), pp. 94-106; J. Farrelly & C. O'Brien, An unrecorded stone circle in North Tipperary in *THJ* (1997), pp. 107-11; C. Power, Clonmel Excavations in *THJ* (1997), pp. 112-23; T.E. Collins, The Medieval Town Defences of Cashel in *THJ* (1997), pp. 124-30; D. O'Keeffe, 18th century decorated gravestones: the Kilsheelan-Kilmurry group in *THJ* (1998), pp. 198-214; T. Collins, Hore Abbey Cashel: the archaeological record in *THJ* (1998), pp. 234-40; B. Hodkinson, Excavations in the gatehouse of Nenagh Castle 1996-97 in *THJ* (1999), pp. 162-82; M.G. O'Donnell, Excavations of a Section of the Rian Bó Phadraig near Ardfinnan in *THJ* (1999), pp. 183-89; E. O'Riordan, A second "Sheela" at Shanrahan in *THJ* (1999), pp. 197-98; R. Clutterbuck, Graystown: a later medieval settlement near Fethard in *THJ* (2000), pp. 157-72; J. O'Neill, A summary of investigations by the Lisheen Archaeological Project in *THJ* (2000), pp. 173-90; R. O'Brien, New archaeological finds at Killea Graveyard in *THJ* (2000), pp. 191-93; D. O'Keeffe, Instruments of the Passion on the gravestones of South Tipperary in *THJ* (2001), pp. 155-74; R. O'Brien, Nenagh bye-pass excavations, 1998-99 in *THJ* (2001), pp. 175-88; N. Finlay & P. Woodman, Trial Excavations at Ballybrado House, Cahir in *THJ* (2001), pp. 189-96; E. O'Donovan & S. Duffy, A deserted medieval village at Ballysheehan, Co Tipperary in *THJ* (2002), pp. 33-44; R. O'Brien, The Benedictine Priory of Kilcommon in *THJ* (2003), pp. 1-8; P. Stevens, 'The Munster Hotel' Cathedral Street, Thurles: Archaeological excavations 1998-99 in *THJ* (2003), pp. 9-30; E. O' Donovan et al, Excavations at Friar Street, Cashel: a story of urban settlement in *THJ* (2004), pp. 3-90.

Ballysheeda Castle, Courtesy of the Irish Architectural Archive

in 2004. The key archaeological event in the county was the discovery of the Derrynaflan treasures in 1980.[252]

In 1987, a year prior to the first issue of *Tipperary Historical Journal*, a new archaeology journal *Archaeology Ireland* came on the market. This is directed at the general reader and Tipperary Studies has a comprehensive holding. Apart from a host of general articles, all superbly illustrated, some material of specific Tipperary interest has been published.[253]

Holycross from Tour in Ireland (Holmes)

Due to more stringent planning regulations in recent years, archaeologists investigate a large number of sites.[254] Since 1999, an annual report or "excavations bulletin" has been published.[255] In 2000 for example, some sixty sites were listed for Tipperary.

The first report of the "Discovery Programme", a concerted archaeological investigation of various parts of the country, was published in 1992 and details the Emly region.[256] The survey of megalithic tombs in Tipperary was published in 1982.[257] While archaeology is not treasure hunting, the word "hoard" has a certain resonance.[258] The most common archaeological feature on the Irish landscape is the ringfort and the definitive work is Matthew Stout's monograph.[259] Round towers have received scholarly attention in recent years.[260] Peter Harbison's work is definitive on high crosses.[261] There is a very detailed work on 'inscribed stones' from six of Tipperary's best-known early church sites.[262] For

---

[252] Tipperary Studies has a comprehensive file of newscuttings and photographs. Also a copy of the 1987 Supreme Court judgement.

[253] Examples include 'The Prehistoric Dark Ages in North Munster' and 'Heritage Guide No. 6: Lackeen – c. Lorrha a late medieval settlement in Tipperary NR' in *Archaeology Ireland* 24 (1993); 'The archaeology of hurling' in *Archaeology Ireland* 45 (1998); 'A sight for sore eyes: a Hiberno-Roman curative cult at Golden Co Tipperary in *Archaeology Ireland* 60 (2002).

[254] For example: *Catalogue of artifacts and ecofacts: the Munster Hotel Cathedral Street Thurles* (Margaret Gowen & Co. Ltd, 2001).

[255] I. Bennett (ed.), *Excavations Bulletin – Excavations 1999: summary accounts of archaeological excavations in Ireland* (Wordwell, Bray, 2000), Tipperary Numbers 813-839; Bennett, *Excavations 2000* (Bray, 2002), Tipperary Numbers 909-970; Bennett, *Excavations 2001* (Bray, 2003), Tipperary Numbers 1188-1232; Bennett, *Excavations 2002*, (Bray, 2004), Tipperary Numbers 1683-1776.

[256] *Discovery Programme Reports 1 – Project Results 1992*.

[257] R. de Valera & S. Ó Nualláin, *Survey of Megalithic Tombs of Ireland – Vol. IV Counties Cork, Kerry. Limerick and Tipperary* (Dublin, 1982).

[258] G. Eogan, *Hoards of the Irish Later Bronze Age* (Dublin, 1983). See M. Ryan (ed.), *The Derrynaflan Hoard 1 – a preliminary account* (Dublin, 1983).

[259] M. Stout, *The Irish Ringfort* (Dublin, 1997). Also V.B. Proudfoot, *The Economy of the Irish Rath in Medieval Archaeology*, v, (1960-61), pp. 94-122. An older work is T.J. Westropp, *The Ancient Forts of Ireland* (Dublin, 1902).

[260] G.L. Barrow, *The Round Towers of Ireland* (Dublin, 1979); B. Lalor, *The Irish Round Tower: origins and architecture explored* (Collins, 1999); T. O'Keeffe, *Ireland's Round Towers* (Tempus, 2004).

[261] P. Harbison, *The High Crosses of Ireland* (Bonn, 1992) 3 volumes. Less academic: H. Richardson & J. Scarry, *An Introduction to Irish High Crosses* (Dublin, 1990) and R. Stalley, *Irish High Crosses* (Dublin, 1996).

[262] E. Kasha & K. Forsyth, *Early Christian Inscriptions of Munster: a Corpus of the Inscribed Stones* (Cork UP, 2001).

many years the standard general work on ancient man-made features on the Irish landscape was that of Sean P. O'Riordan.[263] Tipperary Studies has a number of older excavation reports.[264] A more popular and superbly illustrated book is also available.[265]

Sheela-na-Gigs are among the most intriguing artifacts from the medieval period. The theft of the Fethard example in 1990 aroused a great deal of interest.[266] Terence Barry's work on medieval settlement has valuable Tipperary material.[267] With reference to Tipperary, the north of the county has been better served.[268] Denise Maher discusses medieval grave slabs in the county and a summary of the work of Conrad Cairns on Tipperary tower houses has been published as a pamphlet. The thesis on which this is based is also available.[269] A more recent guide to Tipperary castles has been published.[270]

Pillar Stone, Powerstown, I.T.A. Survey

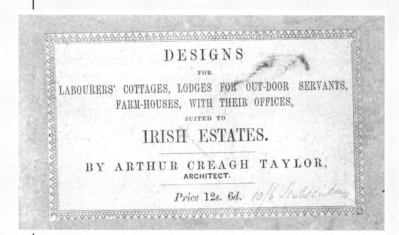

[263] S.P. O'Riordan, *Antiquities of the Irish Countryside* (1st ed. London, 1942). See also M.J. O'Kelly, *Early Ireland: an introduction to Irish Prehistory* (Cambridge UP, 1989); G. Cooney & E. Grogan, *Irish Prehistory: a social perspective* (Bray, 1994); J. Waddell, *The Prehistoric Archaeology of Ireland* (Galway UP, 1998); M.A. Monk & J. Sheehan (eds.), *Early Medieval Munster: archaeology, history and society* (Cork UP, 1998); T. O'Keeffe, *Medieval Ireland: an archaeology* (Tempus, 2000); M.J. O'Kelly, *Newgrange: Archaeology, Art & Legend* (London, 1982).

[264] H.G. Leask & R.A.S. Macalister, The partial excavation of a site at Liathmore or Leigh, Co Tipperary in *PRIA*, li (1951); R.A.S. Macalister & H.G. Leask, On some excavations recently conducted on Friar's Island, Killaloe in *JRSAI*, (1929); C. McNeill, Monaincha, Co Tipperary: Historical Notes in *JRSAI*, (1920); M.J. O'Kelly, A Horned-Cairn at Shanballyedmond, Co Tipperary in *JCHAS*, lxiii, 198, (1958), pp. 37-70; M.J. O'Kelly, A Wedge-Shaped gallery grave at Baurnadomeeny, Co Tipperary in *JCHAS*, lxv, 202 (1960), pp. 85-114; P.F. Wallace, A Prehistoric Burial Cairn at Ardcrony, Nenagh Co Tipperary in *N. Munster Arch. Jn.*, xix, (1977), pp. 3-19.

[265] J. O'Brien & P. Harbison, *Ancient Ireland* (London, 1996).

[266] J. O'Connor, *Sheela na Gig* (Fethard Historical Society, 1991); B. Freitag, *Sheela-na-Gigs: unravelling an enigma* (London, 2004); M. Concannon, *The Sacred Whore: Sheela Goddess of the Celts* (Collins Press, 2004); J. Andersen, *The Witch on the Wall* (London, 1977). Also a file on Thurles Sheela-na-Gig (J.Condon).

[267] T.B. Barry, *The Medieval Moated Sites of South-Eastern Ireland: Counties Carlow, Kilkenny, Tipperary and Wexford* (BAR 35, 1977); T.B. Barry, *The Archaeology of Medieval Ireland* (London, 1987); T. Barry (ed.), *A History of Settlement in Ireland* (London, 2000). See also K.D. O'Conor, *The Archaeology of Medieval Rural Settlement in Ireland* (RIA, Dublin, 1998) and A. O'Sullivan, *The Archaeology of Lake Settlement in Ireland* (RIA, Dublin, 1998).

[268] G. Cunningham, *The Anglo-Norman Advance into the South-West Midlands of Ireland 1185-1221* (Roscrea, 1987); G.T. Stout, *Archaeological Survey of the Barony of Ikerrin* (Roscrea, 1984); C. Manning (ed.), *Excavations at Roscrea Castle* (Dublin, 2003).

[269] D. Maher, *Medieval Grave Slabs of County Tipperary, 1200-1600* (BAR 262, 1997); C.T. Cairns, *Irish Tower Houses: a Co. Tipperary case study* (Dublin, 1987).

[270] M. Salter, *The Castles of North Munster* (Folly Publications, 2004).

Section Eight: Heritage

"Heritage" is a much-abused word. At its most debased it can mean the packaging for quick sale of a spurious version of Irish culture. At its best, the word refers to our inheritance from the past, both material and cultural: language, landscape, buildings, and the arts. At a deeper level, heritage encompasses what we see in our environment and how we react to what we see. In other words, heritage provides the context within which we find and express our identity. The most comprehensive discussion of all aspects of Irish heritage is *The Heritage of Ireland*.[271] Topics covered include archives, archaeology, architecture, art, conservation, dance, film, folklore,

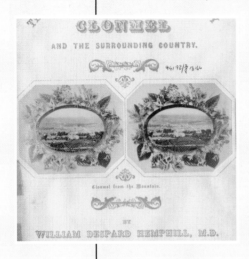

genealogy, history, language, libraries, museums, music, place-names, science, sport, and storytelling. While its regional case studies do not deal with Tipperary, the *Atlas of the Irish Rural Landscape* is an excellent introduction to all aspects of the countryside: bogs, forests, fields, buildings, towns and villages, demesnes, communications and mining, power and water.[272]

John Feehan provides the best introduction to the impact of farming on the landscape.[273] The 1907 royal commission on canals and waterways has evidence about the navigation of the Suir.[274] The relationship between heritage and tourism is discussed in a study from 1995.[275] Tipperary Studies has

---

[271] N. Buttimer, C. Rynne, H. Guerin, *The Heritage of Ireland* (Cork, 2000).

[272] F.H.A. Aalen, K. Whelan & M. Stout (eds.), *Atlas of the Irish Rural Landscape* (Cork UP, 1997). Also, Lord Killanin & M.V. Duigan (eds.), *Shell Guide to Ireland* (London, 1962 and subsequent eds.); P. Harbison, *Guide to National and Historic Monuments of Ireland* (Dublin, 1992 ed.); A.G. Moore, *Contributions towards a Cybele Hibernica, being outlines of the geographical distribution of plants in Ireland* (2nd ed., London 1898); J. Feehan & G. O'Donovan, *The Bogs of Ireland* (UCD, 1996).

[273] J. Feehan, *Farming in Ireland: History, Heritage and Environment* (UCD, 2003).

[274] *Royal commission on canals and waterways, vol ii, part ii* [Cd. 3717], 1907. For the Suir see anonymous article Irish Rivers No. IX: The Suir in *Dublin University Magazine*, xlii, pp. 208-16, 323-37.

[275] K.A. Griffin, *The Operation and Organisation of Irish Tourism: Lough Derg – a Local Study* (Typescript, 1995).

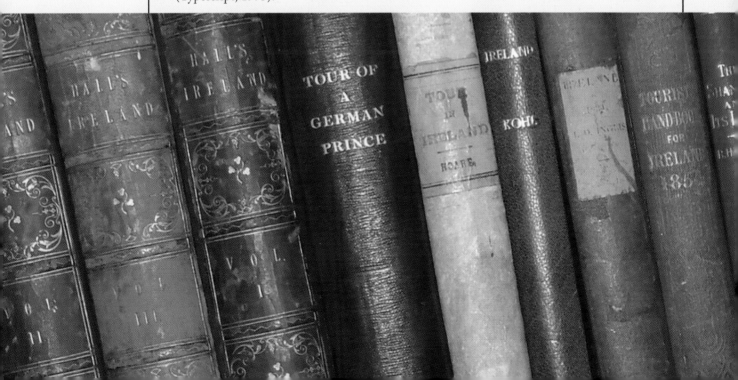

one volume of a late nineteenth-century Irish tourism journal.[276] Perhaps its greatest treasure is a two-volume reproduction of the *Book of Kells*.[277]

There are some useful guides to Irish buildings, especially Williams who has a valuable section on Tipperary.[278] Architectural inventories are available with respect to North and South Tipperary and also two Tipperary towns, Clonmel and Roscrea.[279] Perhaps the most assertive imposition on the landscape is the 'Big House'. Dating from the eighteenth and nineteenth centuries and varying from aggressive statements of status to more comfortable family homes, they were all focal points of an estate system that radically transformed the Irish landscape. The standard guide is by Mark Bence-Jones, which includes entries, with photographs, for most of these houses in Tipperary.[280] Tipperary Studies also holds a number of related books.[281] James Pain was a well-known nineteenth-century architect, especially of church buildings.[282]

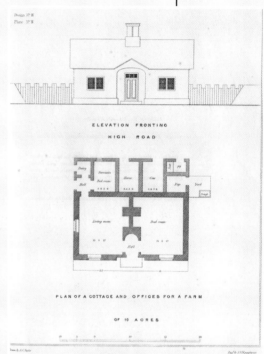

Plans for Killenure from Sketches (Cooper)

While the 'Big House' has attracted a good deal of attention, there are sources with respect to fortified dwellings, an architecture where security mattered much more than comfort.[283] The Library also holds monographs about 'everyday' urban architecture,[284]

Designs (Taylor)

[276] *The Irish Tourist* (Vol.1 no.1 June 1894 to Vol 1 No.6 Oct 1894).

[277] Two volumes, plus Introduction (Bern, 1950).

[278] J. Williams, *A Companion Guide to Architecture in Ireland 1837-1921* (Dublin, 1994); S. Rothery, *A Field Guide to the Buildings of Ireland* (Dublin, 1997).

[279] M. Craig & W. Garner, *National Heritage Inventory: buildings of architectural, historic and artistic interest in Tipperary SR – a preliminary survey* (Unpublished, An Foras Forbartha Teoranta, 1975); Anon., *Buildings of Architectural Interest in Tipperary NR* (Unpublished, An Foras Forbartha, 1972); *Clonmel Architectural Heritage, Study* (Unpublished, Duchas 1997) 2 volumes; *Roscrea Architectural Heritage Study* (Unpublished, Duchas, 2000) 2 volumes.

[280] M. Bence-Jones, *A Guide to Irish Country Houses* (Revised ed. London, 1988).

[281] Knight of Glin, D.J. Griffin, N.K. Robinson, *Vanishing Country Houses of Ireland* (Dublin, 1988); R. MacDonnell, *The Lost Houses of Ireland* (London, 2002); B. de Breffny & R. ffolliott, *The Houses of Ireland* (London, 1975); D. Guinness & W. Ryan, *Irish Houses and Castles* (London, 1971); J. O'Brien & D. Guinness, *Great Irish Houses and Castles* (London, 1992); S. O'Reilly, *Irish Houses & Gardens from the articles of Country Life* (London, 1998); P. Somerville Large, *The Irish Country House* (London, 1995); B. de Breffny, *Castles of Ireland* (London, 1977); E. Malins & Knight of Glin, *Lost Demesnes: Irish Landscape Gardening 1660-1845* (London, 1976); M. Bence Jones, *Life in an Irish Country House* (London, 1996); M. Craig, *Classic Irish Houses of the Middle Size* (London, 1976); F. O'Kane, *Landscape Design in Eighteenth Century Ireland: mixing foreign trees with the natives* (Cork UP, 2004); C.S. Sykes, *Country House Camera* (London, 1980).

[282] D. Lee, *James Pain, Architect* (Limerick Civic Trust, 2005).

[283] H.G. Leask, *Irish Castles and Castellated Houses* (Dundalk, 1941); P.M. Kerrigan, *Castles and Fortifications in Ireland, 1485-1945* (Cork, 1995); D. Sweetman, *The Medieval Castles of Ireland* (Cork, 1999); H. Coleman, *Farney Castle, County Tipperary* (Typescript, 1970); C.T. Cairns, *Irish Tower Houses, a County Tipperary case study* (Dublin, 1987); M. Salter, *The Castles of North Munster* (Folly Publications, 2004).

[284] P. & M. Shaffrey, *Buildings of Irish Towns: treasures of everyday architecture* (Dublin, 1983).

cover illustration, Margaret Leahy

vernacular rural architecture,[285] Cistercian Monasteries,[286] Romanesque architecture.[287] The definitive guide to medieval religious foundations is Gwynn & Hadcock, an indispensable source.[288]

The geographer E. Estyn Evans was one of the first to call academic attention to wide definitions of culture and heritage.[289] For a long time Freeman's was the textbook of Irish geography.[290] More recently, the *Atlas of the Irish Rural Landscape* has wonderfully presented aspects of Irish material culture.[291] An important discussion on sources is found in Toby Barnard's book.[292]

Tipperary Studies has monographs on a variety of topics, all part of our material heritage: dress,[293] windows,[294] holy wells,[295] the festival of Lughnasa,[296] public sculpture,[297] Church of Ireland churches,[298] traditional crafts,[299] mills,[300] railways,[301] distilleries,[302] clockmakers,[303] photographs,[304] coinage,[305] Irish flora.[306]

[285] K. Flynn, *Social Origins of Vernacular Farmhouses in Doon Co Tipperary (sic) Ireland* (Unpublished typescript – presented to the School of Architecture and Landscape, Thames Polytechnic, 1983-84). Of interest also is A. Creagh Taylor, *Designs for Agricultural Building suited to Irish Estates etc.* (Dublin, 1841).

[286] R. Stalley, *The Cistercian Monasteries of Ireland* (Yale UP, 1987).

[287] T. O'Keeffe, *Romanesque Ireland: architecture and ideology in the twelfth century* (Dublin, 2003).

[288] A. Gwynn & R.N. Hadcock, *Medieval Religious Houses Ireland* (1st ed. 1970, Dublin, 1988). See also H.G. Leask, *Irish Churches and Monastic Buildings* (Dundalk, 1996 ed.) 3 volumes.

[289] E. Estyn Evans, *Irish Heritage* (Dundalk, 1958) and *The Personality of Ireland* (Cambridge, 1973).

[290] T.W. Freeman, *Ireland* (London, 1950).

[291] F.H.A. Aalen, K. Whelan & M. Stout (eds.), *Atlas of the Irish Rural Landscape* (Cork UP, 1997).

[292] T. Barnard, *A guide to sources for the history of material culture in Ireland, 1500-2000* (Dublin, 2005).

[293] H.F. McClintock, *Handbook on the Traditional Old Irish Dress* (Dundalk, 1958); M. Dunlevy, *Dress in Ireland* (London, 1989). Much older than these: J.C. Walker, *An historical essay on the dress of the ancient and modern Irish* (Dublin, 1788).

[294] N. Roche, *The Legacy of Light – a history of Irish Windows* (Bray, 1999).

[295] A. Rackard & L O'Callaghan, *Fishstonewater – Holy Wells of Ireland* (Cork, 2001).

[296] M. MacNeill, *The Festival of Lughnasa, a study of the survival of the Celtic festival of the beginning of the harvest* (UCD, 1982).

[297] J. Hill, *Irish Public Sculpture: A History* (Dublin, 1998).

[298] S. Hutchinson, *Towers, Spires and Pinnacles: a history of the cathedrals and churches of the Church of Ireland* (Bray, 2003).

[299] D. Shaw-Smith, *Traditional Crafts of Ireland* (London, 2003).

[300] W.E. Hogg, *The Millers and the Mills of Ireland of about 1850* (Author, 1997).

[301] K.A. Murray & D.B. McNeill, *The Great Southern & Western Railway* (Irish Railway Record Society, 1976); B. Pender, H. Richards, *Irish Railways Today* (Transport Research Associates, 1967); S. Johnson, *Johnson's Atlas & Gazetteer of the Railways of Ireland* (Leicester, 1997); B. Mac Aongusa, *Broken Rails, crashes and sabotage on Irish railways* (Blackrock, 2005).

[302] B. Townsend, *The Lost Distilleries of Ireland* (Glasgow, 1997).

[303] W.G. Stuart, *Watch and Clockmakers in Ireland* (Dublin, 2000); G. Fennell, *A History of Irish Watch and Clock Makers* (Dublin, 1963).

[304] E.E. O'Donnell (ed.), *Father Browne's Images of Tipperary* (Dublin, 2001); Three collections of photographs by Nenagh photographer Pádraig Ó Flannabhra, *Ireland Beyond the Pale* (Dolmen, 1986), *Eire ar an Imeall Ireland on the Fringe* (TAL, 1993), *Turning a Blind Eye: images of Ireland in the 1990s* (TAL, 1997).

[305] Anon, *Coinage of Saorstat Eireann, 1928* (Government Publication, Dublin, n.d.) – features the Percy Metcalfe designs.

[306] C. Nelson, *An Irish Florilegium, wild and garden plants of Ireland* (London, 1983).

MARGUERITE, COUNTESS OF BLESSINGTON

Section Nine: Women's Studies

Even the most casual reading of the preceding eight sections of this Guide reinforces a simple point: there are a great many men and very few women. With the development and growth of women's history over the past few decades, this imbalance is beginning to change. However, at the level of local or regional studies, examination of the role of women is barely underway. One of the key academics contributing to this examination nationally is Clonmel-native Maria Luddy. Her 'agenda for women's history in Ireland' and 'women's history project: some sources for the history of Tipperary' are the best starting points.[307] Maria Luddy has made many other contributions to women's history.[308]

Tipperary Historical Journal has published a number of articles about the role of women in the county.[309] The notorious burning of Bridget Cleary in 1895, which

---

[307] An agenda for women's history in Ireland: M. Mac Curtain & M. O'Dowd, Part 1- 1500-1800; M. Luddy, Part II – 1800-1900 in *Irish Historical Studies* xxviii, 109 (1992), pp. 1-37; M. Luddy, The Women's History Project: some sources for the history of Tipperary in *THJ* (2001), pp. 33-42. See also *A Directory of Sources for Women's History in Ireland* (CD-ROM).

[308] M. Luddy & C. Murphy (eds.), *Women Surviving: studies in Irish Women's History in the 19th & 20th centuries* (Dublin, 1989); M. Luddy (ed.), *The Diary of Mary Mathew* (Co Tipperary Historical Society, 1991); M. Luddy, *Women and Philanthropy in Nineteenth-Century Ireland* (Cambridge UP, 1995); M. Cullen & M. Luddy (eds.), *Women, Power and Consciousness in 19th Century Ireland: eight biographical studies* (Dublin, 1995); M. Luddy, *Hanna Sheehy Skeffington* (Historical Association of Ireland, 1995); M. Luddy (ed.), *Women in Ireland, 1800-1918: A Documentary History* (Cork UP, 1995); M. Cullen & M. Luddy (eds.), *Female Activists: Irish Women and Change 1900-1960* (Dublin, 2001); M. Luddy (ed.), *The Crimean Journals of the Sisters of Mercy 1854-56* (Dublin, 2004); M. Luddy, Women's History in L.M. Geary & M. Kelleher (eds.), *Nineteenth century Ireland; a guide to recent research* (UCD Press, 2005).

[309] E. Bell, Lena Rice of New Inn in *THJ* (1988), pp. 13-14; M. Fitzgerald, Margaret Ryan, Poet of Garrynoe in *THJ* (1991), pp. 129-31; N. Higgins, Julia Kavanagh (1824-1877) – a novelist from Thurles in *THJ* (1992), pp. 81-83; M. Luddy, Presentation Convents in County Tipperary: 1806-1900 in *THJ* (1992), pp. 84-95; M. Luddy, Women & Work in Clonmel: Evidence from the 1881 Census in *THJ* (1993), pp. 95-101; M. Luddy, District Nursing in Ireland, 1815-1974 in *THJ* (1996), pp. 164-70; A. Bourke, The burning of Bridget Cleary: newspapers and oral tradition in *THJ* (1998), pp. 112-27; N. Beary-Ó Cleirigh, Marlfield's coloured embroidery industry and Lady Aberdeen in *THJ* (2000), pp. 20-24; A.M. Chadwick, Alice O'Sullivan, Clonmel missionary and martyr (1836-1870) in *THJ* (2001), pp. 83-88; A. McCan, The Roman Princess from Tipperary in *THJ* (2002), pp. 91-96.

Knockgraffon (Herbert)

took place near Fethard and which seemed a throw-back to an earlier age, has prompted two monographs, the first excellent, the second not so remarkable.[310] Only a handful of women associated with Tipperary have received attention from biographers: Daisy Bates, Clementina Viscountess Hawarden, Agnes Ryan, Anna Doyle Wheeler, Aleen Cust and Catherine Mahon.[311] Not exactly household names. Ranging from anthropology in Australia, photography in London, business in Dublin, female autonomy, female professional education and trade union leadership, the passions of these women were unusual. Similarly, only a handful of Tipperary

women have left us first-hand accounts of their lives, the most important being the journals of Dorothea Herbert.[312]

No group of women had a bigger impact on the country than the various congregations of nuns.[313] Only in one instance has the interaction between convent and local community been examined in detail.[314] Accounts are available of a number of other convents in the county.[315] The Sisters of Mercy, one of the leaders being a sister of Archbishop Croke, played an important role in the Crimea during that war. Apart from the book edited by Maria Luddy mentioned above, there is an older study.[316]

Pharmacy advert
Thurles

---

310 A. Bourke, *The Burning of Bridget Cleary: a true story* (London, 1999); J. Hoff & M. Yeates, *The Cooper's Wife is Missing* (New York, 2000). Also A. Bourke, Reading a Woman's Death: colonial text and oral tradition in 19th century Ireland in *Feminist Studies*, 21, 3 (1995), pp. 553-86. Tipperary Studies has a comprehensive file of contemporary newscuttings about the killing.

311 J. Blackburn, *Daisy Bates in the Desert* (London, 1994); C. Mavor, *Becoming: The Photographs of Clementina, Viscountess Hawarden* (Duke UP, 1999) and V. Dodier, *Clementina, Lady Hawarden: Studies from Life 1857-1864* (V & A Publications, n.d.); I.M. Ní Riain, *The Life & Times of Mrs A.V. Ryan* (Author, n.d.); D. Dooley, Anna Doyle Wheeler in M. Cullen & M. Luddy (eds.), *Women, Power & Consciousness in Nineteenth Century Ireland* (Dublin, 1995) and D. Dooley, *Equality in Community: sexual equality in the writings of William Thompson and Anna Doyle Wheeler* (Cork, 1996); C.M. Ford, *Aleen Cust Veterinary Surgeon: Britain's First Woman Vet* (Author, 1990); S. Chuinneagáin, *Catherine Mahon: first woman president of the INTO* (INTO, 1998).

312 D. Herbert, *Retrospections of Dorothea Herbert 1770-1806* (Dublin, 1988 ed.); M. Luddy (ed.), *The Diary of Mary Mathew* (Thurles, 1991); E. Butler Battle Artist, *Autobiography* (1st ed. 1922, 1993 ed.); E. Gormanston [Butler], *A Little Kept* (London, 1953); M. Healy, *For the Poor and for the Gentry* (Dublin, 1989); M. Quarton, *Breakfast the Night Before: recollections of an Irish Horse Dealer* (Dublin, 2000); H. Cooke, *Rectory Days* (Portlaw, 2002).

313 C. Clear, *Nuns in Nineteenth Century Ireland* (Dublin, 1987). Also T.J. Walsh, *Nano Nagle and the Presentation Sisters* (Dublin, 1959).

314 D.G. Marnane, *'A Lamp Kindled': The Sisters of Mercy and Tipperary Town* (Tipperary, 2000).

315 T. Prior & G. Cunningham (eds.), *The Convent of the Sacred Heart Roscrea 1842-1992* (Roscrea, 1992); Sr M. Lillis, *200 Years Agrowing: the story of the Ursulines in Thurles 1787-1987* (Thurles 1987); Sr C. Meagher, The Presentation Sisters in B. Moloney (ed.), *Times to Cherish: Cashel & Rosegreen Parish History 1795-1995* (Cashel, 1994); Sr Liguori, Presentation Convent Thurles 1817-1917 in W. Corbett & W. Nolan (eds.), *Thurles The Cathedral Town: essays in honour of Archbishop Thomas Morris* (Dublin, 1989); *The Story of St Mary's Secondary School, Nenagh* (Committee, 2000).

316 E. Bolster, *The Sisters of Mercy in the Crimean War* (Cork, 1964).

The Tipperary writer L.M. McCraith wrote a popular work on heroic Irishwomen –from Queen Macha to Anne Devlin.[317] Tipperary Studies has a small collection of books dealing with a variety of related topics, not specifically dealing with Tipperary but all casting light on the role of women in the development of Ireland. Topics include: the revolutionary movement,[318] politics[319] and socio-economic history.[320] There is also a work on the Irish Countrywoman's Association.[321]

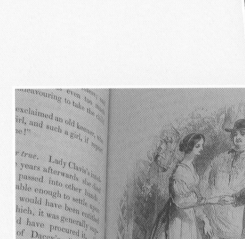

Sketches of Irish Character
(Hall)

---

[317] L.M. McCraith, *The Romance of Irish Heroines* (1st ed. 1913, this ed. Dublin, 1924).

[318] S. McCoole, *No Ordinary Women: Irish Female Activists in the Revolutionary Years 1900-1923* (Dublin, 2003); M. Broderick, *Wild Irish Women: extraordinary lives from history* (Dublin, 2001).

[319] M. McNamara & P. Mooney (eds.), *Women in Parliament: Ireland 1918-2000* (Dublin, 2000); M. Ward, *Hanna Sheehy Skeffington: a life* (Cork UP, 1997).

[320] M. Hill, *Women in Ireland: a century of change* (Belfast, 2003); C. Clear, *Woman of the House: women's household work in Ireland 1922-1961 – discourses, experiences, memories* (Dublin, 2000); J. Robbins, *Nursing and Midwifery in Ireland in the 20th century* (Dublin, 2000); N. Ó Cleirigh, *Hardship and Hard Living: Irish Women's Lives* (Dublin, 2003); R. Cullen Owens, *A Social History of Women in Ireland, 1870-1970* (Dublin, 2005); R.B. Finnegan & J.L. Wiles (eds.), *Women and Public Policy in Ireland: a documentary history, 1922-1997* (Dublin, 2005).

[321] S. McNamara, *Those Intrepid United Irishwomen: pioneers of the ICA* (Author, 1995); D. Duggan & N. O'Malley, *ICA South Tipperary Federation: development and history, 1941-1996* (Tipperary, 1996).

Section Ten:
Leabhair Ghaeilge (Donnchadh Ó Duibhir)

Réamhrá

Toisc nár mhór a líon ní dhearnadh ach cúig roinn de na leabhair Ghaeilge atá sa Leabharlann Tagartha i nDúrlas Éile, mar atá: Ársaíocht, Dúchas, Riail agus Reacht, Litríocht Chruthaitheach agus Foinsí Tagartha. Ina dhiaidh sin, ba dheacair a rá cén roinn a gcuirfí leabhar faoi leith ann, agus, go deimhin, níor lia duine ná tuairim faoi. An té a bheadh ag súil le leabhar áirithe a fháil i roinn amháin, más ea, seans gur i roinn eile a leagfadh sé a lámh air. Tharlódh, leis, an leabhar céanna bheith i liosta an Bhéarla agus i liosta na Gaeilge chomh maith, *Annála Ríoghachta Éireann*, mar shampla.

Séard atá sa chatalóg seo ná áireamh ar na leabhair Ghaeilge a bhaineann le Tiobraid Árann. Áirítear, freisin, leabhair nach bhfuil baint díreach acu leis an gcontae, ach go meastar tábhacht a bheith leo. Tá go leor leabhar Gaeilge eile scaipthe ar fud an chontae ins na leabharlanna áitiúla, ach cloítear go dlúth sa chlár seo leis an Leabharlann Tagartha

Táim buíoch de Mháire Uí Dhiarmada agus d'fhoireann na leabharlainne as ucht a gcineáltais agus a gcabhrach. Táim faoi chomaoin, leis, ag an Dr. Liam Mac Peaircín, Coláiste Mhuire gan Smál, Luimneach, a léigh na profaí dom.

A: Ársaíocht

An té a bheadh ag tóraíocht eolais ar chóras dlí na hÉireann mar a bhí fadó, níor mhór dó an *Senchas Már* a cheadú i dtús báire, nó leabhar a bheadh ag tarraingt as.[322] Seans gurb é an leabhar is luachmhaire sa roinn seo é ó thaobh airgid de, ach *Annála Ríoghachta Éireann* a fhágaint as an áireamh. Macasamhail de lámhscríbhinn atá in Ollscoil na Tríonóide atá ann. Meastar gur i dtuaisceart lár na tíre a breacadh í.

---

[322] R.I. Best, R. Thurneysen (eag.), *The Oldest Fragments of the Senchas Már* (B.Á.C., 1931).

Fada go leor siar, leis, do *Leabhar na hUidhre*,[323] a scríobhadh san 11ú haois. Tá an-iomrá ar an leagan den *Táin* atá ann, é simplí, gonta. Ar ndóigh, is é an *Táin* eipic mhór na Gaeilge agus é ar cheann de na scéalta is luaithe a scríobhadh síos i dteanga na ndaoine san Eoraip. Níor fágadh an leabharlann gan aistriúcháin air,[324] agus is mór go deo an mhaise ar leabhar Mary Hutton léaráidí áille Sheáin Mhic Chathmhaoil. Tá go leor téacsanna eile i *Leabhar na hUidhre:* scéalta Rúraíochta, *Immram Brain, Scéla Laí Brátha, Fís Adomnán*, mar shamplaí. As an leabhar céanna a baineadh *Fled Bricrend*,[325] agus tá athinsint ar *Immram Brain* agus seanscéalta eile in *Scéalaíocht na Ríthe*,[326] ina bhfuil léaráidí taibhseacha le Micheál Mac Liammóir.

Leabhar eile a bhaineann leis an tSeanGhaeilge is ea *Auraicept na nÉces, The Scholars' Primer*,[327] a leagtar ar Cheann Fhaolaidh. Fuair seisean bás sa bhliain 679, de réir an tseanchais. Tráchtas gramadaí is ea é, agus an cuma ar an scéal gur bhain an t-údar feidhm as *Origines*, saothar dá shórt le Naomh Isadóir Seville.

Tugtaí an-aird ar *Lebor Gabála Érenn*[328] tráth, ach ní ghlactar mar fhíorstair anois le cuid mhaith de. Cuntas atá ann ar na hionraí éagsúla a rinneadh ar Éirinn, ar na Fir Bolg, ar Thuatha Dé Danann agus a leithéidí agus cur síos ar ríthe na tíre go haimsir na Normannach. San 11ú haois a cumadh an chéad chuid de.

Bolscaireacht ar mhaithe leis na Brianaigh atá in *Cogadh Gaedheal le Gallaibh*,[329] ach níl fáil sa leabharlann ar stocaireacht Eoghanacht Chaisil, is é sin *Caithréim Chellacháin Chaisil*.

Ba é Cathal Mac Finghuine, rí na Mumhan, a bhí faoi bhroid in *Aislinge Meic Conglinne*.[330] Craosdeamhan a lonnaigh ina bholg a chuir air bheith ag creacadh na tíre le hairc is le hamplacht itheacháin, go dtí gur leigheas Mac Conglinne é. Scanradh a bhfuil de chur síos ar shaghasanna bídh ann, ach is é an aoir is an t-imdheargadh a dhéantar ar an gcléir an gné is suntasaí de, bfhéidir. A mhalairt ar fad de ghalar a bhuail Oengus in aisling eile,[331] galar an ghrá, d'fág claoite, tréith é, gan faobhar ar bith ar a ghoile.

---

[323] R.I. Best, O. Bergin (eag.), *Lebor na hUidre* (B.Á.C., 1929).

[324] Joseph Dunn, *The Ancient Irish Epic Tale, Táin Bó Cualnge* (Londain, 1914); Mary Hutton, *The Táin* (B.Á.C., 1907).

[325] George Henderson (eag.), *Fled Bricrend* (Londain, 1899).

[326] Tomás Ó Floinn (eag.), *Scéalaíocht na Ríthe* (B.Á.C., 1956); K.Meyer, A.Nutt, *The Voyage of Bran* (Londain, 1899).

[327] George Calder (eag.), *Auraicept na n-Éces* (B.Á.C., 1917).

[328] R.A.S. Macalister,(eag.), *Lebor Gabála Érenn* (Londain,1938,1939,1940,1941,1956), 5 iml.

[329] James Henthorn Todd (eag.), *Cogadh Gaedel re Gallaibh* (Londain, 1867).

[330] K. Meyer (eag.), *Aislinge Meic Conglinne* (Nua Eabhrach, 1974) eagrán nua; an chéad eagrán, Londain, 1892.

[331] Francis Shaw S.J.,(eag.), *Aislinge Oenguso* (B.Á.C., 1934).

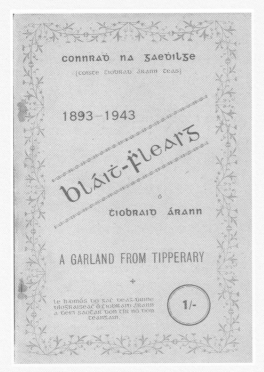

Faighimíd léargas ar luathstair na hÉireann in *Annála Inis Faithleann*.[332] Ceaptar gur ó cháipéisí a bhain le mainistir Imligh a scríobhadh na hannála tosaigh timpeall na bliana 1092, cé gur i mainistir Inis Faithleann i Loch Léin a breacadh an chuid deireannach. Ábhar suime linn roinnt mhaith de, a leithéid seo don bhliain 1192: "Ár mór la hUa Briain ar Gallaib a cath Durlais Ua Fhocarta."

Ar ndóigh, is iad *Annála Ríoghachta Éireann*[333] na hannála is mó atá i mbéal an phobail ó rinne an Donnabhánach eagarthóireacht agus aistriúchán orthu idir 1847 agus 1851, beart a chuir buanchomaoin ar aos staire na tíre. B'é an bráthair bocht Micheál Ó Cléirigh agus a chomhleacaithe a scríobh an bunleagan idir 1632 agus 1636. Thug seisean cuairt ar Chaiseal agus é i mbun taighde. Ba mhór aige approbatio ar a shaothar a fháil ó "Fhlann Mac Cairpre Mic Aedhaccáin, ó Bhaile Mhic Aedhaccáin, i ccontae Thiobrat-Arann," agus chuir i mbrollach na lámhscríbhinne é. Ba le Austin Cooper, tráth, fear ón dtaobh seo tíre ó dhúchas, ba leis ceann de na lámhscríbhinní a raibh an Donnabhánach ag tarraingt as. Tá beathaisnéis an Donnabhánaigh sa leabharlann.[334]

Ní i dtaobh leis na hannála sin atáimíd: tá trí cinn eile againn.[335] Díol suime na *Fragmentary Annals* i ngeall ar fhear a gcóipeála, An Dubhaltach Mac Fhirbhisigh. Deirtear go bhfuair sé scolaíocht i mBaile Mhic Aodhagáin i gContae Thiobraid Árann ó Fhlann agus ó Bhaothghalach Mac Aodhagáin. Is ar shaothar eile, ámh, a sheasann a cháil. In aimsir Chromail is ea chuir an Connachtach léannta seo a mhórshaothar le chéile, *Leabhar Mór na nGenelach*,[336] atá bfhéidir ar chomhchéim le *Annála Ríoghachta na hÉireann*. Craobha ginealaigh is mó atá ann agus cuirtear leo seanchas nó dánta a bhainfeadh le hábhar. Deir Ó Muraíle go bhfuil suas is anuas le 40,000 duine luaite ann. Ós rud é go raibh Mac Fhirbhisigh mór le huaisle, leithéidí Sir James Ware agus Dr John Lynch, bhí teacht aige ar leabhair i mBéarla is i Laidean. Tharraing sé as *Opus Chronologicum Novum* leis an scoláire Ollanach Ubbo Emmius agus é ag cur síos ar ríthe na hAlban. Cé gur bhain sé a ghaisneas as *Foras Feasa* agus as *Annála Ríoghachta na hÉireann* ní fios ar bhuail sé riamh lena n-údair. Aisteach go leor, níl tagairt ar bith ina leabhar don scoláire mór Flann Mac Aodhagáin, dá mhéid de chomaoin is a chuir Clann Mhic Aodhagáin air. Tá réamhrá an Dubhaltaigh ar cheann de na míreanna in *Irish Genealogical Tracts*.[337]

---

332 Seán Mac Airt, (eag.), *The Annals of Innisfallen* (B.Á.C., 1951).
333 John O'Donovan (eag.), *Annála Ríoghachta Éireann* (B.Á.C., 1856), an dara heagrán, 7 iml.
334 Patricia Boyne, *John O'Donovan* (Cill Chainnigh, 1987).
335 Seamus Ó hInnse, *Miscellaneous Irish Annals* (B Á.C., 1947); Joan Newton Radner, *Fragmentary Annals of Ireland* (B.Á.C., 1978); Rev. Denis Murphy S.J., *Annals of Clonmacnoise* (B.Á.C., 1896), Fótóchóip.
336 Nollaig Ó Muraíle (eag.), *Dubhaltach Mac Fhirbhisigh, Leabhar Genealach* (B.Á.C., 2003/4) 5 Iml.
337 Toirdhealbhach Ó Raithbheartaigh (eag.), *Genealological Tracts* (B.Á.C., 1932).

Is iomaí sin údar a ndeachaigh scéal Shuibhne Geilt[338] i gcionn air, Seamus Heaney agus Flann O'Brien ina measc. D'imigh Suibhne bocht le craobhacha; Cath Maighe Rátha agus mallacht sagairt anuas air a chuir dá threoir é. Más gruama féin mar ábhar seachrán an fhir allta, tá an scéal breac le dánta áille a léiríonn an dlúthcheangal ag an duine leis an dúlra, rud fíorGhaelach. Déanann an nádúr a pheacaí a agairt go géar ar Shuibhne, ach

tugann sí sólás dó ina dhiaidh sin. Faoiseamh fós dó aithris na logainmneacha; is geal leis "damh Sléibhe aird Eibhlinne".

Léirítear filíocht an tréimhse 1200-1600, dánta le Giolla Bríde Mac Con Midhe, mar shampla, i leabhair Quiggin,[339] agus Frazer, Grosjean agus O'Keeffe.[340] Tá filíocht ina caise i leabhair an Irish Texts Society: Ó Bruadair,[341] Ó Rathaille,[342] Cearbhallán,[343] Tadhg Dall Ó hUiginn,[344] agus filí na hIomarbhá.[345]

Tá riar maith againn de leabhair sin an Irish Texts Society, Cumann na Scríbheann nGaedhilge, agus is fiú iad a lua. Ar ndóigh, is é *Foras Feasa*[346] an leabhar is mó orthu, dar linne, mar gur chuir an Céitinneach scéal na hÉireann ar fáil ar mhodh taitneamhach soléite, bíodh is go bhfuil go leor finscéalta tríd an insint. Ach dhlúthaigh sé le chéile stair agus seanchas na tíre, is chothaigh mórtas cine, agus bhréagnaigh lucht ár gcáinte. Tá an deilín ann gur fearr an stíl ná an stair aige; ní féidir a shéanadh, ar aon nós, gurb éachtach an cur amach atá aige ar an Laidean, ar an mBéarla, agus ar shaíocht na hEorpa. Scaipeadh an saothar go rábach ar fud na tíre, cóipeáladh go mion minic é, agus fuair uaisle Gall éachtaint air sna haistriúcháin, go háirithe i leabhar Dhiarmaid Uí Chonchubhair. Thug fear Chaisil, Tomás Ó Súilleabháin, fobha faoi, ach sin scéal eile.

As an mbaróchas Eorpach, i dtaca le cráifeacht dúchais na hÉireann, a fáisceadh *Trí Bior-Ghaoithe an Bháis*.[347] Is léir air tionchar exempla agus searmóintí ón ngluaiseacht iarThriontach i Sasana agus san bhFrainc ach go háirithe. Gnáththéama i litríocht na haimsire ab ea díomuaine an bheatha; agus an áibhéil agus an drámatúlacht a chleacht an Céitinneach á léiriú, bhí sin go forleathan thar lear.

[338] J.G. O'Keeffe (eag.), *Buile Suibhne* (Londain, 1913).
[339] E.C. Quiggin, *Prolegomena to the Study of the Later Irish Bards 1200-1500* (Londain, 1911).
[340] J. Frazer, P. Grosjean, J.G. O'Keeffe, *Irish Texts, Fasc.2* (Londain, 1931).
[341] John C MacErlean (eag.), *Duanaire Dháibhidh Uí Bhruadair* (Londain, 1910, 1913, 1917), 3 iml.
[342] Patrick S Dinneen, Tadhg Ó Donoghue (eag.), *Dánta Aodhagáin Uí Rathaille* (Londain, 1911).
[343] Tomás Ó Máille (eag.), *Amhráin Chearbhalláin* (Londain, 1916).
[344] Eleanor Knott (eag.), *A bhfuil againn dár Chum Tadhg Dall Ó hUiginn* (Londain, 1920), 2 iml.
[345] L. McKenna (eag.), *Iomarbhágh na bhFileadh* (Londain, 1920), 2 iml.
[346] D. Comyn, P.S. Dinneen (eag.), *Foras Feasa ar Éirinn* (Londain, 1901, 1908, 1914), 4 iml.
[347] Osborn Bergin (eag.), *Trí Bior-Ghaoithe an Bháis* (B Á.C., 1931).

Ábhar spéise linn anseo *Poems on Marcher Lords*,[348] bunaithe ar lámhscríbhinn a scríobhadh i gCo. Thiobraid Árann i dtús na 16ú haoise. Cuimsítear ann dánta molta ar Sheán Cantúil, Ardeaspag Chaisil, 1452-82, ar Sheamus Puirséal, Barún Luachma, ar Thadhg Ó Cearbhaill Ráth Eine, ar Philib Haicéad Bhaile Uí Shíocháin, agus ar Phiaras Buitléir na Cathrach. Is maith ann iad na léarscáileanna: gach áit a luadh ar ghaibh na taoisigh sin agus iad i mbun caithréime, tá sé marcáilte go cruinn beacht. Is féidir a chur in aon-aicme leis an leabhar seo *Poems on the Butlers*, ina ndéantar móradh ar thiarnaí móra na mBuitléarach, go háirithe ar Thiobóid na Cathrach agus a bhean, Máire Ciomhsóg. Is léir go raibh duanaire mór toirtiúil i gCathair Dhún Iascaigh tráth, ach níl fágtha anois de ach roinnt bheag leathanach.

"Lá aonaigh Bhaile an Gharraí.i. Chille Baoithín.i. an aonaigh is coirpthe i gCúige Mumhan ná i gCúige Laighean." Sin tuairisc ag Amhlaoibh Ó Súilleabháin ó Chalainn sa bhliain 1828.[349] Tá mórchuid eolais le fáil sa chínlae iomráiteach seo, cúntas beo ar shaol a linne, agus ní hannamh dó spleáchadh a thabhairt thar teorainn ar Thiobraid Árann.

Léirítear cumas na nGael sa Laidean in *Imtheachta Aeniasa*,[350] aistriúchán ar *Aeneid* Virgil agus stiallíní suimiúla curtha leis. I *Leabhar Bhaile an Mhóta* a fuarthas é. Más fíor an scéal scríobhadh cuid den leabhar sin i gCeapach Raitin, láimh le Ceapach na bhFaoiteach sa chontae seo. Aistriúchán eile is ea *Gabháltais Shearlais Mhóir*,[351] a scríobhadh c. 1400.

Eibhlín agus Seamus

Le Cúige Uladh a bhaineann *Tóruigheacht Gruaidhe Griansholus*[352] agus *Caithréim Congail Cláiringhnigh*;[353] Ultach mór eile atá faoi thrácht in *Beatha Aodha Ruaidh Uí Dhomhnaill*.[354] B'aoibhinn le Gaeil riamh scéalta ar nós *Giolla an Fhiugha*[355] agus na heachtraí atá ar fáil in *Two Irish Arthurian Romances*.[356] Bhíodh an-tóir ar an gcéad Romance, ar *Eachtra an Mhadra Mhaoil, The Adventure of the Crop Eared Dog*, agus é go flúirseach ins na lámhscríbhinní. Rinne Eadhmon Puirtéal cóip álainn de i gCathair Dhún Iascaigh sa bhliain 1823.

348 Anne O'Sullivan, Pádraig Ó Riain, *Poems on Marcher Lords* (Londain, 1987); James Carney (eag.), Poems on the Butlers (B.Á.C., 1945).
349 Michael McGrath (eag.), *Cinnlae Amhlaoibh Uí Shúilleabháin* (Londain, 1936, 1937), 4 iml.
350 G. Calder (eag.), *Imtheachta Aeniasa* (Londain, 1907).
351 Douglas Hyde (eag.), *Gabháltais Shearlais Mhóir* (Londain, 1919).
352 Cecile O'Rahilly (eag.), *Tóruigheacht Gruaidhe Griansholus* (Londain, 1924).
353 P.M. MacSweeney (eag.), *Caithréim Conghail Cláiringhnigh* (Londain, 1904).
354 Paul Walsh, Colm Ó Lochlainn, (eag.), *Beatha Aodha Ruaidh Uí Dhomhnaill* (Londain, 1948,1957), 2 iml.
355 Douglas Hyde (eag.), *Giolla an Fhiugha* (Londain, 1899).
356 R.A.S. Macalister (eag.), *Two Irish Arthurian Romances* (Londain, 1908).

Cíortar cúrsaí leighis in *Rosa Anglica*,[357] atá bunaithe ar shaothar John of Geddesden. Déantar leas an anama in *Instructio Pie Vivendi*,[358] aistriúchán ar leabhar cráifeach ón 14ú haois, agus in *Life of St. Declan of Ardmore*.[359] Béaloideas is ábhar do *Sgéalta Thomáis Uí Chathasaigh*.[360]

Níor fágadh an Fhiannaíocht as an áireamh, ní nach ionadh. Faightear *Agallamh na Seanóirí*[361] go mion minic sna lámhscríbhinní. Cuir leis sin *Laoithe na Féinne*[362] agus *Duanaire Finn*,[363] a breacadh in Ostend sa bhliain 1627. I dtaca leis sin fós tá *Poems of Ossian*[364] le Macpherson na hAlban againn, an té a thuill náire is aithis mar gheall ar na bréaglaoithe Fiannaíochta a chum sé féin, bíodh is gur leath a cháil ar fud na hEorpa, is go mbíodh a leabhair á léamh ag Napoleon agus ag Goethe.

Ábhar iontais linn dornán leabhar i nGáidhlig na hAlban a bheith sa leabharlann. Tá trí leabhar againn a thráchtann ar shaothar mórluachmhar Dheán an Leasa Mhóir[365] ón 16ú haois. (Lios Mór na hAlban atá i gceist). Tá Fiannaíocht ann, bairdne, aoir, agus go leor eile ó Éirinn agus ó Albain. Filíocht Uilliam Ros[366] agus Bliain a '45 is ábhar do na leabhair eile.

Sa bhliain 1849 is ea chuaigh cló ar *Miscellany of the Celtic Society*[367] agus an scoláire mór Seán Ó Donnabháin ina bhun. Cuid den mheascra ná *Ginealach Chorca Laidhe*, filíocht, agus *Docwra's Tracts*. Is iomaí duine ó Thiobraid Árann a áirítear i liosta na mball, agus tús áite ag uachtarán an Society, an Dochtúir Labhrás Ó Reineacháin ó Ghort na hUagha, a bhí ina cheann ar Choláiste Mhaighe Nuat san am sin.

Ba gheal leis an nGael riamh an naomhsheanchas. Faightear tuairisc i leabhar Plummer[368] ar iliomad naomh nach bhfuil d'eolas ag mórchuid daoine orthu ach a n-ainmneacha, agus cuireann an saoi ildánach úd[369] George Petrie leis.

SeanGhaeilge agus MeánGhaeilge is mó atá faoi thrácht san iris *Eriu*.[370] Cuirfidh muintir Thiobraid Árann spéis, bfhéidir, ins na haistí leis an ardscoláire Micheál Ó Briain, a rugadh i gCluain Meala. (deartháir leis ba ea Tommy O'Brien, fear craolta

[357] Winifred P. Wulff (eag.), *Rosa Anglica* (Londain, 1929).

[358] J. MacKechnie (eag.), *Instructio Pie Vivendi* (Londain, 1934, 1946), 2 iml.

[359] P. Power (eag.), *Life of St. Declan of Ardmore and Life of St. Mochuda of Lismore* (Londain, 1914).

[360] Douglas Hyde (eag.), *Sgéalta Thomáis Uí Chathasaigh* (Londain, 1939).

[361] P. de Barra (eag.), *Agallamh na Seanóirí* (Cathair na Mart, 1986).

[362] An Seabhac (eag.), *Laoithe na Féinne* (B.Á.C., 1941).

[363] Eoin MacNeill, Gerard Murphy, Anne O'Sullivan, Idris L. Foster, Brendan Jennings, (eag.), *Duanaire Finn* (Londain, 1908, 1933, 1953), 3 iml.

[364] James Macpherson, *Poems of Ossian* (Dún Éideann, 1926), athchló.

[365] E.C. Quiggin (eag.), *Poems from the Book of the Dean of Lismore* (Cambridge, 1937); W.J. Watson (eag.), *Scottish Verse from the Book of the Dean of Lismore* (Dún Éideann, 1937); Rev. T. M' Lauchlan (eag.), *The Dean of Lismore's Book* (Dún Éideann, 1862).

[366] G. Calder (eag.), *Orain Ghaidhealach le Uilliam Ros* (Dún Éideann, 1937); an chéad eagrán 1830; J.L. Campbell (eag.), *Highland Songs of the Forty Five* (Dún Éideann, 1935), athchló.

[367] John O'Donovan (eag.), *Miscellany of the Celtic Society* (B.Á.C., 1849).

[368] Charles Plummer (eag.), *Bethada Náem nÉrenn* (Oxford, 1997); an chéad eagrán, 1922; 2 iml.

[369] George Petrie (eag.), *Christian Inscriptions in the Irish Language* (B.Á.C., 1872, 1878), 2 iml.

[370] *Eriu*, (B Á.C., 1904-1916; 1921-1932).

an cheoil), nó san alt le Joseph O'Neill ar Riail Ailbhe. Tháinig an chéad uimhir den iris ar an saol in 1904, ach cé go bhfuil sé fós ar an bhfód is é eagrán 1932 an chóip is déanaí againn.

veaġ-ḃlas . . . .
lom-ġlaine . . . .
sár-marġaḋ!

Éire 1941

Ní rófhada a sheas an iris léannta eile *Gadelica*,[371] cé go raibh ardmheas air. Bhí ábhar ann le Seamus Ó Casaide, a rugadh i bhFiodh Ard: sleachta as *Cínlae Amhlaoibh Uí Shúilleabháin*, an chéad uair a cuireadh i gcló é. Is san iris sin, leis, a sholáthraigh Osborn Bergin sleachta fada as an aoir phróis úd *Pairlement Chloinne Tomais*. Tá cuntas barrúil i gceann acu ar an raic a ghaibh le baint an fhómhair ar mhacaire Chaisil, agus iníon na scolóige le fáil ag an mbuainí ab fhearr.

Tá go leor leabhar Béarla sa leabharlann a bhfuil a bheag nó a mhór de Ghaeilge iontu, agus cuid eile a bhfuil eolas luachmhar ar ár n-oidhreacht iontu. Ní healaí dúinn iad go léir a áireamh, ach níor mhiste dornán díobh a lua.[372] Más linn eolas a fháil ar réimeas Chaisil, mar shampla, tá sin go flúirseach ag Francis John Byrne in *Irish Kings and High Kings*.

B: Dúchas

Méar ar eolas ar shaíocht an Chontae an tsraith léachtaí a tionóladh faoin dteideal *Dúchas*[373] idir 1983 agus 1991. Faightear ann eolas maith fóinteach, staidéar agus taighde ar an Haicéadach agus ar an gCéiteannach agus tuilleadh nach iad. Tá cur síos cruinn, mar shampla, ag an Athair Valkenberg ar thuismitheoirí Phadraigín Haicéad, eolas nach raibh ar fáil roimhe sin. Tuilleadh feasa anois againn, más ea, ar Liam Dall, ar Dhiarmaid Ó Riain, ar an Athair Micheál Ó hIcí, ar an Athair Mathúin Ó Riain, agus ar chúrsaí na Gaeilge.

Is é *The Poets and Poetry of Munster*[374] an leabhar ceoil is seanda dá bhfuil againn i Roinn na Gaeilge cé nach mar leabhar ceoil a scríobhadh é. An-leabhar ar fad é: tá focail na n-amhrán ann, agus aistriúchán orthu, ceol na n-amhrán maraon le cúntas ar lucht a gcumtha. An gnáthcheol a ghabhann le "Seán Ó Duibhir a' Ghleanna" faoi láthair is dócha gur ón leabhar seo a scaipeadh é. Trí leabhar ceoil eile atá againn agus tábhacht leo: *Amhráin Mhuighe Seola*,[375] *Londubh an Chairn*[376] agus *Ceol ón Mumhain*.[377]

---

[371] T.F. O'Rahilly (eag.), *Gadelica* (B.Á.C., 1912-1913).

[372] Alfred P. Smith (eag.), *Seanchas* (B.Á.C., 2000); Brian Ó Cuív, *Seven Centuries of Irish Learning* (B Á.C., 1961); K.W. Nicholls, *Gaelic and Gaelicised Ireland in the Middle Ages* (B.Á.C., 2003), athchló; Donnchadh Ó Corráin, *Irish Antiquity* (Corcaigh, 1981); John & Phil Flood, *Kilcash* (B.Á.C., 1999); W.J. Hayes (eag.), *Tipperary Remembers* (Achadh Úr, 1976); Eugene O'Curry, *On the Manners and Customs of the Ancient Irish* (B.Á.C., 1996), athchló; an chéad eagrán, 1873; 3 iml.; Francis John Byrne, *Irish Kings and High Kings* (B Á.C., 2001), athchló; an chéad eagrán, 1973.

[373] L. Prút (eag.), *Dúchas* (B.Á.C., 1986, 1990, 1993), 3 iml.

[374] J. O'Daly, J.C. Mangan, W.M. Hennessy, C.P. Meehan, *The Poets and Poetry of Munster* (B.Á.C., 1884), an chéad eagrán 1849.

[375] Mrs. Costello, *Amhráin Mhuighe Seola* (B.Á.C., 1923).

[376] S. Clandillon, M. Hannagan, *Londubh an Chairn* (Oxford, 1927).

[377] L. de Noraidh, *Ceol ón Mumhain* (B.Á.C., 1965).

Má ghabhaimíd cúpla céim thar teorainn an Chontae gheobhaimíd éachtaint ar theanga na nDéise atá ar aon dul lenár gcanúint féin. Leabhar mórluachmhar isea *An Sléibhteánach*,[378] scéal a bheatha á insint ag Seamus Ó Caoimh ó cheantar Mhellerí. Éamon Ó Conchúir a scríobh síos é i Ros Cré. "Tá samhlaíocht, cuimhne, agus cumas inste sa

Sléibhteánach,"adeir an t-Ollamh Pádraig Ó Fiannachta sa réamhrá, "agus mar mhaise orthusan tá saibhreas éigse béil, foclóra, pictiúr, agus meafar." Má's mian linn tuilleadh eolais a fháil ar an saghas Gaeilge a bhíodh á labhairt i dTiobraid Árann ceadaímís *Sean-Chaint na nDéise.*[379]

Gaeilge na nDéise, leis, a labhartaí i gCill Chainnigh, a fhianaise sin an fótóchóip de lámhscríbhinn ó cheantar Chalainn. B'é Piaras Grás ó Cheapach Éidín a scríobh í sa bhliain 1809.[380] B'í Mrs. Angela Greene, Cnoc na Croiche, Ráth Ó gCormaic, Co.Phort Láirge sealbhóir na lámhscríbhinne, agus chuir Michael Briody réamhrá agus innéacs leis an bhfótóchóip. Tráchtann an Grásach ar cheart na Gaeilge agus ar mhodh a scríofa, agus faightear uaidh filíocht Mhuimhneach, Faoisidin Sheamuis Paor na Srón, An Sotach agus a Mháthair, agus go leor eile.

"Tabharfaidh an staidéar seo thíos léargas ar leith dúinn ar an saol Gaelach i gceantar beag, nár mhó ná ceithre pharóiste, in aice le Sliabh na mBan, ar dhá thaobh den teorainn idir Cúige Mumhan agus Osraí." "Gleann an Óir" a thugtaí ar an gceantar sin, agus is é is teideal do leabhar Eoghain Uí Néill.[381] An rud a chuir sé roimhe a dhéanamh d'éirigh thar barr leis. Saol Phádraig Uí Néill as Ónainn (1765-1832) ar an dtaobh thall den Ghleann (Buaile Uí Eoghain Fhinn an leagan ceart, dar leis an údar.) is mó a léiríonn é, chomh maith le cur síos ar a mhuintir i Lios Ruanach agus i mBaile Uí Néill ar an dtaobh i bhfus. Duine ildánach ba ea an Niallach: fear deisiúil, feirmeoir, muilleoir, ceoltóir, scríobhnóir, bailitheoir lámhscríbhinní, file. Ba ghnáthach an ainnise is an dealús a shamhlú leis an Ghaeilge, agus is amhlaidh a bhí, go minic. Os a choinne sin, is léir ón leabhar go raibh daoine saibhre agus oideachas orthu ar lucht a labhartha, leis, daoine, fearacht an Niallaigh, ná raibh dall ar na claisicí ná ar shaíocht na hEorpa.

---

[378] Seamus Ó Caoimh; Eamonn Ó Conchúir (eag.), *An Sléibhteánach* (Maighe Nuad, 1989).
[379] Rev. M. Sheehan, *Sean-Chaint na nDéise* (B.Á.C., 1906); R.B. Breatnach, *Seana-Chaint na nDéise 2* (B.Á.C., 1984).
[380] Piaras Grás, *Lámhscríbhinn ó Challainn*, 1809 (fótóchóip); Micheál Briody (réamhrá).
[381] Eoghan Ó Néill, *Gleann an Óir* (B.Á.C., 1988).

Gné thábhachtach d'oideas na Gaeilge na hagallaimh beirte agus na ceapóga a chuir le scléip is sult na ndaoine i gcónaí riamh. Tá cuntas cumasach tugtha ag Seán Ó Morónaigh ar an rannaireacht seoigh seo ina leabhar *Agallamh na hÉigse*.[382] Sa bhliain 1993 rianaigh Eibhlín Uí Mhorónaigh scéal Chonradh na Gaeilge in Aonach Urmhumhan (1901-1993).[383] Ba mhór le rá ann Pádraig Ó Meára mar gheall ar a dhíograis agus a dhúthracht; tugtar a dhíol ómóis dó.

Níl ach an t-aon leabhar amháin againn a bhaineann le cluichí faiche, agus cá hionadh linn gurb é *Scéal na hIomána*[384] é, cuntas cumasach ar "chluiche uasal ársa is aithnid dúinn ó ré na Tána agus an tSeanchais Mhóir, díol ceana is imeartha ag ridire is rídhamhna, cluiche dea-oird, dea-eagair, a d'imrítí faoi smacht i bhfaichí iata le breis is míle bliain".

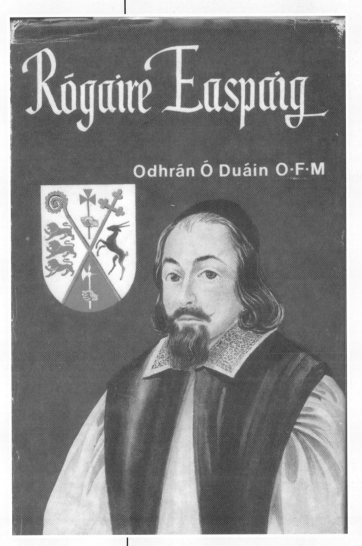

Is deacair a shamhlú anois cé chomh mór is a chuaigh leabhair an "Chraoibhín Aoibhinn"(Dubhghlas de hÍde) i bhfeidhm ar éigse na tíre. Ba gheal le Synge, mar shampla, *Abhráin Ghrádha Chúige Connacht*.[385] Nuair a thiomsaigh An Craoibhín dánta diaga na ndaoine ba mhór an t-ionadh ag an aos léinn é gné folaithe den dúchas bheith á léiriú dóibh.[386]

Minic go leor a chastar le cléir na hEaglaise Caitlicí gur thugadar droim láimhe leis an nGaeilge, ach ná síntear méar i dtreo an Ardeaspaig Uí Bhré i bhfianaise na Statuta[387] a d'eisigh sé do dheoise Chaisil agus Imligh. Ordaíonn sé an Ghaeilge a úsáid de réir mar is gá é agus chuige sin cuireann sé an leagan Gaeilge ar fáil go cruinn cáiréiseach ar phaidreacha agus ar theagasc, cab ar chab leis an leagan Béarla. Cuma foghrúil atá ar an nGaeilge agus an cló Rómhánach air. A leithéid seo: "Anis eireoig an Sagart, poaguig an altoir, agus a touirt eigh air a bpobul, bearhig se an beannacha uaig, ag raa: Siochawn agus beannaght De uille-choaghtaigh, an Athar, an Mhic, agus an spirrid naovha orrib uille ar feag uar saoil. Amen"

Tráchtar ar easpag eile dár gcuid, ar an "Rógaire Easpaig", is é sin Maoilir Mac Craith, i leabhar Uí Dhubháin.[388] An creideamh sinseartha a chleacht sé idtús a shaoil, agus dhein easpag Caitliceach de, nó gur iompaigh sé agus gur ceapadh ina

382 Seán Ó Morónaigh, *Agallamh na hÉigse* (Camus, 2001).
383 Eibhlín Uí Mhorónaigh (eag.), *Ó Ghlúin go Glúin* (B.Á.C., 1993).
384 Liam P. Ó Caithnia, *Scéal na hIomána* (B.Á.C., 1980).
385 Douglas Hyde, *Abhráin Grádh Chúige Connacht* (Sionainn, 1969), athchló; an chéad chló, 1893.
386 Douglas Hyde, *Abhráin Diadha Chúige Connacht* (Sionainn, 1972), athchló; an chéad chló, 1906.
387 Thomas Bray, *Statuta Synodalia pro Unitis Dioecesibus Cassel. et Imelac.* (B.Á.C., 1813). Bearnach.
388 Odhrán Ó Duáin, O.F.M., *Rógaire Easpaig* (B.Á.C., 1975).

Ardeaspag Protastúnach ar Chaiseal é mar luach saothair. Rinne Eoghan Ó Dubhthaigh é a aoradh: "A Mhaoil gan Mhuire ataoi leamh, dul ar neamh ní hé do thriall". Thuig Maoilir tábhacht na Gaeilge; mhol sé don bhanríon Eilís ábhar cráifeach a chur ar fáil sa teanga sin deich mbliana sar ar cuireadh cló ar Thiomna Nua Uí Dhomhnaill. Len ár linn féin chuir An t-Athair Colmcille ábhar spioradálta ar fáil do Chaitlicigh sa Ghaeilge.[389]

Bunaíodh An Cumann le Béaloideas Éireann in 1927 agus tá siad ar a dtáirm ó shin i leith ag bailiú is ag caomhnú is ag foilsiú bhéaloideas na tíre. *Béaloideas*[390] is teideal dá n-iris. Ba liosta le háireamh a bhfuil ann idir scéalta is rannta is orthaí, paidreacha is piseoga. Sraith bhearnach atá againn, ach is maith ann í. I dtaca leis sin de ní miste a rá go bhfuil fáil ar an stór luachmhar a bhailigh scoláirí bunscoile an chontae i dtriochaidí na haoise seo caite; tá sé ar mhiocrascannán sa leabharlann.

I dtreo dheireadh an chogaidh in 1943 chuir Connradh na Gaeilge leabhar beag amach, *Bláith-Fhleasg ó Thiobraid Árann*.[391] Tá rudaí fiúntacha ann, aistí staire leis na seanundúirí Micheál Mac Carrthaigh, Seamus Ó Bric, Tomás de Bhial; filíocht le hÁine Ní Fhoghludha agus le Pádraig de Brún; cur síos ag Pilib Ó Foghludha ar a imeachtaí agus é ina thimire Gaeilge sa chontae; turas a thug "Máire" ar Chaiseal. Tugann na fógraí léargas dúinn ar na tionscail bheaga atá imithe le gaoith: "Leanbh-Charranaí Cluain Meala Déanta i gCluain Meala i monarchain atá 100% Éireannach." "Láimhíní Chlú is Cháil "Dhuragh" Tiobraid Árann Déanta de Leathar." Ach maireann "Ó Ceallaigh" fós mar fhógra siopa i mbaile Thiobraid Árann, mar a ndíoltar fós "earraí éaduigh do gach cineul d'fhearaibh is do mhnáibh". Dá mbfhíor d'fhógra eile sa *Bhláith-Fhleasg* níor ghá duit tart ná ocras a bheith ort i nDúrlas Éile-chuirfí cóir mhaith chaoin ort i Sráid Pharnell "i dtigh Sheamuis Uí Mheachair na Féile".

C: Riail agus Reacht

Níorbh é an dea-theist a bhí ar an gcontae seo ó thaobh na coiriúlachta agus na mí-réire de tráth dá raibh. Cá hionadh mar sin muintir Thiobraid Árann bheith líonmhar i leabhar Thomáis de Bhial: Éamonn an Chnoic, Ó hÓgáin Fia-Mharcach, Cos Mhéiscreach, "Cut" Coinnleán, gan trácht ar ropairí móra ár gcomharsan, Fréiní agus Ó Crotaigh.[392] Níor bhuan dá réim. "An chríoch chéanna a bhí i ndán dóibh go léir. Thiteadar le gad an chrochaire".

Bhí Séamas Ó Maoileoin[393] ar a choimeád, leis, le linn Chogadh na Saoirse, ach thug sé na cosa leis: níor doirteadh a chuid fola. Bhain eachtraí corraitheacha dó i dTiobraid Árann agus in oirthear Luimnigh, mar a raibh an chéad cholún reatha sa

[389] An t-Ath. Colmcille, O.C.S.O., *Deoraí Chríost* (B.Á.C., 1960); *Urnaí na hOíche* (B.Á.C., 1974).
[390] *Béaloideas* (B.Á.C., 1927-29, 1931-33, 1947-49, 1951-52, 1961-66).
[391] Connradh na Gaedhilge, *Bláith-Fleasg ó Thiobraid Árann* (gan log luaite, 1943).
[392] Tomás de Bhial, *Tóraithe agus Ropairí* (B.Á.C., 1955).
[393] Seamus Ó Maoileoin, *B'fiú an Braon Fola…* (B.Á.C., 1972), athchló; an chéad eagrán, 1958.

tír. Cuntas bríomhar corraitheach a thugann Colm Ó Labhra (An tAthair Colmcille O.C.S.O.) ar an gcogadh céanna;[394] go deimhin, shílfeá ar uairibh gur scéal Fiannaíochta a bhí á aithris aige: "Ansan is ea a thosnaigh an gleo agus an gleithearán. D'éirigh an príosúnach de léim, á theilgean féin i gcoinne an Chonstábla Uí Rinn gur bhuail a dhá lámh gona nglas cruaí le feidhm uile a nirt ar a aghaidh is ar a éadan, agus mar d'éirigh, baineadh tuairt as corp an Chonstábla Mac Ionrachtaigh anuas den tsuíochán gur teilgeadh ar lár agus ar lántalamh é". Na blianta roimhe sin agus na toscaí ba chúis leis an gcogadh, táid pléite ag Pádraig Ó Snodaigh.[395]

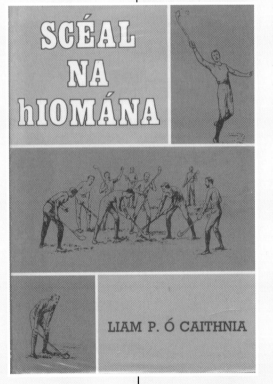

D: Litríocht Chruthaitheach

"Tá sé ar cheann de na haistí spóirt is fearr sa Ghaeilge; tá greann, searbhas, áibhéil, ealaín, agus réalaíocht seoigh ina n-orlaí tríd. Ealaíontóir den scoth ab ea Diarmaid sa Ghaeilge."[396] Ardmholadh é sin, gan dabht ar bith ach cad é an saothar a thuill é? Barántas Dhiarmaid Uí Riain na Báinsí ina ndéantar aoir agus imdheargadh ar "Thadhg Mac Finghín Mheic Cárthaigh Hiberno-waterlouse" atá i gceist. Séard is barántas ann ná aithris mhagaidh i bprós agus i bhfilíocht ar *arrest warrants* an Bhéarla; tá Barántas Dhiarmada le léamh sa leabhar *An Barántas*.[397] Is mó cáil an Rianaigh as an amhrán Béarla *"The Peeler and the Goat"* ach gan a dhíol aitheantais fachta fós aige mar fhile Gaeilge.

Faighimíd léas ar an oidhreacht a d'imigh uainn in *Duanaire Thiobraid Árann*,[398] fuíoll áir, faraoir, amhráin a bhailigh Seán Ó Duinn agus Seamus Ó Braonáin ar theorainn Thiobraid Árann agus Chill Chainnigh i seascaidí na 19ú haoise. Tá leaganacha suimiúla de ghnáthamhráin ann, *"Iníon an Fhaoitigh ón nGleann"*, *"Cill Chaise"*, *"A Bhuachaillí Chroí"*, ach is iad na hamhráin eile na seoda, amhráin na ndaoine a bheadh imithe gan tuairisc murach dúthracht na mbailitheoirí. Tá duanairí eile againn[399] agus is é an ceann is mó slacht ná *An Duanaire*.[400] Chuir na heagarthóirí rompu "caoi a thabhairt dár muintir ar fad dul i seilbh a n-oidhreacht liteartha ath-uair". Roghnaigh siad dánta ó ré na filíochta aiceanta (1600-1900) agus chuireadar nua-aistriúcháin leo, saothar an Chéitinnigh agus an

[394] Colm Ó Labhra, *Trodairí na Treas Briogáide* (Aonach Urmhumhan, 1955).
[395] Pádraig Ó Snodaigh, *Comhghuaillithe na Réabhlóide 1913-1916* (B Á.C., 1966).
[396] P. Ó Fiannachta, "Diarmaid Ó Riain agus a Bharántas", *Dúchas 1986-89*, (B.Á.C., 1990).
[397] P. Ó Fiannachta, *An Barántas* (Maigh Nuad, 1978).
[398] D. Ó hÓgáin (eag.), *Duanaire Thiobraid Árann* (B.Á.C., 1981).
[399] N. Tóibín (eag.), *Duanaire Déiseach* (B.Á.C., 1979), an dara cló; C.Ó Coigligh, *Cuisle na hÉigse* (Cathair na Mart, 1986), eagrán nua; Éamon Cuirtéis a chruinnigh an chéad eagrán, 1920.
[400] S. Ó Tuama, T. Kinsella, *An Duanaire, Poems of the Dispossessed* (B.Á.C., 1979), an dara cló.

Haicéadaigh ina measc. Mar leis an Haicéadach céanna is mór an áis leabhar Mháire Ní Cheallacháin.[401] Thug Pádraigín, an Doiminiceánach ó Chaiseal, gean dá chairde, do mhná, do na Buitléaraigh, agus grá thar chuimse d'Éirinn. Fear faobhair a bhí ann nuair a bhí an Confederation i mbarr a réime agus is é a bhí géar ar an dream ná raibh ar aon-bhuille leis, ach, gheobhadh amhrán álainn a scríobh do Mháire Tóibín, "Dála an nóinín".

Rinne Risteárd Ó Foghludha eagarthóirtheacht ar dhánta Liam Inglis.[402] D'áitigh sé gurbh as Tiobraid Árann don bhfile, ach is dóigh le hÚna Nic Éinrí ina leabhar ar Inglis gur dóichí baint a bheith aige le teorainn Luimnigh agus Tiobraid Árann. (Úna Nic Éinrí, *Canfar an Dán* (An Daingean, 2003)). Rinne Ó Foghludha an beart céanna do Liam Dall Ó hIfearnáin.[403] I dtaca leis sin níor mhiste an trialóg a bhunaigh Liam Ó Catháin ar shaol an fhile a lua.[404] B'é Máirtín Ó Corrbuí a chuir Gaeilge ar an dtríú leabhar, ar *Ceart na hUaighe*. Cogadh na Saoirse ba chúlra d'úrscéal eile leis an gCathánach, *Eibhlín an Ghleanna*.[405]

Rinneadh trácht cheana ar *Poets and Poetry of Munster* (Dúchas). Tá leabhar beag eile againn le Seán Ó Dálaigh, *The Irish Language Miscellany*.[406] Más beag féin é níl sé gan tábhacht; tá dánta ann atá coitianta go leor ins na lámhscríbhinní, ach gur dheacair teacht orthu i gcló, "A chór an uird úd Mhalladh", "Eachtra Sheamuis Gray," "Beo-chaoine Mhártuin Uí Chredáin", mar shampla.

Mar le filí an lae inniu is ábhar maoite linn iad seo a bhfuil baint acu le Tiobraid Árann, An t-Athair Pádraig de Brún, Máire Mhac an tSaoi,[407] iníon deirféar dó, Nuala Ní Dhomhnaill, Áine Ní Ghlinn,[408] Liam Prút,[409] Seán Ó hÓgáin,[410] Deirdre Brennan.[411] Faightear cuid dá saothar ins na hirisí liteartha e.g. *Innti*[412] agus in *Duanaire Nuafhilíochta*.[413] Tá an chéad eagrán de *Eireaball Spideoige*[414] againn, leis an bhfile mór Seán Ó Ríordáin, agus réamhrá spreagúil leis-"Cad is filíocht ann? Aigne linbh?" Leabhar go bhfuil slacht agus maise air is ea *Miserere*,[415] pictiúirí le Roualt, filíocht le Pádraig de Brún, agus aistriúchán le Máire Mhac an tSaoi. An té ar ghile leis filíocht níos seanaimseartha, Ó Rathaile, Ó Bruadair, is a leithéid, bheadh riar a

[401] M. Ní Cheallacháin, *Filíocht Phádraigín Haicéad* (B.Á.C., 1962).
[402] R. Ó Foghludha (eag.), *Cois na Bríde* (B.Á.C., 1937).
[403] R. Ó Foghludha (eag.), *Ar Bruach na Coille Muaire* (B Á.C., 1939).
[404] L. Ó Catháin, *Ceart na Sua* (B.Á.C., 1964); *Ceart na Bua* (B.Á.C., 1968); *Ceart na hUaighe* (B.Á.C.,1986) – Máirtín Ó Corrbuí a chuir Gaeilge air; *Eibhlín an Ghleanna* (B.Á.C.,1954).
[405] Liam Ó Catháin, *Eibhlín a' Ghleanna* (B.Á.C., 1954).
[406] J. O'Daly, *The Irish Language Miscellany* (B.Á.C., 1876).
[407] M. Mhac an tSaoi, *Margadh na Saoire* (B.Á.C., 1956).
[408] Á. Ní Ghlinn, *An Chéim Bhriste* (B.Á.C., 1984).
[409] L. Prút, *Asail* (B.Á.C., 1982); *Sean-Dair agus Scéalta Eile* (B.Á.C., 1985); *An Dá Scór* (B.Á.C.,).
[410] S. Ó hÓgáin, *Diascáin* (B.Á.C., 1987).
[411] Deirdre Brennan, *I Reilig na mBan Rialta* (B Á.C., 1984).
[412] Micheál Davitt (eag.), *Innti 8* (B Á.C., 1984.
[413] F. O'Brien, *Duanaire Nuafhilíochta* (B.Á.C., 1969).
[414] S. Ó Ríordáin, *Eireaball Spideoige* (B.Á.C., 1952).
[415] P. de Brún, M. Mhac an tSaoi, G. Roualt, *Miserere* (B.Á.C., 1971).

cháis aige i leabhair an "Irish Texts Society", ar deineadh trácht orthu cheana faoin gceannteideal "Ársaíocht".

Bíonn an-tóir ar an gcéad eagrán de ghnáth, go háirithe nuair is leabhar mór le rá é. Tá an chéad eagrán den *Béal Bocht*[416] i gcomhad againn, leabhar a chosnódh pingin mhaith anois. Tá, leis, againn, an chéad eagrán d'úrscéal éachtach Mháirtín Uí Chadhain, *Cré na Cille*.[417] B'é an Cadhnach a d'aistrigh *Sally Cavanagh*[418] le Charles Kickham. Áirítear *Fiche Blian ag Fás*[419] ar cheann de chlaisicí na Gaeilge; tá an chéad eagrán againn.

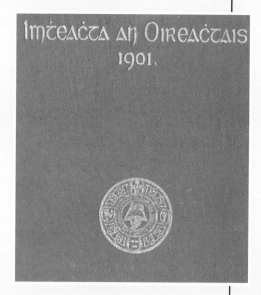

Ní iomadúlacht go scríbhinní Mháirtín Uí Chorrbúí.[420] Scríobh sé carn leabhar don aos óg, ach scríobh sé roinnt eile d'fhóinfeadh don duine fásta. Is dócha gurb é *Seantéada ar Crith* an ceann is mó aithne orthu siúd. Luadh cheana gurbh é a chuir Gaeilge ar *Ceart na hUaighe* le Liam Ó Catháin.

Tá *Sliabh na mBan bhFionn*[421] againn leis an Athair Peadar Ó Laoghaire, agus *Forbhas Chluain Meala*[422] le Sinéad de Valéra. Tugann Tomás Ó Duinn[423] léargas ar a shaol dúinn. Cineál féinbheathaisnéise, leis, ach é i gcrot úrscéil, is ea leabhar Sheamuis Uí Mhaolchatha, *An Gleann agus a raibh ann*.[424] Leabhar tábhachtach atá ann, ar dhá chúis; tugann sé léas ar shaol na Gráinsí fé tháinig an Béarla in uachtar ann, agus tugann sé léas ar chanúint Gaeilge na háite. Chuir Pádraigín Riggs ó bhaile Thiobraid Árann beathaisnéis léannta ar fáil ar Dhonncha Ó Céilleachair.[425]

Ós rud é nach mórán de dhifríocht atá idir Ghaeilge Thiobraid Árann agus Gaeilge Phort Láirge níor mhiste féachaint ar na leabhair bheaga ós na Déise do pháistí, *Gile na mBláth*[426] agus *Arthrach an Óir*,[427] mar shampla, agus is deas iad léaráidí Ailbe Uí Mhonacháin ar *Eachtra na Beiche*[428] agus ar *Eachtra an Phortáin*.[429] Is cuidsúlach go maith iad roinnt des na léaráidí eile ar leabhair

[416] Myles na gCopaleen (Brian Ó Nualláin), *An Béal Bocht* (B Á.C., 1941).
[417] M. Ó Cadhain, *Cré na Cille* (B.Á.C., 1949).
[418] M. Ó Cadhain, (aist.), *Saile Ní Chaomhánaigh* (B.Á.C.,1932).
[419] M. Ó Súilleabháin, *Fiche Blian ag Fás* (B Á C., 1933).
[420] M. Ó Corrbuí, *Máistir an Bhaile* (B Á.C., 1991); *Rí na gCnoc* (B.Á.C., 1966); *Cé Mharaigh an Cunta?* (B.Á.C., 1965); *An t-Éan Cluana* (Indreabhán, 1985); *Seantéada ar Crith* (B.Á.C., 1965).
[421] An t-Ath. P. Ua Laoghaire, *Sliabh na mBan bhFionn agus Cúán Fithise* (B.Á.C., 1914).
[422] S. de Valéra, *Forbhas Chluain Meala* (B.Á.C., 1941).
[423] T. Ó Duinn, *Ar mo Chonlán Féin* (B.Á.C., 1980).
[424] S. Ó Maolchathaigh, *An Gleann agus a raibh ann* (B.Á.C., 1963).
[425] P. Riggs, *Donncha Ó Céilleachair: Anailís stíleach* (B.Á.C., 1978).
[426] Rev. M. Sheehan, *Gile na mBláth* (B.Á.C., 1912).
[427] Rev. M. Sheehan, *Árthach an Óir* (B.Á.C., 1912).
[428] M. Ó Cionnfhaolaidh, *Eachtra na Beiche* (B.Á.C., 1941).
[429] M. Ó Cionnfhaolaidh, *Eachtra an Phortáin agus Scéalta eile* (B.Á.C., 1940).

don aos óg. Jack B. Yeats a mhaisigh an chéad eagrán de *Sean-Eoin*;[430] Nano Reid a mhaisigh *Rí na gCat*.[431] Chítear rian láimhe George Altendorf ar *Eibhlín agus Seamus*[432] agus K.Maidment ar *Scéalta an Domhain*.[433] Is fiú féachaint, leis, ar *Tír na Deo*,[434] *Scéalta Munchausen*,[435] agus ar *Scéal Mhóirín*.[436] Leabhar ana-shuimiúil isea an leabhar áirithe sin, mar gurb í an cailín atá i lár an aonaigh ann, agus is iontach mar a thug An Seabhac a haigne is a leagan intinne leis, mar shampla í bheith mí-shásta lena cuid gruaige, nó an mionchur síos a rinne sí ar ghúna brídeoige. Tá an greann agus an spraoi céanna ann is atá in *Jimín*, ach, ar chuma éigin, déantar dearmad ar *Mhóirín*, cé gurb é sin an chéad leabhar sa Ghaeilge a léiríonn aigne an chailín scoile go sonraíoch.

E: Foinsí Tagartha

Níl aon scanradh ach an éacht oibre a rinne Diarmaid Breathnach agus Máire Ní Mhurchú agus *Beathaisnéis*[437] idir lámha acu. Cuntas achomair a sholáthar ar Ghaeilgeoirí aitheanta ó 1560 go 2002, ar mhúnla *Dictionary of National Biography* an Bhéarla, b'shin a gcuspóir, agus chuireadar i gcrích go buach é, tuilleadh is milliún focal ann. Is mór a bhí an saol Gaelach ina phráinn. Is de bhunadh Thiobraid Árann Diarmaid Breathnach, agus tá leabhar tagartha eile leis sa leabharlann, *Almanag Éireann*.[438]

Cuirfear suim san dá leabhar beathaisnéise eile,[439] *Ceannródaithe*[440] ach go háirithe, mar go bhfuil cur síos ann ar Liam P. Ó Riain, iriseoir, údar, sóisialaí agus fealsamh ón dTeampall Mór. Ar chuma éigin, déantar neamhshuim anois den cheannródaí cumasach, meabhrach, liobrálach úd, agus gan oiread is leabhar amháin scríofa faoi, go bhfios dom, cé go bhfuil fótóchóip anseo de thráchtas ollscoile air.

"Ní réitíonn cumar domhain mar chliabhán di agus níl de bhuime aici agus í ag sileadh as broinn a toibrín ach sceach bheag gorta." Abha na Siúire i dtús a haistir chun na farraige síos atá i gceist ag Annraoi Ó Liatháin[441] agus a cúrsa á rianadh aige ó Bhearnán Éile go Cumar na dTrí Uisce. Más linn leagan ceart logainmneacha an Chontae a aimsiú níl dul thar leabhar Phádraig Uí Chearbhaill,[442] fear eile de bhunadh Thiobraid Árann, cúpla glúin siar. Chuir an t-Athair Éamonn Ó hÓgáin comaoin mhór ar na scoláirí lena shaothar léannta féin.[443] Is amhlaidh a thiomsaigh sé na logainmneacha as na seanleabhair, agus rinne iad a shuíomh ina n-ionaid soaitheanta féin ar fud na tíre.

---

[430] M. Ní Chriagáin, T. Ó Faoláin, *Sean-Eoin* (B.Á.C., 1938), an chéad eagrán.
[431] B. Ní Loingsigh, *Rí na gCat* (B.Á.C., 1949).
[432] M. Nic Mhaicín, *Eibhlín agus Seamus* (B.Á.C., 1942).
[433] Gan údar luaite, Scéalta an Domhain, *Léightheoirí Teamhrach* (B.Á.C., gan dáta).
[434] M. Ní Ghráda, *Tír na Deo* (B.Á.C., 1938).
[435] P. Ó Bróithe, *Scéalta ó. Eachtraibh an Bharúin Munchausen* (B.Á.C., gan dáta).
[436] An Seabhac (P. Ó Siochfhradha), *Leabhar Mhóirín* (B.Á.C., 1934).
[437] D. Breathnach, M. Ní Mhurchú, *Beathaisnéis* (B.Á.C., 1986, 1990, 1992, 1994, 1997, 1999, 2001, 2003), 8 iml.
[438] D. Breathnach, *Almanag Éireannach* (B.Á.C., 1981).
[439] E. O'Reilly, *A Chronological Account of nearly Four Hundred Irish Writers* (Sionainn, 1970), athchló; an chéad eagrán, 1820.
[440] R. Ó Glaisne, *Ceannródaithe* (B. Á. C., 1974); Martin J. Waters, *W.P. Ryan and the Irish Ireland Movement* (Tráchtas Ph.D., Ollscoil Connecticut, 1970).
[441] A. Ó Liatháin, *Cois Siúire* (B.Á.C., 1982).
[442] P. Ó Cearbhaill, (eag.), *Liostaí Logainmneacha Tiobraid Árann* (B.Á.C., 2004).
[443] Edmund Hogan, S.J., *Onomasticon Goedelicum* (B.Á.C., 1910).

Brainse Logainmneacha na Suirbhéireachta Ordanáis a d'eisigh an leabhar úd le Pádraig Ó Cearbhaill. Sa tsraith chéanna tá againn Luimneach,[444] Port Láirge,[445] Cill Chainnigh agus Uibh Fhailí. Go deimhin, tá carn leabhar againn ar an ábhar. Is dócha gurb é leabhar an tSeoighigh[446] an ceann is fearr aithne air. Sar a dtáinig Coimisiún na Logainmneacha ar an bhfód b'é ba mhó a ghéilltí dó i gcúrsaí dinnseanchais, cé gur léir anois ná bíodh iomlán an chirt i gcónaí aige. Leagan simplí dá leabhar is ea *Irish Local Names Explained*. Níor dhein an Paorach dhá leath dá dhícheall agus é ag gabháil do *The Place-Names of Decies*.[447] Chaith sé na blianta ag cruinniú na logainmneacha; thaisteal sé an dúthaigh de shiúl cos, ar rothar, ar an dtraein; scríobh sé na céadta litir; cheistigh sé daoine barrántúla ar fud na nDéise, leithéidí Sheamuis Uí Mhaolchatha. Ina dhiaidh sin is uile bhí d'umhlaíocht ann a rá gur chinnte botúin a bheith ann i ngan fhios dó. Rinne údair na leabhar eile a ndícheall cóir agus cruinneas a bheith acu.[448] Dála an tSeoighigh b'as Luimneach don Athair Pádraig de Bhulbh, agus tá ráchairt fós ar a leabhar ar shloinnte na hÉireann.[449]

Cé go dtugtar tús áite anois d'Fhoclóirí de Bhaldraithe agus Uí Dhomhnaill, agus roimhe sin arís d'Fhoclóir an Duinnínigh, ba mhaith ann ina aimsir féin an *English-Irish Phrase Dictionary*[450] a chuir an t-Ath. Láimhbheartach Mac Cionnaith dá pheann sa bhliain 1911. Cor na Gaeilge ó shin agus dúnghaois an rialtais ina leith, tá siad cíortha ag Seán Ó Riain.[451]

móirín
6

Scéal Mhóirín

Cuireadh tús le *Feasta*, iris Chonradh na Gaeilge in 1948. "Is iris liteartha í *Feasta* sa chiall is leithne-reviú den smaointeachas Éireannach, litríocht, eolaíocht, polaitíocht", adúirt an t-eagarthóir sa bhliain 1999. Filí agus scríobhnóirí móra na Gaeilge, tá a saothar le fáil inti, gualainn ar ghualainn le léirmheastóirí agus iriseoirí meabhracha. Bhí géarghá le hinnéacs; agus nuair a chuir Liam Mac Peaircín sin ar fáil fearadh na mílte fáilte roimis, mar áis thaighde thar a bheith fóinteach.[452]

caoine chille cais.*

Cread déanfamaoid feasda gan adhmad,
Atá deire na g-coillte ar lár?
Níl trácht ar Chill Chais ná a teaghlach,
'S ní bainfear a cling† go bráth!
An áit úd 'na g-comhnuigheac an Dia-bhean,
Fuair gairm 'r meidhir tar mná,
bhídheac iarlaidhe‡ ag tarruing tar toinn ann,
'S an t-aifrionn binn dá rádh.

[444] Art Ó Maolfabhail (eag.), *Logainmneacha na hÉireann Contae Luimnigh* (B.Á.C., 1990).
[445] *Liostaí Logainmneacha Contae Phort Láirge* (B.Á.C., 1991); *do. Contae Chill Chainnigh* (B.Á.C., 1993), *do. Contae Uibh Fhailí* (B.Á.C., 1994).
[446] P.W. Joyce, *Irish Names of Places* (B.Á.C., 1995) athchló; P.W. Joyce, *Irish Local Names Explained* (B.Á.C., 1979), athchló.
[447] P. Canon Power, *The Place-Names of Decies* (Corcaigh, 1952), an dara heagrán.
[448] Risteárd Ó Foghludha, *Log Ainmneacha* (B.Á.C., gan dáta); *Ainmneacha Gaeilge na mBailte Poist* (B.Á.C., 1969); Breandán Ó Cíobháin, Toponomiae Hiberniae 2, 3 (B.Á.C., 1984), 2 iml.
[449] Rev. Patrick Woulfe, *Sloinnte Gaedheal is Gall* (B.Á.C., 1922) .
[450] Lambert McKenna, S.J., *English-Irish Phrase Dictionary* (B.Á.C., 1911).
[451] Seán Ó Riain, *Pleanáil Teanga in Éirinn* (B.Á.C., 1994).
[452] Liam Mac Peaircín, *Feasta, Innéacs 1948-2000* (B.Á.C., 2003).

Irlandois et Irlandoise comme ils alloyent accoustres estans au seruice de feu Roy Henry

3. WATERCOLOUR PAINTING BY LUCAS DE HEERE OF IRISH PEOPLE " AS THE
WENT ATTIRED IN THE REIGN OF HENRY VIII "

Section Eleven: Early and Medieval Irish History

This and the following two sections indicates the books and collections of articles on Irish history in Tipperary Studies under the general headings: Early and Medieval, Early Modern and Modern. Much of this material, while not specifically dealing with Tipperary, contains relevant information.

A useful starting point is the authoritative and mammoth *A New History of Ireland*, published by Oxford University Press under the auspices of the Royal Irish Academy.

There are seven volumes, from prehistory to 1984 and each volume has contributions from a variety of specialists. There are also two companion volumes with a chronology, maps, genealogies and various lists. The publishing history of the *New History* has been drawn-out. Volume III covering early modern Ireland was first to appear, published in 1976. Volume I, dealing with prehistory and early Ireland, was last to be published, only appearing in 2005.[453]

Ireland's Ancient Schools and Scholars Healy, 1902

Apart from many archaeological reports (**see Section Seven**), *Tipperary Historical Journal* has published little on Tipperary medieval history.[454] *Tipperary: History & Society* contains five important articles, discussing archaeology, urban development, parochial organisation, Gaelic landownership and the impact of the Normans.[455] On

---

[453] Relevant to this Section are: D. Ó Cróinín (ed.), *A New History of Ireland I Prehistoric and Early Ireland* (Oxford UP, 2005) and A. Cosgrove (ed.), *A New History of Ireland II Medieval Ireland 1169-1534* (Clarendon Oxford, 1987). Each volume has a comprehensive bibliography.

[454] D.G. Marnane, English Law in Tipperary 1295-1314 in *THJ* (2003), pp. 41-64. See also D. Cowman, The Silvermines: Sporadic Workings 1289-1874 in *THJ* (1988), pp. 96-115; P. Conlan OFM, The Fransciscans in Clonmel 1269-1998 in *THJ* (1999), pp. 98-110.

[455] R. Raleigh, The archaeology of prehistoric Tipperary; J. Bradley, The medieval towns of Tipperary; M. Hennessy, Parochial organisation in medieval Tipperary; C.A. Empey, The Norman period 1185-1500; K. Nicholls, Gaelic landownership in Tipperary from the surviving Irish deeds in W. Nolan & T.G. McGrath (eds.), *Tipperary: History & Society* (Dublin, 1985).

History of the Irish Confederation (Gilbert)

this latter topic the impact of the Normans on the county, the key articles are by C.A. Empey.[456]

George Cunningham's study is important with respect to the early experiences of Normans in North Tipperary.[457] This is one of a very small number of modern monographs discussing the early and medieval history of some Tipperary regions.[458] The best-known contemporary partisan witness is Giraldus Cambrensis.[459] The classic text is Orpen's study.[460] Subsequent narrative histories are by Curtis and Otway-Ruthven.[461] An important source for Norman settlement in Aherlow is the *Calendar of the Gormanston Register*.[462] There is a ground-breaking monograph on agricultural practices in the county.[463]

History did not begin with the Normans and one of the most noted figures in early Ireland was Cormac Mac Cuilennain, king of Cashel in the early 10th century and also an ecclesiastic. His name is linked to a famous glossary and also a psalter.[464] The early church could have an intensely spiritual element.[465] Two important studies of

---

[456] C.A. Empey, The cantreds of medieval Tipperary in *N. Munster Antiq. Jn.*, xiii (1970), pp. 22-29; C.A. Empey, The settlement of the kingdom of Limerick in J. Lydon (ed.), *England & Ireland in the Later Middle Ages* (Dublin, 1981), pp. 1-25; C.A. Empey & K. Simms, The ordinances of the White Earl and the problem of coign in the later middle ages in *R.I.A. Proc.*, lxxv (1975), pp. 161-87; C.A. Empey, Conquest and Settlement: patterns of Anglo-Norman settlement in North Munster and South Leinster in *IESH*, xiii (1986), pp. 5-31; C.A. Empey, The Anglo-Norman settlement in the cantred of Eliogarty in J. Bradley (ed.), *Settlement & Society in medieval Ireland* (Kilkenny, 1988); C.A. Empey, The Anglo-Norman community in Tipperary and Kilkenny in the middle ages: change and continuity in G. MacNiocaill & P. Wallace (eds.), *Keimelia: Studies in medieval archaeology and history* (Galway, 1988), pp. 449-67; D. Edwards & A. Empey, Tipperary Liberty ordinances of the 'Black' earl of Ormond in D. Edwards (ed.), *Regions & Rulers in Ireland 1100-1650* (Dublin, 2004), pp. 122-45.

[457] G. Cunningham, *The Anglo-Norman Advance into the South-West Midlands of Ireland 1185-1221* (Roscrea, 1987). Tipperary Studies has typescripts of some summer schools organised by George Cunningham and dealing mainly with early and medieval history, 1977-79. See also M. Hennessy, Manorial Organisation in early 13th century Tipperary in *Irish Geography*, 29 (2), (1996), pp. 116-25; M. Hennessy, Manorial agriculture and settlement in early fourteenth-century Co Tipperary in H.B. Clarke, J. Prunty & M. Hennessy (eds.), *Surveying Ireland's Past: multidisciplinary essays in honour of Anngret Simms* (Dublin, 2004), pp. 99-118 and B.J. Graham, *Medieval Irish Settlement: A Review* (Historical Geography Research Series 3 (1980); B.J. Graham, *Anglo-Norman Settlement in Ireland* (Irish Settlement Studies 1(1985) and T. Barry (ed.), *A History of Settlement in Ireland* (London, 2000).

[458] E. Ó Neill, *The Golden Vale of Ivowen – between Slievenamon and Suir* (Dublin, n.d.); D.G. Marnane, *Land & Settlement: a history of West Tipperary to 1660* (Tipperary, 2003).

[459] T. Wright (ed.), *The Historical Works of Giraldus Cambrensis* (London, 1913). This includes both the Topography and the Conquest. More recent editions have been published.

[460] G.H. Orpen, *Ireland Under the Normans, 1169-1333* (Oxford, 1911-20) 4 volumes. (Orpen was educated in the Abbey Grammar School, Tipperary town).

[461] E. Curtis, *A history of medieval Ireland from 1086 to 1513* (London, 1938); A.J. Otway-Ruthven, *A history of Medieval Ireland* (London, 1968).

[462] J. Mills & M.J. McEnery, *Calendar of the Gormanston Register* (Dublin, 1916).

[463] I. Leister, *Peasant openfield farming and its territorial organisation in County Tipperary* (Marburg/Lahn, 1976).

[464] W. Stokes, *Three Irish Glossaries [Cormac's Glossary, Codex A from a manuscript in the library of the RIA]* (London, 1862).

[465] (Anon), Irish Culdees and their Abbey of Monaincha in *Dublin University Magazine*, 76 (1870), pp.706-16; P. O'Dwyer, *Ceili De: Spiritual Reform in Ireland, 750-900* (Dublin, 1981). Also J. O'Neill, The Rule of Ailbe of Emly in *Ériu*, 3 (1907), pp. 92-115.

[466] F.J. Byrne, *Irish Kings and High-Kings* (London, 1973); K. Nicholls, *Gaelic and Gaelicised Ireland in the Middle Ages* (Dublin, 1972). Older studies about pre-Norman Ireland are E. MacNeill, *Phases of Irish History* (Dublin, 1920) and T.F. O'Rahilly, *Early Irish History and Mythology* (Dublin, 1946).

Gaelic Ireland are by F.J. Byrne and Kenneth Nicholls.[466] Important texts on Gaelic Ireland are *The Book of Rights and An Leabhar Muimhneach*.[467]

Two books examine the Cistercians.[468] Holy Cross, described by Roger Stalley, as 'the most distinguished monument of fifteenth-century Ireland' is a Cistercian foundation.[469] A number of older books, now collector's items, look at aspects of the medieval history of parts of the county.[470] These scholars also published articles of value.[471] Probably the most prolific writer of articles on the early and medieval history of North Tipperary was D.F. Gleeson.[472] With regard to early church history, the most useful guide is Kenney.[473] The standard guide to ecclesiastical sites and religious foundations is Gwynn & Hadcock.[474] The classic work on ancient place-names and territories is Hogan.[475] The story of Brian Boru and the victory against the Danes at the Battle of Solohead is told in a famous propaganda poem.[476] Fr John Ryan discussed the politics of the O'Briens before the Normans.[477] The most important published records with respect to the medieval history of Tipperary

467 J. O'Donovan, *Leabhar na Gceart, The Book of Rights* (Dublin, 1847); T. O Donnchadha, *An Leabhar Muimhneach* (Dublin, n.d.)

468 Colmcille O Conbhuidhe OCSO, *The Cistercian Abbeys of Tipperary* (Dublin, 1999); R. Stalley, *The Cistercian Monasteries of Ireland* (Yale UP, 1987). Also Rev. P. Power, The Cistercian Abbeys of Munster in *JCHAS*, xliii 157 (1938).

469 Rev. D. Murphy, *Triumphalia Chronologica Monasterii Sanctae Crucis in Hibernia* (Dublin, 1891) and the best of the modern works: G. Carville, *The Heritage of Holy Cross* (Belfast, 1973). Also, Sr M. Brennan, *The Historical-Geography of the Cistercian Abbey of Holy Cross County Tipperary* (Unpublished B. Ed. Thesis, Limerick, 1986). Some official reports are of interest: 74th and 81st annual reports of the Commissioners of Public Works.

470 P.F. Flynn, *The Book of the Galtees and the Golden Vein* (Dublin, 1926); W.P. Canon Burke, *History of Clonmel* (Waterford, 1907); Rev. St John D. Seymour, *The Diocese of Emly* (Dublin, 1913); Rev. J. Gleeson, *History of the Ely O'Carroll Territory or Ancient Ormond* (1st ed. 1915, reprint Kilkenny, 1982) 2 volumes; Rev. J. Gleeson, *Cashel of the Kings* (Dublin, 1927); Rev. A. Gwynn & D.F. Gleeson, *A History of the Diocese of Killaloe* (Dublin, 1962).

471 For example: Rev. St John D. Seymour, Loughmoe Castle and its legends in *JRSAI*, (1909); Rev. St John D. Seymour, Liath-Mor-Mochoemog in *JNMAS*, ii, 3 (1912), pp. 126-33; Rev. St John D. Seymour, Family Papers belonging to the Purcells of Loughmoe Co Tipperary in *JNMAS*, I, 3 (1913-15), pp. 124-29, 191-203; H.S. Crawford, The Ruins of Loughmoe Castle, Co Tipperary in *JRSAI*, (1909), pp. 234-41; H.S. Crawford, The Dolmens of Tipperary in *JRSAI*, (1910); Rev. St John D. Seymour, Notes on a Temporary parish (Donohill) in *JCHAS*, (1916); Rev. P. Power, The Rian Bó Phadruig (the ancient highway of The Decies) in *JRSAI*, (1905); Rev. J. Everard, Everard's castle now Burntcourt castle near Cahir Co Tipperary in *JRSAI*, (1907); W.F. Butler, Clan and settler in Ormond in *JCHAS*, xx (1914), pp. 1-16; H.F. Berry, The antiquities of the parish of Kilcomenty, near Birdhill Co Tipperary in *JRSAI* (1904), pp. 99-110; E. St John Brooks, The Family of Marisco in *JRSAI*, (1931), pp. 89-112; P. Lyons, Kilfeacle and Knockgraffon Motes Co Tipperary in *JRSAI*, (1950)

472 The Ormond Freeholders of the Civil Survey in *JRSAI*, lxvi (1936), pp. 130-53; The Castle and manor of Dromineer Co Tipperary in *N. Munster Antiq. Jn.*, (1936); An Unpublished Cromwellian Document in *N. Munster Antiq. Jn.*, (1936-39); The Silver Mines of Ormond in *JRSAI*, lxvii (1937), pp. 101-16; The Manor of Ardcrony in *Molua* (1937); The Episcopal Succession of Killaloe, AD 1317-1616 in *N. Munster Antiq. Jn.*, (1940), pp. 51-62; The Manor of Ballinaclogh in Ormond in *N. Munster Antiq. Jn.*, (1943), pp. 129-43; Parish Boundaries in the Killaloe Diocese in *N. Munster Antiq. Jn.*, (1949), pp. 1-8; Some Learned Men of Killaloe Diocese in *Molua* (1950); The River of Geogh in *N. Munster Antiq. Jn.*, (1959). Also his typescript notes on the OS maps of Co Tipperary, sheets 1-33 and a file of newspaper articles.

473 J.F. Kenney, *The Sources for the Early History of Ireland Ecclesiastical: an introduction and guide* (Columbia UP, 1929). Also K. Hughes, *Early Christian Ireland: Introduction to the Sources* (London, 1972) and her *The Church in Early Irish Society* (London, 1966).

474 A. Gwynn & R.N. Hadcock, *Medieval Religious Houses Ireland* (London, 1970).

475 E. Hogan, S.J., *Onomasticon Goedelicum: an index with identifications to the Gaelic names of places and tribes* (Dublin, 1910). See also Rev. P. Power, *The Place-Names of Decies* (London, 1907).

476 J.H. Todd (ed.), *Cogadh Gaedhel re Gallaibh* (London, 1867).

477 Rev. J. Ryan, The Dalcassians in *N. Munster Antiq. Jn.*, iii, 4 (1943), and The O'Briens in Munster after Clontarf in *N. Munster Antiq. Jn.*, ii, 4 (1941).

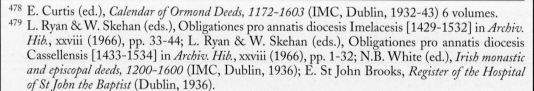

A CROMWELLIAN DEBENTURE.

are the *Ormond Deeds*.[478] There are a number of important collections of church records relevant to the medieval history of the county.[479]

Various annals, especially the *Four Masters* and *Inisfallen* are vital primary sources.[480] An important literary source touching on the Cantwells, Purcells, O Carrolls, Hacketts and Butlers in the fifteenth-century is a collection of poems.[481] With reference to the early church, Fr Ryan's book is a classic text.[482]

One wonders how some of the older books in Tipperary Studies came to be there? Perhaps they were part of a nineteenth century urban library. A case in point is a document edited by the Kilkenny antiquarian the Rev. James Graves.[483] In the 1870s and '80s, five volumes of "documents relating to Ireland" were published in summary form and covered the late 12th to the early 14th centuries. While this series is a calendar, and ideally the complete document should be used; "Sweetman" has been an important source for medieval Irish history.[484]

Cromwellian Settlement of Ireland
John P. Prendergast.
London, 1865

Down Survey Map of Slieveardagh reprinted in Ordnance Survey Letters, 1840

---

[478] E. Curtis (ed.), *Calendar of Ormond Deeds, 1172-1603* (IMC, Dublin, 1932-43) 6 volumes.

[479] L. Ryan & W. Skehan (eds.), Obligationes pro annatis diocesis Imelacesis [1429-1532] in *Archiv. Hib.*, xxviii (1966), pp. 33-44; L. Ryan & W. Skehan (eds.), Obligationes pro annatis diocesis Cassellensis [1433-1534] in *Archiv. Hib.*, xxviii (1966), pp. 1-32; N.B. White (ed.), *Irish monastic and episcopal deeds, 1200-1600* (IMC, Dublin, 1936); E. St John Brooks, *Register of the Hospital of St John the Baptist* (Dublin, 1936).

[480] S. Mac Airt (ed.), *The Annals of Inisfallen* (Dublin, 1951); S. O hInnse (ed.), *Miscellaneous Irish Annals, 1114-1437* (Dublin, 1947); J.N. Radner (ed.), *Fragmentary Annals of Ireland* (Dublin, 1978); J. O'Donovan (ed.), *Annals of the Kingdom of Ireland* (2nd ed., Dublin, 1856) 7 volumes; Very Rev. R. Butler (ed.), *The Annals of Ireland by Friar John Clyn* (Dublin, 1849).

[481] A. O'Sullivan (ed.), *Poems on Marcher Lords* (Irish Texts Society, 1987).

[482] Rev. J. Ryan, *Irish Monasticism: origins and early development* (Dublin, 1931).

[483] Rev. J. Graves (ed.), *A roll of the proceedings of the king's council in Ireland for a portion of the 16th year of the reign of Richard 11, AD 1392-3* (London, 1877).

[484] H.S. Sweetman (ed.), *Calendar of Documents relating to Ireland* (five volumes, 1171-1251, 1252-84, 1285-92, 1293-1301, 1302-1307).

Tipperary Studies holds a number of collections of essays, all with valuable material for anyone interested in early and medieval history and in some instances with information relevant to Tipperary.[485] For example, the Stephens & Glasscock volume has articles on 'moated sites and deserted boroughs and villages' and 'town and *baile* in Irish place names'; the Rynne volume has an article on 'the rise of the Dál Cais' while the Edwards volume has an article on 'the synod of Cashel'. Similarly with respect to a number of monographs and articles, there are Tipperary references.[486] Two books covering the medieval period and extending into modern times are a compilation of documents and a work on judges.[487]

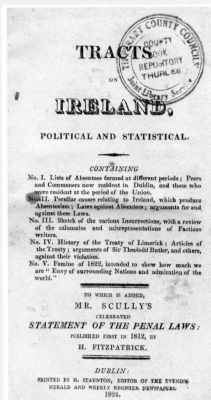

The taking of the Earl of Ormond April 10, 1600

---

[485] C. Manning (ed.), *Dublin and Beyond the Pale: studies in honour of Patrick Healy* (Bray, 1998); J. Littleton & T. O'Keefe (eds.), *The Manors in Medieval & Early Modern Ireland* (Dublin, 2005); D. Edwards (ed.), *Regions & Rulers in Ireland 1100-1650* (Dublin, 2004); A.P. Smyth (ed.), *Seanchas: Studies in Early & Medieval Irish Archaeology, History and Literature in honour of F.J. Byrne* (Dublin, 2000); N. Stephens & R.E. Glasscock (eds.), *Irish Geographical Studies in honour of E. Estyn Evans* (Belfast, 1970); E.Rynne (ed.), *North Munster Studies* (Limerick, 1967).

[486] M.D. O'Sullivan, *Italian Merchant Bankers in Ireland in the Thirteenth-Century* (Dublin, 1962); D Ó Cróinín, *Early Medieval Ireland 400-1200* (London, 1995); T. O'Keeffe, *Romanesque Ireland: architecture and ideology in the twelfth century* (Dublin, 2003); T. McNeill, *Castles in Ireland: feudal power in a Gaelic World* (London, 1997); G.O. Sayles (ed.), *Documents on the affairs of Ireland before the King's Council* (IMC, Dublin, 1979); H.G. Richardson & G.O. Sayles, *Parliament in Medieval Ireland* (DHA, 1964); A. Thomas, *The Walled Towns of Ireland* (Dublin, 1992) 2 volumes; H. Jager, Land Use in medieval Ireland in *IESH*, x (1983), pp. 51-65.

[487] E. Curtis & R.B. McDowell (eds.), *Irish Historical Documents 1172-1922* (London, 1943); F. E. Ball, *The Judges in Ireland 1221-1921* (New York, 1927), 2 volumes.

The Arrest of a Whiteboy by the Yeomen

W. J. Scanlon
The United Irishmen

Section Twelve:
Early Modern Irish History

The volume in *A New History of Ireland* covering the early modern period was the first of the series published.[488] In the thirty years since, a good deal has been published on this period, including in the pages of *Tipperary Historical Journal*.[489]

A number of older works are useful with respect to the sixteenth and seventeenth-centuries. Paul Flynn's book is a readable account of the Desmond wars, especially around Aherlow.[490] Much of Sir Michael O'Dwyer's 'history of an Irish sept' concentrates on the seventeenth-century and has

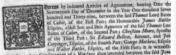

An ACT *for Sale of Part of the Estate of* Thomas Lord Baron *of* Caher, *in the Kingdom of* Ireland, *towards discharging the Debts and Incumbrances affecting the same, and other Purposes therein mentioned.*

---

[488] T.W. Moody, F.X. Martin, F.J. Byrne (eds.), *A New History of Ireland III Early Modern Ireland 1534-1691* (Clarendon, Oxford, 1976).

[489] A. McClintock, Tipperary's role in the governing of Ireland (1603-1641) in *THJ* (1988), pp. 159-72; J.G. Simms, The Cromwellian Settlement of Tipperary in *THJ* (1989), pp. 27-34; H. A. Taatgen, Thomas McDonough's 'Middle Country': The Norman and Cromwellian Plantations in *THJ* (1990), pp. 133-48; W.J. Smith, Towns and Town Life in Mid-17th Century Co. Tipperary in *THJ* (1991), pp. 163-70; R. Gillespie & B. Cunningham, Holy Cross Abbey and the Counter Reformation in Tipperary in *THJ* (1991), pp. 171-80; C. Breathnach, Archbishop John Brenan (1625-1693): his life and work in *THJ* (1993), pp. 148-59; M. Boland, The decline of the O'Kennedys of Ormond in *THJ* (1994), pp. 129-41; E. Ó hAnnracháin, Irish veterans in the Invalides: the Tipperary contingent in *THJ* (1998), pp. 158-89; D. O Riain-Raedel, A German visitor to Monaincha in 1591 in *THJ* (1998), pp. 223-34; M. O'Donnell, Parliamentary Representation for County Tipperary, 1560-1800 in *THJ* (2000), pp. 136-48; I. Fennessy OFM, The theft of the relic of Holy Cross Abbey in *THJ* (2000), pp. 149-56; M. O'Donnell, Parliamentary Representation for County Tipperary, 1560-1800 (Part 2) in *THJ* (2001), pp. 97-110; C. Manning, The two Sir George Hamiltons and their connections with the castles of Roscrea and Nenagh in *THJ* (2001), pp. 149-54; M. O'Donnell, Parliamentary Representation for County Tipperary, 1560-1800 (Part 3) in *THJ* (2002), pp. 45-58; B. Cunningham, Geoffrey Keating's family connections in *THJ* (2002), pp. 59-68; M. O'Donnell, Parliamentary Representation for County Tipperary, 1560-1800 (Part 4) in *THJ* (2003), pp. 65-80; J. Morrissey, Kilnamanagh and the Frontier: surviving the New English of the early seventeenth century in *THJ* (2004), pp. 101-14; M. O'Donnell, Parliamentary Representation for County Tipperary, 1560-1800 (Part 5) in *THJ* (2004), pp. 135-50.

[490] P.J. Flynn, *The Book of the Galtees and the Golden Vein* (Dublin, 1926). For a recent study see, A.M. McCormack, *The Earldom of Desmond, 1463-1583: the decline and crisis of a feudal lordship* (Dublin, 2005).

Glen of Aherlow

been reprinted. John Morrissey's work on the O'Dwyers of Kilnamanagh, is very academic and deals with this same topic.[491] David Butler's study of "religion, land and rivalry" in South Tipperary is both academic and readable.[492] Dermot Gleeson's study of North Tipperary in the seventeenth-century also dates from the 1930s and has been republished with a deal of additional notes.[493] Also published in the 1930s was Martin Callanan's study of the O'Kennedys, O'Dwyers, O'Mulryans (Ryans) and O'Meaghers.[494]

A number of important sources for sixteenth century Irish history have been published. The most detailed are the Tudor Fiants, collections of government orders, appointments and grants which, fortunately had been calendared and published prior to the destruction of the Public Record Office in 1922.[495] ['Fiant' or 'Let' such and such be done, from the opening word of the usual formula heading these documents.] Tipperary Studies has some volumes of the *Calendar of the State Papers relating to Ireland*, an important indexed summary of official documents.[496] The Library has four of the six volumes of the Carew Manuscripts.[497] Tipperary Studies also has a number of volumes in the Domestic (English) series of state papers.[498]

Two collections of documents dealing with ecclesiastical history are especially useful with respect to the impact of the Reformation on religious houses.[499] The material in the first volume listed below came from the Ormond MSS originally in Kilkenny Castle, while the second collection was taken from the Public Record Office in London and refers to property in Tipperary held by nineteen religious foundations. Previous reference was made to the six volumes of the calendar of Ormond deeds, a treasury of Tipperary information. The final three volumes

---

[491] Sir M. O'Dwyer, *The O'Dwyers of Kilnamanagh the history of an Irish sept* (London, 1933, reprint Limerick 2000); J. Morrissey, *Negotiating Colonialism: Gaelic-Irish reaction to New English expansion in Early Modern Tipperary, c.1541-1641* (Galway, 2003). Also his Searching for Common Ground: Colonialism and Collaboration in Early Modern Ireland in *THJ* (2005), pp. 25-30.

[492] D.J. Butler, *South Tipperary 1570-1841 Religion, Land & Rivalry* (Dublin, 2006).

[493] D.F. Gleeson, *The Last Lords of Ormond* (London, 1938; revised edition by D.A. Murphy, Relay, Nenagh, 2001).

[494] M. Callanan, *Records of Four Tipperary Septs* (Galway, 1938, reprinted 1995).

[495] *The Irish Fiants of the Tudor Sovereigns during the reigns of Henry VIII, Edward VI, Philip & Mary and Elizabeth I* (Edmund Burke, Dublin, 1994) 4 volumes.

[496] *Calendar of the State Papers relating to Ireland*. Tipperary Studies holds the following volumes: 1509-73; 1574-85; 1586-88; 1603-06; 1606-08; 1608-10; 1611-14; 1615-25; 1647-60 with addenda 1625-60. See also 15th report HMC, ...*acts of the privy council in Ireland*, 1556-1571 [C- 8364] (London, 1897).

[497] Calendar of the Carew Manuscripts preserved in the archiepiscopal library at Lambeth, 1515-74; 1575-88; 1589-1600; 1601-03 (London, 1867-73).

[498] *State Papers Henry VIII*, vols 2-11; *State Papers Elizabeth, 1547-80; State Paper James I, 1603-10, 1611-18, 1619-23, 1623-25; State Papers Charles 1, 1625-26, 1627-28, 1628-29, 1629-31; State Papers Charles II, 1660-61.*

[499] N.B. White (ed.), *Irish Monastic and Episcopal Deeds A.D. 1200-1600* (IMC, Dublin, 1936); N.B. White (ed.), *Extents of Irish Monastic Possessions, 1540-1541* (IMC, Dublin, 1943).

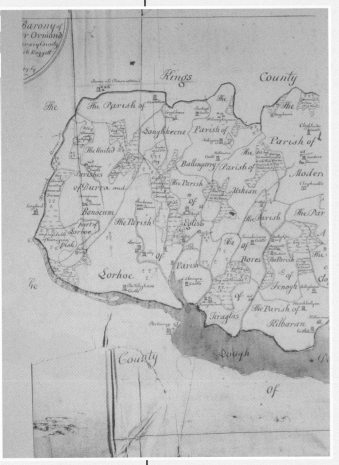

Down Survey Map

cover the Tudor period.[500] Sir James Perrott was an important player in the drama of the Geraldine rebellions.[501] Edmund Spenser lived for a time in the shadow of the Galtees and wrote his views on Ireland.[502] A contemporary source is *Holinshed's Chronicle*.[503]

Two important collections of seventeenth-century sources have been published for the county: a land survey of the 1650s and taxation records of the 1660s.[504] The originals of these taxation records were destroyed in 1922. Heads of households are listed. The *Civil Survey* gives proprietors of land in 1640, together with many topographical, geographical and economic details. The *Civil Survey* for County Limerick is of value because part of what is now Tipperary was then Limerick.[505] The Civil Survey for Waterford is also in Tipperary Studies.[506] A related source gives the proprietors of the later seventeenth-century. This has not been published but Tipperary Studies has a manuscript copy.[507] Another source, relating to the whole country, including Tipperary is a so-called 'census' c.1659.[508] These sources have been used as the basis of discussions about seventeenth-century Tipperary.[509] A study of the transplantation to Connacht has information about Tipperary dispossessed.[510] Information is available on Cashel & Emly and Killaloe for the early seventeenth-century.[511]

The archives of the Butlers of Ormond(e) collected and (then) kept at Kilkenny Castle also cast light on seventeenth-century Tipperary and were published over

---

[500] E. Curtis (ed.), *Calendar of Ormond Deeds*, vols. iv – vi (IMC, Dublin, 1937-43).

[501] H. Wood (ed.), *The Chronicle of Ireland 1584-1608 by Sir James Perrott* (IMC, Dublin, 1933).

[502] W. Renwich (ed.), *Edmund Spenser, A View of the Present State of Ireland* (Oxford, Clarendon, 1970).

[503] L. Miller & E. Power (eds.), *Holinshed's Irish Chronicle* (Dolmen, 1979).

[504] R.C. Simington (ed.), *The Civil Survey A.D. 1654-1656 County of Tipperary Eastern and Southern Baronies* (IMC, Dublin, 1931) and *Western and Northern Baronies* (IMC, Dublin, 1934); T. Laffan, *Tipperary's Families: being the Hearth Money Records for 1665-6-7* (Dublin, 1911).

[505] R.C. Simington (ed.), *The Civil Survey County of Limerick* (IMC, Dublin, 1938).

[506] R.C. Simington (ed.), *The Civil Survey County of Waterford* (IMC, Dublin, 1942).

[507] *Book of Survey and Distribution, County Tipperary*.

[508] S. Pender (ed.), *A Census of Ireland, c.1659* (IMC, Dublin, 1939).

[509] W. Smyth, Property, patronage and population – reconstructing the human geography of mid-seventeenth century County Tipperary in Nolan & McGrath (eds.), *Tipperary: History & Society* (Dublin, 1985); W.J. Smyth, Making the documents of conquest speak: the transformation of property, society and settlement in seventeenth-century counties Tipperary and Kilkenny in M. Silverman & P.H. Gulliver (eds.), *Approaching the Past: Historical Anthropology through Irish Case Studies* (New York, 1992); W.J. Smyth, Land Values, Landownership and Population Patterns in County Tipperary for 1641-60 and 1841-50: some comparisons in L.M. Cullen & F. Furet (eds.), *Ireland and France, 17th-20th Centuries: towards a comparative study of rural history* (Paris, 1980). These sources have also been used with respect to Clanwilliam in mid-west Tipperary; see D.G. Marnane, *Land and Settlement: a history of West Tipperary to 1660* (Tipperary, 2003).

[510] R.C. Simington, *The Transplantation to Connacht, 1654-58* (Dublin, 1970).

[511] M.A. Murphy, The Royal Visitation, 1615, Cashel & Emly in *Arch. Hib.*, I (1912), pp. 272-311 and Killaloe in *Arch. Hib.*, III (1914), pp. 210-26.

several decades in the late 19th and
early 20th centuries. Tipperary
Studies holds some of these
volumes.[512] One of the best known
of an earlier generation of
historians of this period was a
Tipperaryman, Richard Bagwell of
Marlfield near Clonmel who wrote
a series of books on the impact of
both the Tudors and Stuarts on
Ireland.[513] The Rev. St John D.
Seymour, also with a county
connection, wrote on the puritans
in Ireland.[514] Another writer on this
period with Tipperary connections
was William Butler.[515] The most
important member of the Butler

Bookplate from
Sir William Butler's
Autobiography

family in the seventeenth-century was James, 1st duke of Ormonde and Tipperary
Studies has a copy of the classic 'life' by Thomas Carte.[516] Sir John Davies was Irish
Attorney General in the early 1600s and his "A Discovery of the true causes why
Ireland was never entirely subdued" is an important text.[517] Another view of the
condition of Ireland from the same period is of interest.[518] The classic monograph
on the 'Cromwellian Settlement' is Prendergast.[519] Tipperary Studies has a number
of important texts (including the oldest book, 1680, in the collection) with respect
to the upheavals of the seventeenth-century; including Hickson's work using the
1641 Depositions.[520] Toby Barnard has contributed hugely to our understanding of
the creation of the Ascendancy.[521]

[512] *10th report HMC, MSS Marquis of Ormonde [C-4576-1* (London, 1885); *14th report HMC, MSS
Marquis of Ormonde [C-7678]* (London, 1895); *Report MSS Marquis of Ormonde [C-9245]*
(London, 1899); *Calendar of the manuscripts of the Marquess of Ormonde, preserved at Kilkenny
Castle* (HMC, London, 1902-1912) volumes i-vii.

[513] R, Bagwell, *Ireland Under the Tudors* (London, 1885-90) 3 volumes and Ireland Under the Stuarts
and during the interregnum (London, 1909-16) 3 volumes. (The third volume is missing). See
also R. Dunlop, *Ireland under the Commonwealth* (Manchester, 1913).

[514] St. John D. Seymour, *The Puritans in Ireland*, 1647-1661 (Oxford, 1921).

[515] W.F.T. Butler, *Confiscation in Irish History* (2nd ed., Dublin, 1918); W.F.T. Butler, *Gleanings from
Irish History* (London, 1925).

[516] T. Carte, *An History of the Life of James Duke of Ormonde* (London, 1736) 2 volumes. See also T.
Barnard & J. Fenlon (eds.), *The Dukes of Ormonde 1610-1745* (Boydell Press, 2000); Lady
Burghclere, *The Life of James First Duke of Ormonde, 1610-1688* (London, 1912) 2 volumes.

[517] Included in *Historical Tracts: By Sir John Davies* (Dublin, 1787). Tipperary Studies also has a
separate edition of A Discovery (London, 1747).

[518] G. O'Brien (ed.), *Advertisements for Ireland being a description of the state of Ireland in the reign of
James I, contained in a manuscript in the library of TCD* (Dublin, 1923).

[519] J.P. Prendergast, *The Cromwellian Settlement of Ireland* (London, 1865). See also his *Ireland from
the Restoration to the Revolution, 1660-1690* (London, 1887).

[520] J.T. Gilbert (ed.), *The history of the Irish Confederation and the war in Ireland (1641-9)* (Dublin,
1882-91) 7 volumes; J. Hogan (ed.), *Letters and papers relating to the Irish Rebellion between 1642-
46* (IMC, Dublin, 1936); *The History of the Execrable Irish Rebellion traced from many preceding acts
to the grand eruption the 23 October 1641* (London, 1680); *The History of the War of Ireland from
1641 to 1653 by a British Officer* (Dublin, 1873); J.T. Gilbert (ed.), *A Jacobite narrative of the war
in Ireland, 1688-91* (Dublin, 1892); Sir W. Petty, *Political Survey of Ireland* (2nd ed. London,
1719); Sir W. Petty, *The Political Anatomy of Ireland* (1st ed. 1691, IUP Shannon, 1970); E.
Ludlow, *Memoirs of Edmund Ludlow* (Vevey Switzerland, 1698-9) volumes 1 and 2. Volume 3 is
missing. These are among the oldest books in Tipperary Studies; M. Hickson, *Ireland in the 17th
century or the massacres of 1641* (London, 1884) 2 volumes.

[521] T. Barnard, *A New Anatomy of Ireland – the Irish Protestants, 1649-1770* (Yale UP, 2003).

Listed below relating to the sixteenth and seventeenth-centuries are monographs on people and topics, in most cases having some Tipperary connections. Richard Heaton was a scholar living near Roscrea,[522] William Tirry OSA was a Fethard-based catholic martyr,[523] Patrick Sarsfield was Patrick Sarsfield,[524] Erasmus Smith was a Cromwellian Adventurer.[525] Among the topics are the Dominicans,[526] Franciscans,[527] administration,[528] social history,[529] economic history,[530] plantation,[531] religious dissent,[532] Quakers,[533] Huguenots,[534] synods,[535] politics[536].

Monasticon Hibernicum

[522] L. Walsh O Cist, *Richard Heaton of Ballyskenagh, 1601-1666* (Roscrea, 1978).

[523] J. O'Connor OSA, *A Priest on the Run: William Tirry OSA, 1608-1654* (Dublin, 1992).

[524] P. Wauchope, *Patrick Sarsfield and the Williamite War* (Dublin, 1992).

[525] M.V. Ronan, *Erasmus Smith Endowment: a romance of Irish Confiscation* (Dublin, 1937) and for a different view see W.J.R. Wallace, *Faithful To Our Trust: a history of the Erasmus Smith Trust and The High School, Dublin* (Columba Press, 2004).

[526] T. Flynn OP, *The Irish Dominicans 1536-1641* (Dublin, 1993).

[527] Rev. C.P. Meehan, *The rise and fall of the Irish Franciscan Monasteries & memories of the Irish hierarchy in the 17th century* (Dublin, 1872); J.F. O'Donnell, *Memories of the Irish Franciscans* (Dublin, 1871)

[528] J. Ohemeyer & E. O Ciarda (eds.), *The Irish Statute Staple Books, 1596-1687* (Dublin, 1998).

[529] E. MacLysaght, *Irish Life in the 17th century* (Dublin, 1939).

[530] G. O'Brien, *The Economic History of Ireland in the Seventeenth-Century* (1st ed. 1919, reprint 1972).

[531] M. MacCarthy-Morrogh, *The Munster Plantation – English Migration to Southern Ireland* (Oxford 1986); K.S. Bottigheimer, *English Money and Irish Land: The "Adventurers" in the Cromwellian Settlement of Ireland* (Oxford, Clarendon, 1971).

[532] K. Herlihy (ed.), *The Irish Dissenting Tradition, 1650-1750* (Dublin, 1995).

[533] T. Wight, *A history of the rise and progress of the people called Quakers, in Ireland from the year 1653 to 1700* (4th ed. London, 1811).

[534] G.L. Lee, *The Huguenot Settlement in Ireland* (London, 1936).

[535] A. Forrestal, *Catholic Synods in Ireland, 1600-1690* (Dublin, 1998).

[536] A. Clarke, *The Old English In Ireland, 1625-42* (London, 1966); A. Clarke, *Prelude to Restoration in Ireland: the end of the Commonwealth 1659-60* (Cambridge UP, 1999); J.G. Simms, *The Jacobite Parliament of 1689* (DHA, 1966); J.G. Simms, *The Treaty of Limerick* (DHA, 1961); J.G. Simms, *Jacobite Ireland 1685-91* (London, 1969).

TENANT RIGHT
IN
TIPPERARY

HUMOROUS SKETCHES
OF
IRISH LIFE AND CHARACTER
(ILLUSTRATED).

"I say Molly, here comes the Landlord. Hand me down the owld blunderbuss till I pay the dacent gintleman his rint!?"

GLASGOW: WILLIAM LOVE, 226 ARGYLE STREET.
EDINBURGH: JOHN MENZIES & CO.
DUBLIN: HODGES, FIGGIS, & CO.
LONDON: HOULSTON & SONS, 7 PATERNOSTER BUILDINGS.
MELBOURNE AND SYDNEY: GEO. ROBERTSON.

[ENT. STA. HALL.]

PRICE ONE SHILLING

Section Thirteen: Modern Irish History

The *New History of Ireland* covered the early modern period in one volume. The modern period is covered in four hefty volumes.[537] Three ancillary publications dealing with population statistics and election results are very useful works of reference.[538] Because Tipperary Studies holds a great deal of material dealing with modern history, especially the nineteenth[539] and early twentieth centuries, this section is divided into the following subject areas: Land, The Famine, Law and Order, Politics, Religion & Education.

Famine Pot located outside Nenagh library

---

[537] T.W. Moody & W.E. Vaughan (eds.), *A New History of Ireland IV Eighteenth-Century Ireland 1691-1800* (Clarendon Oxford, 1986); W.E. Vaughan (ed.), *A New History of Ireland V Ireland Under the Union 1801-70* (Clarendon Oxford, 1989); W.E. Vaughan (ed.), *A New History of Ireland VI Ireland Under the Union 1870-1921* (Clarendon Oxford, 1996); J.R. Hill (ed.), *A New History of Ireland VII Ireland 1921-1984* (Oxford UP, 2003). Note that these volumes have comprehensive bibliographies.

[538] B.M. Walker (ed.), *Parliamentary election results in Ireland, 1801-1922* (RIA Dublin, 1978); B.M. Walker (ed.), *Parliamentary election results in Ireland, 1918-1992* (RIA Dublin, 1992); W.E. Vaughan & A.J. Fitzpatrick (eds.), *Irish Historical Statistics Population 1821-1971* (RIA Dublin, 1978).

[539] See L.M. Geary & M. Kelleher (eds.), *Nineteenth Century Ireland: a guide to recent research* (UCD Press, 2005).

A: Land

Matters relating to land especially landlord-tenant relations have been the subjects of numerous articles in the *Tipperary Historical Journal*.[540] This has not been an 'equal opportunity' source. Reflecting available evidence, landlords receive most attention and agricultural labourers, least. **Section One** lists the parish histories held by Tipperary Studies and most of these contain information on local struggles for land. Since 1998, the parish of Boherlahan-Dualla near Cashel has published an annual historical journal. Many of the articles relate to the land issue, especially two series: one on Nodstown, a townland owned by a Dublin charity, the Bluecoat School: the other an analysis of the Smith-Barry estate in Boherlahan.[541]

Tipperary: History and Society has some articles on the topic, those by Willie Nolan and T. Jones Hughes being of particular interest.[542] Dealing with Tipperary town and its hinterland, Des Marnane's narrative and discussion is the most comprehensive treatment of the topic for a region within the county.[543] The best and only monograph on a Tipperary estate deals with Castle Otway in North

---

[540] D.G. Marnane, Land and Violence in Tipperary in the 1800s in *THJ* (1988), pp. 53-89; S. O Seanóir, Tipperary and the evicted tenants: the John Dillon Papers in *THJ* (1988), pp. 90-95; J. O'Donoghue, The Scullys of Kilfeakle: Catholic Middlemen of the 1770s in *THJ* (1989), pp. 38-51; D.G. Marnane, New Tipperary: a centenary perspective in *THJ* (1989), pp. 80-81; J. Condon, The Inch Correspondence: a selection in *THJ* (1989), pp. 126-36; G. Carpentier, Kickham's Panorama of rural Ireland 1840-1870 in *THJ* (1990), pp. 63-74; D. Fitzpatrick, News from home: letters from Golden to Sydney 1851-1859 in *THJ* (1990), pp. 75-94; D. Fitzpatrick, 'The Galling Yoke of Oppression': Images of Tipperary and Australia, 1853-1868 in *THJ* (1991), pp. 83-108; D.G. Marnane, A Tipperary Landlord's Diary of the 1860s in *THJ* (1991), pp. 121-28; W. Neely, The Protestant Community of South Tipperary, 1660-1815: Part 1 in *THJ* (1991), pp. 132-40; G. Moran, William Scully and Ballycohey: a fresh look in *THJ* (1992), pp. 63-74; W. Neely, The Protestant Community of South Tipperary, 1660-1815: Part 2 in *THJ* (1992), pp. 132-39; J. Hackett, Mullinahone 1789-1917: Hackett Land Holdings in *THJ* (1992), pp. 140-47; D.G. Marnane, Samuel Cooper of Killenure (1750-1831): a Tipperary land agent and his diaries in *THJ* (1993), pp. 102-27; D.G. Marnane, The Diary of Frederick Armitage of Noan for 1906 in *THJ* (1994), pp. 48-65; C. Ó Gráda, The Wages book of a Fethard Farmer, 1880-1905 in *THJ* (1994), pp. 67-72; N. O'Donoghue, Thomas Crowe of Mount Bruis: a note in *THJ* (1994), p. 96; Sir A.F. Baker, The Bakers of Lismacue: a family chronicle in *THJ* (1994), pp. 115-28; P. Bracken, Ballydavid House, Littleton in *THJ* (1996), pp. 108-09; M. O'Dwyer, 18th century Cashel rental in *THJ* (1996), pp. 173-74; P. Holland, A Portrait of Cornwallis Maude in *THJ* (1999), pp. 140-44; P. Ó Drisceoil, Charles Kickham: current critical attitudes in *THJ* (2000), pp. 38-40; W. Jenkins, The nineteenth century butter markets of South Tipperary in *THJ* (2000), pp. 44-54; A. Carden, 'Woodcock' Carden: a balanced account in *THJ* (2000), pp. 120-31; J. Heuston, The weavers of Shronell 250 years ago in *THJ* (2002), pp. 97-114; A. Carden, Templemore houses and castles: drawings by Robert Smith in *THJ* (2002), pp. 115-30; W.A. Maguire, The murder of Constantine Maguire, 1834 in *THJ* (2003), pp. 103-20; N. Higgins, A survey of Thomastown Castle ruins, 2003 in *THJ* (2003), pp. 185-90; M. Ahern, The Fennells of Cahir in *THJ* (2004), pp. 91-100; D.G. Marnane, 'Such a Treacherous Country': a land agent in Cappawhite, 1847-52 in *THJ* (2004), pp. 233-48; D. Dromey, A labourer's life in mid-twentieth century County Tipperary in *THJ* (2004), pp. 261-62; D.G. Marnane, White v. Gill: Tipperary Famine Clearances Revisited in 1863 in *THJ* (2005), pp. 137-154; G. Sutton, New Tipperary Revisited: the case of Arthur Hugh Smith-Barry in *THJ* (2005), pp. 155-172.

[541] P. O'Dwyer, Nodstown articles in *Boherlahan-Dualla Historical Journal* (1998-2005 and ongoing); D.G. Marnane, Smith-Barry Estate articles in *Boherlahan-Dualla Historical Journal* (2001-2005 and ongoing).

[542] W. Nolan, Patterns of living in Tipperary, 1750-1850 and T. Jones Hughes, Landholding and settlement in County Tipperary in the nineteenth-century in Nolan & McGrath (eds.), *Tipperary: History & Society* (Dublin, 1985), pp. 288-324 and 339-366.

[543] D.G. Marnane, *Land & Violence: a history of West Tipperary from 1660* (Tipperary, 1985). For New Tipperary, see D.G. Marnane, Fr David Humphreys and New Tipperary in Nolan & McGrath (eds.), *Tipperary: History & Society* (Dublin, 1985), pp. 367-78.

CASHEL UNION.

HAY WANTED.

The Board of Guardians of Cashel Union will, at their Meeting to be held on THURSDAY, 13th OCTOBER, 1921, consider Tenders for supplying the Workhouse immediately with

TWO TONS

Best BAWN HAY at   per ton.

To be delivered at the Workhouse in good condition, free of charge for carriage, within four days from above date, or within such time as may be specified in tender.

Tipperary.[544] Mary Murphy has examined the Cole-Bowen estate in North Tipperary, and the role of John Trant of Dovea in two unpublished works.[545] In comparison to the nineteenth-century, little has been published with reference to the previous century. There is one important book, Tom Power's groundbreaking study.[546] Twenty of Tipperary's landed families are described in *The Tipperary Gentry*.[547]

Over some twenty years, the mid-1840s to the mid-1860s, the Tenement Valuation under the supervision of Richard Griffith valued all farms and houses in the country. The work was completed for County Tipperary by around 1850 and used the standard territorial units of townland, civil parish and barony.[548] In towns, streets were used but the town-land remained the key unit. This source is of enormous importance. For each 'tenement', variously land, land and houses and in towns, houses and gardens, an occupier was listed, together with the individual from whom the property was held. Also, the acreage and valuations of both land and houses are given. Apart from its importance as a source of genealogical information, *Griffith's Valuation* is a vital record with respect to land ownership and relative land values within the county. This source also has map references and Tipperary Studies has copies of the relevant maps for the county.[549] Three publications provide guidance to Griffith and his valuation.[550]

A quarter century after this source revealed the proprietorship of Irish land mid-century, another official publication gives an alphabetical list of owners, together with aggregate acreage and valuation, for each county.[551] Arising from this source are well-known commercially published listings of 'great landowners'.[552] The 18th century wit Horace Walpole reacted to the death of the hugely unpopular Frederick Prince of Wales in 1751 with the following verse: "Here lies Fred/ who was alive and is dead/ Had it been his father/I had much rather/ Had it been his brother/ still better than another/ Had it been his sister/ no one would have missed her/ Had it been the whole generation/ still better for the nation/ But since 'tis only Fred/ who was alive and is dead/ There's no more to be said." The point is of course that individuals of status and property were never going to disappear from the record. Such families and individuals in Tipperary dominated political, social and economic

---

544 M. Lambe, *A Tipperary Landed Estate: Castle Otway 1750-1853* (Maynooth Studies in Local History, 1998). Tipperary Studies has a file of material on Castle Otway.

545 M. B. Murphy, *From Bowen's Court to Ballymackey: landlord, tenants and community, 1841-88* (Unpublished BA thesis, UL, (1999); M.B. Murphy, *John Trant of Dovea, Co Tipperary: an improving landlord, 1838-87* (Unpublished MA (Local Studies) thesis, UL, 2004).

546 T.P. Power, *Land, Politics, and Society in Eighteenth-Century Tipperary* (Clarendon Oxford, 1993).

547 W. Hayes & A. Kavanagh, *The Tipperary Gentry Volume 1* (Dublin, 2003).

548 *The Primary Valuation of Tenements (Griffith's Valuation) for County Tipperary*. Tipperary Studies has this source for each of the twelve baronies in County Tipperary.

549 *Archive Maps Tipperary County* (Valuation scanned maps database, Griffith's and cancelled town plans supplied by the Valuation Office, Dublin). C.D.

550 W. Nolan, *Tracing the Past* (Dublin, 1982) and W.E. Vaughan, Richard Griffith and the tenement valuation in G.L. Herries Davies & R.C. Mollan (eds.), *Richard Griffith 1784-1878* (RDS, 1980), pp. 103-22; J. Prunty, *Maps and Map-Making in Local History* (Dublin, 2004).

551 *Return of owners of land of an acre and upwards, in the several counties, counties of cities, and counties of towns in Ireland* [C 1492], HC 1876, lxxx.

552 J. Bateman, *The Great Landowners of Great Britain and Ireland* (4th ed. Reprint, New York, 1970); U.H. de Burgh, *The Landowners of Ireland* (Dublin, 1878).

life for several hundred years and are recorded in standard sources such as Lodge and Burke.[553] The transmission of property was at the heart of the survival of such families, hence the importance of wills.[554] Although it has nothing to do with Tipperary, Maguire's examination of the Downshire estates in the early nineteenth-century is a classic study of estate management.[555]

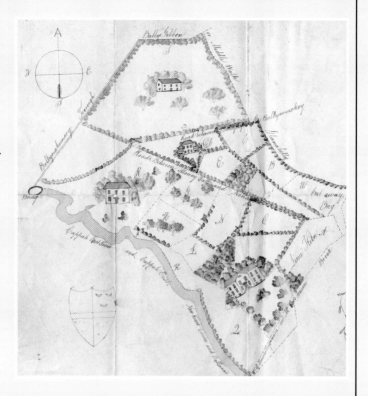

Estate of Wm. Poe, Donnybrook, Nenagh 1810

Tipperary Studies has a range of older sources on Land, many of which are essential. Agricultural societies were attempts to bring landlords and more substantial tenants together and improve agricultural practice.[556] One of the most comprehensive bodies of information on rural Ireland on the eve of the Great Famine is the evidence gathered by the government commission of inquiry 'in respect to the occupation of land in Ireland' known after its chairman as the *Devon Commission*. Witnesses were heard from all over the country, including from Tipperary: landlords, agents, bailiffs, tenants and clergy, including for example: John Chaytor, Edwin Taylor, Thomas Bolton and John Stewart, agents respectively to the Cahir, Clogheen, Ballykisteen and Dundrum estates, some of the biggest in the county. Other voices, such as the parish priest of Clonoulty and Michael Doheny, were also heard. Much of the Tipperary evidence was gathered in 1844 and published the following year.[557]

The two volumes of the *Topographical Dictionary*, a well known pre-Famine source, describes each civil parish in the country, including land proprietorship and land usage.[558] A similar source from the eve of the Great Famine is the *Parliamentary Gazetteer*.[559] The older publications in the Library dealing with aspects of land ownership and usage include contemporary observations and recollections by

---

[553] Burke (still being published) has appeared in many editions. Listed is the Library's holding: Burke, *Landed Gentry of Ireland* (1904); Burke, *Peerage* (1909) 2 volumes; Burke, *Peerage* (1949); Burke, *Landed Gentry of Ireland* (1958); Burke, *Irish Family Records* (1976); Lodge, *Peerage of Ireland* (Dublin, 1789) 7 volumes; Walford, *County Families* (1860).

[554] Sir A. Vicars, *Index to the Prerogative Wills of Ireland, 1536-1810* (Dublin, 1897). See also *Index to Irish Wills, 1484-1858* [in NAI] (CD-ROM). Of particular Tipperary interest is *An Act for vesting in trustees certain lands etc. estate of Francis Mathew of Thomastown County Tipperary* [Bound volume].

[555] W.A. Maguire, *The Downshire Estates in Ireland, 1801-1845: the management of Irish landed estates in the early nineteenth-century* (Oxford, Clarendon, 1972).

[556] *1st Annual Report of the Thurles Union Agricultural Society* (Thurles, 1812).

[557] *[Devon Commission] Law and Practice in respect to the occupation of land in Ireland*, 4 volumes. There is also a *Digest of Evidence* (Dublin, 1847) 2 volumes.

[558] S. Lewis, *Topographical Dictionary of Ireland* (Dublin, 1837) 2 volumes, plus a volume of maps.

[559] *Parliamentary Gazetteer of Ireland, 1844-45* (Dublin, 1846) 10 volumes.

A TREATISE

Richard on *Long*

𝕿𝖍𝖊 𝕷𝖆𝖜

Longfield OF *Cashel*

LANDLORD AND TENANT

visitors and natives and, naturally, are not confined to these topics but refer to many aspects of Irish life.[560] All of these books have something to offer, not least entertainment. Glimpses are allowed into hidden lives and forgotten ways. How else will one learn that in the 'best society' about Clonmel, whiskey punch was much preferred to wine (Inglis, p.137) or that you risked serious injury if you asked someone in Cahir where he was going (Kohl, p.192). Other older books deal with more technical matters.[561] Towards the end of the nineteenth century, much of the conflict in Ireland was about land and both sides, landlord and tenant, produced propaganda. Tipperary Studies has a small

---

[560] Arranged chronologically.
J. Kelly (ed.), *The Letters of Lord Chief Baron Edward Willes to the Earl of Warwick, 1757-1762: an account of Ireland in the mid-18th century* (Boethius, 1990); A. Young, *A Tour in Ireland 1776-1779* (1st ed. 1780, reprint Shannon, 1979) 2 volumes; T. Campbell, *A Philosophical Survey of the South of Ireland, in a series of letters* (London, 1777); W.W. Seward, *Topographia Hibernica* (Dublin, 1795); J. Stevenson (ed.), *Jacques-Louis de Latocnaye, A Frenchman's Walk Through Ireland, 1796-7* (Dublin, 1917); G. Holmes, *Sketches of some of the Southern Counties of Ireland collected during a tour in the Autumn 1797 in a series of letters* (London, 1801); S. Grimes (ed.), *Ireland in 1804* (Dublin, 1980); J. Carr, *The Stranger in Ireland or a tour in the South and West parts of that country in 1805* (1st ed. 1806, this ed. IUP Shannon, 1970); Sir R. Colt Hoare, *Journal of a tour in Ireland A.D. 1806* (London, 1807); E. Wakefield, *An Account of Ireland Statistical and Political* (London, 1812) 2 volumes; J. Gough, *A Tour in Ireland in 1813 and 1814* (Dublin, 1817); T. Cromwell, *Excursions through Ireland* [The Irish Tourist], (London, 1820); *Tracts on Ireland, Political and Statistical including Mr Scully's celebrated statement of the Penal Laws* (Dublin, 1824); JKL (Bishop James Doyle), *Letters on the State of Ireland* (Dublin, 1825); [Prince von Puckler-Muskau], *Tour in England, Ireland and France in the years 1828 and 1829 etc.* (Philadelphia, 1833); [C. Cochrane], *Journal of A Tour made by Senor Juan de Vega the Spanish Minstrel of 1828-9, through Great Britain and Ireland, a character assumed by an English gentleman* (London, 1830) 2 volumes; H.D. Inglis, *A Journey throughout Ireland during the Spring, Summer and Autumn of 1834* (3rd ed., London, 1835) 2 volumes; Lady Chatterton, *Rambles in the South of Ireland during the year 1838* (London, 1859); W.L. Taylor (ed.), *Ireland: Social, Political and Religious by Gustave de Beaumont* (London, 1839) 2 volumes; H.S. Thompson, *Ireland in 1839 and 1869* (London, 1870); Mr & Mrs S.C. Hall, *Ireland, its scenery, character etc.*, (London, 1841-43); Mrs S.C. Hall, *Sketches of Irish Character* (London, 1844); A. Nicholson, *The Bible in Ireland* [1844-5] (London, n.d.); J.G. Kohl, *Travels in Ireland* (London, 1843); Mrs Frederic West, *A Summer's Visit to Ireland in 1846* (London, 1847); Anon. *Sketches of Ireland Sixty Years Ago* (Dublin, 1847); W.H. Smith, *A Twelve-Months Residence in Ireland* (London, 1848); C. MacKay, *Ireland in 1849: the great Irish exodus* (London, 1877); Sir F.B. Head, *A Fortnight in Ireland* (London, 1852); T.C. Foster, *Letters on the condition of the People of Ireland* (2nd ed. London, 1857); *The Tourist's Illustrated Hand-Book for Ireland* (3rd ed., London, 1854); [S. Reynolds Hole], *A little tour in Ireland …by an Oxonian* (new ed. London, 1892, first published 1859); W. Steuart Trench, *Realities of Irish Life* (London, 1868); J.E. Walsh, *Ireland One Hundred and Two Years Ago, being a new and revised edition of Ireland sixty years ago* (Dublin, 1911); A.M. Sullivan, *New Ireland* (2nd ed., London, 1877); W.H. (Bullock) Hall, *Gleanings in Ireland after the Land Acts* (London, 1883) – this work is dedicated to William Spaight of Derry Castle Tipperary "a model Irish landlord"; M. Banim, *Here and There Through Ireland* (Dublin, 1891); W.R. Le Fanu, *Seventy Years of Irish Life* (London, 1893); M. Davitt, *The Fall of Feudalism in Ireland* (London, 1904); L. Paul-Dubois, *Contemporary Ireland* (Dublin, 1908); W. Bulfin, *Rambles in Eirinn* (Dublin, 1929 ed.); S. O Faolain, *An Irish Journey* (London, 1940); C. Graves, *Ireland Revisited* (London, 1949).

[561] Taylor & Skinner, *Maps of the Roads of Ireland* (1st ed., 1778, Shannon, 1969); Rev. M. Sleater, *Introductory Essay to a new system of civil and ecclesiastical topography and itinerary of counties of Ireland* (Dublin, 1805); J. Finlay, *A Treatise on the law of Landlord and Tenant in Ireland* (Dublin, 1825); E. Burroughs, *The Irish Farmers' Calendar etc.* (Dublin, 1835); W. Stewart, *The Law of Distress for Rent in Ireland* (Dublin, 1844); A. Leet, *A Directory to the market towns, villages, gentlemen's seats and other noted places in Ireland* (Dublin, 1844); I. Butt, *Land Tenure in Ireland: a plea for the Celtic Race* (2nd ed., Dublin, 1866); W.P. Coyne (ed.), *Ireland Industrial and Agricultural* (Dept. of Agriculture and Technical Instruction, 1902); J.D. Dardis, *The Occupation of land in Ireland in the first half of the 19th century* (London, 1920).

collection of this material.[562] Hammond on Gladstone is a classic work.[563]

Of modern publications in the Library on the topic of land, perhaps the most useful, though it does not deal with Tipperary, is Vaughan's important study of mid-Victorian landlord-tenant relations.[564] With reference to Tipperary, specifically the Clogheen area, W.J. Smyth's article is seminal.[565] Willie Nolan has written about the landlord settlement, New Bermingham.[566] Also of importance is Donnelly's groundbreaking study of Cork in the nineteenth century.[567] The 'Big House' has received a deal of attention, the most scholarly work being Terence Dooley's.[568] The most useful reference work is *Burke's Guide to Country Houses*, an alphabetical listing with brief histories and illustrations.[569] Of interest is the auction catalogue for the 1862 sale of "Cahir Park House".[570] A number of books on the 'Big House', all well illustrated, have been published.[571]

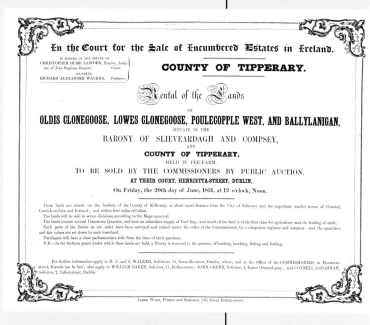

---

[562] J. Godkin, *The Land-War in Ireland* (London, 1870); *The Land Question (in) Ireland. Pamphlets 1879-1881* (The Irish Land Committee); R.J.M., *Days of the Land League* (London, 1882) [Verse]; *Tenant Right in Tipperary: Humorous Sketches of Irish Life and Character* (Glasgow, 1886); *Notes from Ireland* (Irish Loyal & Patriotic Union, 1887, 1888, 1889) 3 volumes; J.J. Clancy (ed.), *Mr Dillon and the Plan of Campaign being Mr Dillon's speech before the Queen's Bench* (Dublin, 1887); W.H. Hurlbert, *Ireland Under Coercion: the diary of an American* (Edinburgh, 1888) 2 volumes; E. Dwyer Gray, *The Treatment of political prisoners in Ireland* (Dublin, 1889); *The Plan of Campaign. The Smith-Barry Estate Tipperary* (Liberal Union of Ireland, June 1890); Also the *Freeman's Journal* Special Correspondent [William O'Brien] investigation of conditions on the Buckley estate: *Christmas on the Galtees* (Dublin, 1878).

[563] J.L. Hammond, *Gladstone and the Irish Nation* (London, 1938).

[564] W.E. Vaughan, *Landlords & Tenants in Mid-Victorian Ireland* (Clarendon, Oxford, 1994). Also Rev. T.A. Finlay, *The Occupation of Land in Ireland in the first half of the nineteenth-century* (Dublin, 1920); B.L. Solow, *The Land Question and the Irish Economy, 1870-1903* (Harvard UP, 1971); P.J. Drudy (ed.), *Irish Studies 2 Ireland: Land, Politics and People* (Cambridge UP, 1982).

[565] W.J. Smyth, Landholding changes, kinship networks and class transformation in rural Ireland: a case study from Co Tipperary in *Irish Geog.* xvi (1983), pp. 16-35.

[566] W. Nolan, 'A public benefit': Sir Vere Hunt, Bart and the town of New Bermingham, Co Tipperary, 1800-1818 in H.B. Clarke, J. Prunty & M. Hennessy (eds.), *Surveying Ireland's Past* (Dublin, 2004), pp. 415-54.

[567] J.S. Donnelly, Jr., *The Land and the People of Nineteenth Century Cork: the rural economy and the land question* (London, 1975).

[568] T. Dooley, *The Decline of the Big House in Ireland* (Dublin, 2001).

[569] M. Bence Jones (ed.), *Burke's Guide to Country Houses Ireland* (revised ed. London, 1988).

[570] Auction 26 March 1862, "Battersby & Co."

[571] B. de Breffny & R. ffolliott, *The Houses of Ireland* (London, 1975); E. Malins & Knight of Glin, *Lost Demesnes: Irish landscape Gardening, 1660-1845* (London, 1976); M. Craig, *Classic Irish Houses of the Middle Size* (London, 1976); Knight of Glin, D.J. Griffin, N.K. Robinson, *Vanishing Country Houses of Ireland* (Dublin, 1988); J. O'Brien & D. Guinness, *Great Irish Houses and Castles* (London, 1992); P. Somerville Large, *The Irish Country House* (London, 1995); M. Bence Jones, *Life in an Irish Country House* (London, 1996); S. O'Reilly, *Irish Houses and Gardens from the articles of Country Life* (London, 1998); R. MacDonnell, *The Lost Houses of Ireland* (London, 2002).

Listed below are some other relevant studies dealing with a variety of topics: fairs and markets,[572] the Co-Operative Movement,[573] anthropology,[574] the Board of Works,[575] the rural economy,[576] 18th century catholic landownership,[577] James Fintan Lalor,[578] William O'Brien MP,[579] Trinity College estates,[580] the ordnance survey,[581] the Land League,[582] land policy in independent Ireland,[583] the Department of Agriculture (T.P. Gill from Nenagh was an important figure in the early history of this department).[584] Finally, a case study showing what went wrong when tradition collided with 'progress'.[585]

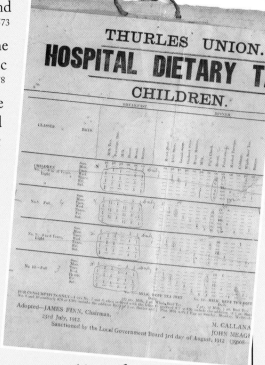

B: The Famine

Prior to the 150th anniversary of the Famine, very little was published on this catastrophic period in Irish history. There was nothing of specific Tipperary interest and essentially a handful of books covered the topic, Woodham-Smith's being the best known.[586] Also available was a related book, written in the mid-nineteenth century by the architect of the poor law system in Ireland.[587]

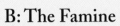

Halls Ireland

[572] P.J. O'Connor, *Fairs and Markets of Ireland: a cultural geography* (Newcastle West, 2001); P. Logan, *Fair Day: the story of Irish fairs and markets* (Belfast, 1986).

[573] P. Bolger, *The Irish Co-Operative Movement: its history and development* (Dublin, 1977).

[574] C.M. Arensberg, *The Irish Countryman: an anthropological study* (London, 1937).

[575] A.R.G. Griffiths, *The Irish Board of Works, 1831-1878* (London, 1987).

[576] T.W. Guinnane, *The Vanishing Irish: households, migration and the rural economy in Ireland, 1850-1914* (Princeton UP, 1997); R.D. Crotty, *Irish Agricultural Production: its volume and structure* (Cork UP, 1966).

[577] C.C. Trench, *Grace's Card: Irish Catholic Landlords 1690-1800* (Mercier, 1997). Of interest also K. Whelan, An Underground Gentry? Catholic Middlemen in 18th Century Ireland in J.S. Donnelly Jr & K. A. Miller (eds.), *Irish Popular Culture 1650-1850* (Dublin, 1999).

[578] L. Fogarty (ed.), *James Fintan Lalor, Patriot & Political Essayist: collected writings* (Dublin, 1947 ed.)

[579] S. Warwick Haller, *William O'Brien and the Irish Land War* (Dublin, 1990).

[580] R. MacCarthy, *The Trinity College Estates, 1800-1923: corporate management in an age of reform* (Dundalgan Press, 1992).

[581] *An Illustrated Record of Ordnance Survey in Ireland* (Dublin, 1991); G.M. Doherty, *The Irish Ordnance Survey: History, Culture and Memory* (Dublin, 2004).

[582] N.D. Palmer, *The Irish Land League Crisis* (Yale UP, 1940).

[583] T. Dooley, *'The Land for the People' the land question in independent Ireland* (Dublin, 2004).

[584] D. Hoctor, *The Department's Story – a history of the Department of Agriculture* (Dublin, 1971). Also of interest and leading to the founding of the Department: *Report of the Recess Committee on the establishment of a Department of Agriculture and Industries for Ireland* (2nd ed. Dublin, 1896). Also *Ireland Industry and Agriculture: Handbook for the Irish Pavilion, Glasgow International Exhibition, 1901* (Dept. of Agriculture and Technical Instruction, 1901).

[585] J. O'Callaghan, *The Red Book: the Hanrahan Case v. Merck, Sharp & Dohme* (Dublin, 1992).

[586] C. Woodham-Smith, *The Great Hunger* (London, 1962); R.D. Edwards & T.D. Williams (eds.), *The Great Famine* (Dublin, 1956); Rev. J. O'Rourke, *A History of the Great Irish Famine of 1847, with notices of earlier famines* (Dublin, 1875).

[587] Sir G. Nicholls, *A History of the Irish Poor Law* (London, 1856, reprint 1967). About the act see: *Act for the more effectual relief of the Destitute Poor in Ireland, with notes, forms and an index* (London, 1839).

Beginning in 1995, *Tipperary Historical Journal* published a great deal of material on the topic, especially a series of articles dealing with South Tipperary by Des Marnane.[588] A selection of other articles is listed below.[589] The Famine in North Tipperary was comprehensively discussed by Danny Grace.[590] The Famine in Nodstown near Cashel and in Clogheen has been given some attention.[591] Similarly the Callan Poor Law Union, which included part of County Tipperary.[592] The Library also holds a number of unpublished studies of aspects of the Famine in the county.[593] A select committee of the mid-1820s allows a view of pre-Famine Ireland.[594] Information on population is available for Templebredin in 1834.[595]

---

[588] D.G. Marnane, South Tipperary on the eve of the Great Famine in *THJ* (1995), pp. 1-53; The Famine in South Tipperary: Part One in *THJ* (1996), pp. 1-42; The Famine in South Tipperary: Part Two in *THJ* (1997), pp. 131-50; The Famine in South Tipperary: Part Three in *THJ* (1998), pp. 56-75; The Famine in South Tipperary: Part Four in *THJ* (1999), pp. 1-24; The Famine in South Tipperary: Part Five in *THJ* (2000), pp. 73-119.

[589] N. Beary Ó Cleirigh, Glimpses of South Tipperary during the Great Famine in *THJ* (1993), pp. 76-81; C. O'Mahony, Emigration from Thurles Workhouse 1848-58 in *THJ* (1993), pp. 82-87; C. O'Mahony, Emigration from Tipperary Workhouse 1848-58 in *THJ* (1994), pp. 105-09; A. Lanigan, Tipperary Workhouse Children and the Famine in *THJ* (1995), pp. 54-80; Memories of the Famine from the Irish Folklore Commission in *THJ* (1996), pp. 43-8; M. O'Donnell, The Great Famine in Fethard, 1845-50 in *THJ* (1996), pp. 49-70; G. Smith, The health and medical aspects of the Famine in Tipperary in *THJ* (1996), pp. 71-83; D. Grace, Crime in pre-Famine North-West Tipperary in *THJ* (1996), pp. 84-95; E. O'Riordan, The Famine in the Clogheen area in *THJ* (1996), pp. 96-100; L.M. Geary, The Great Famine and Fethard Temporary Fever Hospital in *THJ* (1997), pp. 151-65; J. Walsh, The Butlers of Ballyslatteen: two Famine notebooks in *THJ* (1997), pp. 166-77; D. Grace, Priests who died in the Great Famine in *THJ* (1997), pp. 178-79; S. O'Donnell, Some aspects of the Famine in Clonmel in *THJ* (1998), pp. 76-80; M. O Corrbuí, An Gorta I bParóiste I dTuaisceart Thiobraid Árann in *THJ* (1998), pp. 81-86; H. Kennally, North Tipperary famine orphans 'exported' to Yorkshire in *THJ* (1999), pp. 25-37; M. Ryan, Sir William Butler and that Famine eviction in *THJ* (1999), pp. 38-42; E. O'Riordan, Black (and White) '47 in *THJ* (2001), pp. 89-96.

[590] D. Grace, *The Great Famine in Nenagh Poor Law Union Co. Tipperary* (Relay, Nenagh, 2000).

[591] P. O'Dwyer, Nodstown in Famine Times in *Boherlahan-Dualla Historical Journal* (2000), pp. 10-25; E. O'Riordan, *Famine in the Valley* (Galty Vee Valley Tourism, 1995).

[592] The Authors, *The Famine in the Kilkenny/Tipperary Region: a history of the Callan Workhouse and Poor Law Union, 1845-1852* (Callan, 1998).

[593] T.E. Nyhan, *An Examination of the Socio-Economic Structure of Pre-famine Society in Thurles PLU* (B.A., 1978); M. Hough, *Famine in the Union of Borrisokane, 1846-52* (B. Ed., Limerick 1981); J.B. Fogarty, *The Impossible Burden: Thurles Poor Law Union 1847-1848* (M.A., NUI, 1999); H. Carew, *Cashel Workhouse in Famine Times: A study from 1845 to 1855* (M.Phil. NUI, 1995); M. Lyons, *The Work of Thurles Board of Guardians, 1848-1851: public duty or self-interest* (M.A. in Local History, UL, 2004).

[594] *Inquiry into the state of Ireland, 1824-25* (Dublin, 1825).

[595] F. O'Ferrall, The population of a rural Pre-Famine parish, Templebredin Counties Tipperary and Limerick in 1834 in *N. Munster Antiq. Jn.*, (1975), pp. 91-101.

Tipperary Studies has a selection of the huge volume of material published about the Famine.[596] And also some related material.[597] There are also eight volumes of parliamentary papers on the Famine.[598] This series is a vital source with respect to the official reaction to the crisis and has information about workhouses in the county. Given below, is a brief reference to each of the eight volumes.

(The second number (in Roman) refers to the original sequencing, followed by the year and finally the number of the individual paper.)

British Parliamentary Papers: The Famine

Volume I	lv (1847) 766 790 863	Correspondence regarding workhouses
Volume II	liv (1847-48) 896	Relief of distress
	lv (1847-48) 919	Relief of distress
Volume III	lvi (1847-48) 955	Relief of distress
Volume IV	liv (1847-48) 999	Relief of distress
	xlviii (1849) 1042	Relief of distress
Volume V	xxxvii (1846) 735	Relief of distress
	li (1847) 761	Relief of distress
	li (1847) 56	Index
Volume VI	l (1847) 764	Relief of distress
	l (1847) 80	Index
Volume VII	lii (1847) 797	Relief of distress
	lii (1847) 80 – ii	Index
	lii (1847) 796	Relief of distress
	lii (1847) 56 – ii	Index
Volume VIII	xxxvii (1846) 28	Playfair & Lindley Report
	xxxvii (1846)	33 Failure of potato crop
	xxxvii (1846)	171 Instructions to Relief Committees
	xxxvii (1846)	615 Expenditure on relief
	li (1850) 423	Cattle exports Ireland to Britain 1846-49
	xvii (1847) 799	1st Report Relief Commissioners
	xvii (1847) 819	2nd Report
	xvii (1847) 836	3rd Report
	xvii (1847) 859	4th Report

[596] H. Burke, *The People and the Poor Law in 19th Century Ireland* (Dublin, 1987); J. O'Connor, *The Workhouses of Ireland: the fate of Ireland's poor* (Dublin, 1995); J. Killen (ed.), *The Famine Decade: contemporary accounts 1841-1851* (Belfast, 1995); S.J. Campbell, *The Great Irish Famine* (Strokestown Museum, 1994); C. Póirtéir, *Famine Echoes* (Dublin, 1995); J. Hill & C. Ó Grada (eds.), *'The Visitation of God'? The potato and the great Irish Famine Austin Bourke* (Dublin, 1993); J. Keating, *Irish Famine Facts* (Teagasc, 1996); P. Gray, *Famine, Land and Politics: British Government and Irish Society 1843-1850* (Dublin, 1999); D.A. Kerr, *A Nation of Beggars: Priests, People and Politics in Famine Ireland, 1846-1852* (Oxford, 1994); C. Kinealy, *This Great Calamity: the Irish Famine 1845-52* (Dublin, 1994); C. Kinealy, *A Death-Dealing Famine: the Great Hunger in Ireland* (London, 1997); L. Kennedy, P.S. Ell, E.M. Crawford & L.A. Clarkson, *Mapping the Great Irish Famine* (Dublin, 1999); R. Haines, *Charles Trevelyan and the Great Irish Famine* (Dublin, 2004).

[597] E. Malcolm & G. James (eds.), *Medicine, Disease and the State in Ireland, 1650-1940* (Cork UP, 1999). Also S. Kierse, The Cholera of 1832-33 in the parish of Killaloe in *The Other Clare*, 5 (1981) pp. 49-56.

[598] *The Famine Union Workhouses in Ireland* (Irish University Press Series of British Parliamentary Papers) 8 volumes. The Library has a copy of the *Poor Law Act (Ireland) 1838*. Worth noting is the 1909 Report from the Royal Commission on the Poor Laws and Relief of Distress [Cd. 4499] which has a useful historical review.

xxix (1847-48) 876	5th 6th 7th Reports
xxix (1847-48) 956	Supplementary appendix to 7th Report
xvii (1847) 834	Reports from Board of Works
xvii (1847) 860	Reports from Board of Works
xxiii (1849) 1047	Final Report from Board of Works
xxxvii (1846) 120	Representations from medical officials
xli (1852-53) 1562	

Comparisons between the 1841 census and that of 1851 highlight the scale of the Famine and the enormous loss of population. The easiest way to access census data, not for the county as a whole but for the diocese of Cashel & Emly, is the townland by townland and parish-by-parish compilation produced under the direction of the late Archbishop Thomas Morris. The number of houses, together with the number of males and females is given for each townland.[599] Also available for Cashel & Emly are annual baptism and marriage statistics, 1835-55, for each parish, including those in Limerick.[600] Tipperary Studies has other relevant sources.[601] The Quakers were exceptional in their response.[602] Records available with respect to emigrants to the United States are of great genealogical interest.[603]

The most unique records on the Famine in Tipperary held by Tipperary Studies are the minute books and some other original records produced by the various Poor Law Unions in the county. Through these records may be seen something of the workhouse administrations, officials and poor law guardians, as they tried to cope with an extraordinary crisis. (See **Part Three** of *Finding Tipperary*.)

C: Law and Order

In 1842 the famous novelist William Makepeace Thackeray paid a three-months visit to Ireland. Everything he saw fascinated him, but equally, much appalled him, not least the connection between the occupancy of land and the use of violence. Describing one set of tenants, he wrote that they maintained the occupancy of their farms "in Tipperary fashion, by simply putting a (bullet) into the body of any man who would come to take a farm over any one of them" [*The Irish Sketch Book 1842* (London, 1843)]. Thackeray was reflecting the widespread view within the United Kingdom that Tipperary was synonymous with violence. Sometimes this violence was politically motivated (discussed in subsection **D**) but agrarian violence, stretching from the Whiteboys in the 1760s to the seizure of farms during the Troubles, seemed like a Tipperary specialty.

THE
LIFE AND ADVENTURES
OF
JEREMIAH GRANT,
COMMONLY CALLED
CAPTAIN GRANT;
WHO WAS TRIED, FOUND GUILTY, AND EXECUTED
AT THE
SUMMER ASSIZES, 1816,
HELD AT
MARYBOROUGH, IN THE QUEEN'S COUNTY;
WITH A FAITHFUL
REPORT OF HIS TRIAL,
AND CONDUCT AT THE PLACE OF EXECUTION.

THE NARRATIVE TAKEN FROM HIS OWN DETAIL,
AFTER HIS CONVICTION.

---

[599] *Pobal Ailbe: Cashel & Emly Census of Population 1841-1971* (Thurles, 1975).
[600] D.G. Marnane, The Famine in South Tipperary: Part Five, appendix 2 in *THJ* (2000), pp. 108-17.
[601] *Reports of the Commissioners appointed to take the Census of Ireland for the year 1841.* 1843 (504) xxiv; *Reports 1851 Census.* 3 volumes (Volume 3 has reports on Tipperary SR and NR).
[602] *Transactions of the Central Relief Committee of the Society of Friends during the Famine in Ireland 1846 & 1847* (Dublin, 1852).
[603] I.A. Glazier (ed.), *The Famine Immigrants – lists of Irish immigrants arriving at the port of New York 1846-51* (Baltimore, 1983) 7 volumes.

AN EXACT
ABRIDGMENT
OF ALL
The Irish Statutes,
FROM

The First Session of PARLIAMENT in the Third Year of the Reign of King *EDWARD* II. to the End of the Eighth Year of His Present MAJESTY King *GEORGE* II.

TOGETHER WITH

An ABRIDGMENT of All the **English** STATUTES, in Force in *IRELAND*, from **Magna Charta**, to the End of the Eighth Year of His Present MAJESTY King *GEORGE* II.

With the following TABLES, *viz.*

A TABLE of the Titles of the Statutes, shewing under what General Heads they are Abridged.

A TABLE of such Statutes as are either Wholly, or in Part, taken from any **English** Statutes ; together with the **English** Statutes from which they were taken.

A TABLE of such **English** Statutes, since **Poyning's Law,** as bind *IRELAND*.

A TABLE of such Statutes as are to be given in Charge at the Assizes.

A TABLE of such Statutes as are to be given in Charge at the General Quarter-Sessions.

A TABLE of such Statutes as are enjoined to be Read by Ministers in their Churches.

A General TABLE to the Whole, according to the Plan of Mr. *Keeble's* Tables to the **English** Statutes.

Whereunto are likewise added,

Several Marginal NOTES, and New REFERENCES to the *Reports in Law* ; With the Resolutions of the JUDGES upon 28 **Hen.** 8. *Of Administrations ; The Stat. of Distributions.* 10 **Car.** 2. *for ending Differences by Arbitration* : 8 **Ann.** *Concerning Bills of Ex-*

A guide to sources for crime in Ireland is very useful.[604] Tipperary Studies has some sources dealing specifically with the county, including a Ph.D. thesis about 'rural conflict' in the county prior to the Famine.[605] Of particular value are the Library's rare copies of legal proceedings arising from notable examples of agrarian crime.[606] Lover (1848) is especially interesting as it covers the trials of John Lonergan for the murder of William Roe of Rockwell; Harry and Philip Cody for the murder of Edmund Madden; and Edward Roughan and John Daly for the attempted murder of R.U. Bayly. Equally rare is the magistrate's diatribe from 1842 on the lawless state of the county.[607] One of those who gave evidence before a select committee in the mid-1820s on the state of the country was Richard Willcocks, perhaps the first policeman in Tipperary.[608] From the land agitations of the 1880s, the Library holds collections of propaganda pamphlets putting the landlord's case and emphasising tenant violence.[609] The constabulary was on the front line and it is worth remembering that the police service was first established in Tipperary (around Cashel). Older works on the RIC are of interest, especially Brophy which has a section on Ballingarry and '48.[610]

Agrarian crime in Tipperary is discussed in various articles in the *Tipperary Historical Journal*.[611] The county was particularly associated with the growth of massed agrarian protest movements in the 18th century, commonly known as

---

604 B. Griffin, *Sources for the study of crime in Ireland, 1801-1921* (Dublin, 2005).

605 J. Shankleman, *Agricultural Change and Rural Conflict in County Tipperary, 1800-1845* (Unpublished Ph.D. thesis, Essex University, Dept of Sociology, 1978-79). For mid-west Tipperary see D.G. Marnane, *Land & Violence: a history of West Tipperary from 1660* (Tipperary, 1985).

606 W. Ridgeway, *A Report of the trial of George Lidwell and Thomas Prior* (Dublin, 1800); A. Brewster (ed.), *A report of Trials at the Clonmel Summer Assizes of 1829, including those which arose out of the occurrences at Borrisokane on the 26th and 28th July 1829* (Dublin, 1830); H.W. Lover, *Report of the trials etc. at the Special Commission for the County Tipperary held at Clonmel 24th Jan – 1st Feb 1848* (Dublin, 1848).

607 A Magistrate of the County, *The Present State of Tipperary as regards agrarian outrages etc.* (Dublin, 1842).

608 *Select committee on the state of Ireland.... disturbances ... minutes of evidence, 1824-5*, 4 volumes.

609 *Notes from Ireland 1887, 1888, 1890* (Irish Loyal and Patriotic Union) 3 volumes; *The Plan of Campaign – The Smith-Barry Estate Tipperary* (Liberal Union of Ireland, June 1890).

610 R. Curtis, *The History of the Royal Irish Constabulary* (2nd ed. Dublin, 1871); M. Brophy, *Tales of the Royal Irish Constabulary* (Dublin, 1896).

611 D.G. Marnane, Land and Violence in Tipperary in the 1800s in *THJ* (1988), pp. 53-89; M. Luddy, Whiteboy Support in Co. Tipperary, 1761-89 in *THJ* (1989), pp. 66-79; Rev. C. O'Dwyer, Archbishop Leahy and Faction Fighting (1861-74) in *THJ* (1989), pp. 20-26; G. Carpentier, Kickham's Panorama of Rural Ireland, 1840-1870 in *THJ* (1990), pp. 63-74; M. Barrett CSSR, Ballagh Revisited: the 1815 'Protest' in *THJ* (1991), pp. 63-72; T. Bartlett, An Account of the Whiteboys from the 1790s in *THJ* (1991), pp. 141-48; G. Moran, William Scully and Ballycohey- a fresh look in *THJ* (1992), pp. 63-74; S. Ua Cearnaigh, Turbulent Days Beneath Galtymore in *THJ* (1993), pp. 88-94; A. Carden, 'Woodcock' Carden – a balanced account in *THJ* (2000), pp. 120-31; W.A. Maguire, The murder of Constantine Maguire, 1834 in *THJ* (2003), pp. 103-20; D.G. Marnane, 'Such a Treacherous Country': a land agent in Cappawhite, 1847-52 in *THJ* (2004), pp. 233-48.

Whiteboys.[612] General works on this topic usually refer to what was happening in Tipperary.[613] A study of agrarian assassinations in pre-Famine Tipperary is especially noteworthy.[614] Of particular interest is a study of the fate of the Cormack Brothers, executed in Nenagh in 1858 for the murder of land agent William Ellis.[615] Marcus Bourke's examination of a more modern murder also raises the question of the innocent being executed.[616] A study of 'rural unrest' in County Kilkenny is of interest.[617]

The mutiny of the North Tipperary Militia in 1856 has been discussed in two articles.[618] Crime provided work for lawyers and the legal profession featured very much in folk stories.[619] A 1948 report from the visiting committee of Clonmel Borstal is a valuable indicator of changed attitudes.[620] Historically, not much difference was seen between criminality and insanity.[621]

REWARD!

WHEREAS, on the forenoon of Saturday, the 2nd October instant, WILLIAM ROE, of Rockwell, Esq., J. P., was shot dead on the High Road, at Boytonrath, Parish of Boytonrath, Barony of Middlethird, and County of Tipperary, by some Person or Persons unknown:

We, the undersigned, for the better apprehending and bringing to justice the Perpetrators and Conspirators of this Murder, do hereby offer the several Sums affixed to our Names, as a Reward, to any person or persons (except the person or persons by whom the said Murder was actually perpetrated) who shall, within Six Months from the date hereof, give such information as shall lead to the apprehension and conviction of the Party or Parties concerned therein.

Government Reward,	£100 0 0	William Quin, J.P.		Stephen Moore, J.P., D.L.	5 0 0
Donoughmore,	50 0 0	William H. Riall, J.P.	10 0 0	J. Sankey,	5 0 0
Glengall,	50 0 0	Godfrey Levinge,	10 0 0	Edward Galway,	5 0 0
Hawarden,	30 0 0	M. Pennefather, J.P., D.L.	10 0 0	Saml. W. Barton, J.P., D.L.	5 0 0
Snirdale,	20 0 0	Richard B.H. Lowe, J.P.	10 0 0	Robert W. White, J.P.	5 0 0
Nicholas V. Maher, M.P.	20 0 0	George Roe,	10 0 0	Leonard Keating, J.P.	5 0 0
Ralph Osborne, M.P.	20 0 0	George P. Prittie, C.P.	10 0 0	Walter Herbert, J.P.	5 0 0
John Vincent,	30 0 0	Theophilus Bennett, Clk.	10 0 0	James A. Butler, J.P.	5 0 0
N. H. Mandeville, J.P.	25 0 0	H. W. Massey, J.P.	5 0 0	William Murphy, J.P.	5 0 0
John Maher, J.P.	20 0 0	H. B. Bradshaw, J.P.	5 0 0	Thomas Scully, J.P.	5 0 0
Richard Pennefather, J.P.	20 0 0	Charles Minchin, J.P.	5 0 0	Thomas Bolton, J.P.	5 0 0
Charles Clarke, J.P.	20 0 0	Samuel Riall, J.P.	5 0 0	John Chaytor, J.P.	5 0 0
William Perry, J.P.	20 0 0	Samuel Perry, J.P.	5 0 0	Robert Prendergast, J.P.	5 0 0
R. P. Roe,	20 0 0	John Stewart, J.P.	5 0 0	James Prendergast,	5 0 0
J. J. Fitzgerald, Bart., J.P.	10 0 0	J. Massy Dawson, Clk.	5 0 0	John Cahill, C.S.	5 0 0
Joseph Cooke, J.P., D.L.	10 0 0	Rodolph Scully, J.P.	5 0 0	W. P. Worrall,	5 0 0
Simon Lowe, J.P.	10 0 0	John Millet, J.P.	5 0 0	Richard Phillips, J.P.	5 0 0

---

[612] Generally T.P. Power, *Land, Politics and Society in Eighteenth-Century Tipperary* (Clarendon, Oxford, 1993) and specifically a series of articles by J.S. Donnelly Jr, The Rightboy Movement, 1785-8 in *Studia Hibernica* 17-18 (1977-78), pp. 120-202; The Whiteboy Movement, 1761-65 in *Irish Historical Studies*, 21 (1978), pp. 20-54; Irish Agrarian Rebellion: The Whiteboys of 1769-76 in *PRIA*, 83 (1983), pp. 293-331; The social composition of agrarian rebellions in early nineteenth-century Ireland: the case of the Carders and Caravats, 1813-16 in P.J. Corish (ed.), *Radicals, rebels and Establishments* (Belfast, 1985), pp. 151-69. Also M.J. Bric, The Whiteboy Movement, 1760-80 in Nolan & McGrath (eds.), *Tipperary: History & Society* (Dublin, 1985), pp. 148-84.

[613] Sir H. McAnally, *The Irish Militia, 1793-1816: a social and military study* (Dublin, 1949); R. Curtis, *The History of the Royal Irish Constabulary* (Dublin, 1869); D.J. O'Sullivan, *The Irish Constabularies 1822-1922: a century of policing in Ireland* (Brandon, 1999); G. Broeker, *Rural Disorder and Police Reform in Ireland 1812-36* (London, 1970); M. Beames, *Peasants and Power: the Whiteboy Movements and their control in Pre-Famine Ireland* (Harvester Press, 1983); S. Clark & J.S. Donnelly Jr (eds.), *Irish Peasants: Violence and Political Unrest 1780-1914* (Manchester UP, 1983); S. Clark, *Social Origins of the Irish Land War* (Princeton UP, 1979); C. Townshend, *Political Violence in Ireland: Government and Resistance since 1848* (Oxford, 1983); S.R. Gibbons, *Captain Rock, Night Errant: the threatening letters of Pre-Famine Ireland*, 1801-1845 (Dublin, 2004).

[614] M. Beames, Rural conflict in pre-Famine Ireland: peasant assassinations in Tipperary 1837-47 in *Past & Present* 81 (1978), pp. 75-91. See also J. Hurst, Disturbed Tipperary in Eire-Ireland, ix, 3 (Sept 1974). There are comprehensive files with respect to two of these murders, that of Richard Chadwick near Holycross in 1827 and Patrick Clarke near Nenagh in 1845.

[615] N. Murphy, *Guilty or Innocent? The Cormack Brothers – trial, execution and exhumation* (Relay, Nenagh, 1997): also Tipperary Studies has a file of correspondence dealing with the exhumation in 1910.

[616] M. Bourke, *Murder at Marlhill: Was Harry Gleeson Innocent?* (Dublin, 1993).

[617] P. Ó Macháin, *Six Years in Galmoy: rural unrest in County Kilkenny 1819-1824* (Dublin, 2004).

[618] E.H. Sheehan, *The Mutiny of the N. Tipperary Militia on 7 July 1856: a full account of the famous outbreak* (Author, n.d.); D. Murphy, "The Battle of the Breeches"; the Nenagh mutiny, July 1856 in *THJ*, (2001), pp. 139-45.

[619] E. Hickey, *Irish Law and Lawyers in Modern Folk Traditions* (Dublin, 1999).

[620] *Notes by the visiting committee 1948: The Borstal Institution at Clonmel* (Government Publications, 1948).

[621] J. Robbins, *Fools and Madness: a history of the insane in Ireland* (Dublin, 1986).

D: Politics

Mindful of the role of the county in the struggle for independence, from its inception, *Tipperary Historical Journal* has published a great deal of material on this topic. Of particular importance are the first-hand accounts of the War of Independence and Civil War periods.[622] However, all episodes of the struggle, from '98, through '48 to '67, are discussed in these articles, not excluding republican activity against the Free State. Vincent Comerford discussed political representation during the Union.[623] In this same compilation is an article on class and politics 1916-24.[624] Of special interest are the Library's rare copies of the Clonmel trial of William Smith O'Brien

[622] Arranged by year of publication.
M. Moroney, George Plant & the Rule of Law: the Devereux Affair (1940-42) in *THJ* (1988), pp. 1-12; D. O Bric, Pierce McCan MP (Part 1) in *THJ* (1988), pp. 121-32 and (Part 2) in *THJ* (1989), pp. 105-17; An tAthair Colmcille O Cist., The Third Tipperary Brigade (1921-23): From Truce to Civil War in *THJ* (1990), pp. 9-26 and (Part 2) in *THJ* (1991), pp. 35-49 and (Part 3) in *THJ* (1992), pp. 23-30; M. O'Donnell, Thomas Francis Bourke (1840-89) Part 1 in *THJ* (1990), pp. 27-38 and Part 2 in *THJ* (1991), pp. 109-20; D. O'Keeffe, 1798 in South Tipperary in *THJ* (1990), pp. 109-20; E. Ó Duibhir, The Tipperary Volunteers in 1916: a personal account 75 years on in *THJ* (1991), pp. 9-18; Lt-Col. T. Ryan, One Man's Flying Column in *THJ* (1991), pp. 19-34 and (Part 2) in *THJ* (1992), pp. 43-56 and (Part 3) in *THJ* (1993), pp. 41-51; D.G. Marnane, The IRA in West Tipperary in 1931: the assassination of Superintendent Curtin in *THJ* (1992), pp. 9-22; A. O'Rahilly, The Civil War: a teenager's recollections 70 years on in *THJ* (1992), pp. 31-42; P.D. O'Keeffe, Clann na Poblachta: its origins and growth (Part 1) in *THJ* (1993), pp. 19-30 and (Part 2) in *THJ* (1994), pp. 1-8; S. Gaynor, With Tipperary No. 1 Brigade in North Tipperary 1917-21 (Part 1) in *THJ* (1993), pp. 31-40 and (Part 2) in *THJ* (1994), pp. 26-37; M. Neenan, The death of Dinny Lacey in *THJ* (1993), pp. 54-55; W. Grogan, The day Dinny Lacey died in *THJ* (1993), p.56; J. Duff, A Free State soldier's memories of the Civil War in *THJ* (1993), pp. 57-8; P.C. Power, Tipperary Courtmartials: 1798 to 1801 in *THJ* (1993), pp. 135-47; N. Sharkey, The Third Tipperary Brigade: a photographic record in *THJ* (1994), pp. 9-25; F. Campbell, Nationalism in Transformation: Local Government in Co. Tipperary 1912-1920 in *THJ* (1994), pp. 38-47; G. Moran, The Fenians and Tipperary Politics, 1868-1880 in *THJ* (1994), pp. 73-90; P. Kinane, My Part in the War of Independence (Part 1) in *THJ* (1995), pp. 87-93 and (Part 2) in *THJ* (1996), pp. 101-07; C.C. Murphy, North Tipperary in the Year of the Fenian Rising (Part 1) in *THJ* (1995), pp. 108-16 and (Part 2) in *THJ* (1996), pp. 136-44; J. Augusteijn, The operations of South Tipperary IRA, 1916-21 in *THJ* (1996), pp. 145-63; M. Bourke, Shooting the messenger: Col. Costello and the Murray case in *THJ* (1997), pp. 42-59; Fr P. Gaynor, The Sinn Fein Ard-Feis of 1917: a North Tipperary priest's account in *THJ* (1997), pp. 60-64; K. O'Dwyer, The Third Tipperary Brigade: its guerrilla campaign 1919-21 in *THJ* (1997), pp. 65-73; P. Ó Snodaigh, The impact of the 1848 insurrection in *THJ* (1998), p. 1; W. Nolan, The Irish Confederation in County Tipperary in 1848 in *THJ* (1998), pp. 2-18; T. Ó Fiaich, The North and Young Ireland in *THJ* (1998), pp. 19-31; G. Owens, Patrick O'Donohoe's narrative of the 1848 Rising in *THJ* (1998), pp. 32-45; R. Davis, The Reluctant Rebel: William Smith O'Brien in *THJ* (1998), pp. 46-55; S. Sharkey, My role as an Intelligence Officer with the Third Tipperary Brigade 1919-21 in *THJ* (1998), pp. 95-104; J. Maher, Dan Breen looks back 50 years from 1967 in *THJ* (1998), pp. 105-11; R. O'Donnell, Philip Cunningham: Clonmel's insurgent leader of 1798 in *THJ* (1998), pp. 150-57; Fr P. Gaynor, The Dean of Cashel and the 1918 general election in *THJ* (1999), pp. 52-58; S. Gallagher, P.J. Meghen and South Tipperary County Council (1934-42) in *THJ* (2000), pp. 1-10; E. Ó Duibhir, My years in the National Movement before 1916 in *THJ* (2000), pp. 25-30; B. Ó Cathaoir, John Blake Dillon and the '48 Rising in *THJ* (2000), pp. 55-63; M. O'Donnell, Parliamentary Representation for County Tipperary, 1560-1800 (Part 1) in *THJ* (2000), pp. 136-48 and (Part 2) in *THJ* (2001), pp. 97-110 and (Part 3) in *THJ* (2002), pp. 45-58 and (Part 4) in *THJ* (2003), pp. 65-80 and (Part 5) in *THJ* (2004), pp. 135-50; P. Lonergan, Tipperarymen in Spain (1936-37) in *THJ* (2001), pp. 27-32; M. Bourke, The fight to save Sean Allen in *THJ* (2001), pp. 53-6; D.G. Marnane, Tipperary Town one hundred years ago: issues of identity in *THJ* (2002), pp. 173-98; P. Lonergan, Tipperary TDs in *THJ* (2002), pp. 227-32; T. Crowe, Life with a Flying Column, 1919-21 in *THJ* (2004), pp. 249-60; B.J. Sayers, Attempted Rising- July 1848 in *THJ* (2005), pp. 105-136.
[623] R.V. Comerford, Tipperary representation at Westminster, 1801-1918 in Nolan & McGrath (eds.), *Tipperary: History & Society* (Dublin, 1995), pp. 325-38.
[624] D.R. O'Connor Lysaght, County Tipperary: class struggle and national struggle, 1916-24 in *Tipperary: History & Society*, pp. 394-410.

in 1848 and the Dublin trials of Fenians suspects, including Thomas F. Burke.[625] Tipperary Studies has a copy of the government investigation of the 1916 Rising.[626] The *Nationalist* newspaper ran a series of articles on the Fenians.[627]

MEMOIRS

OF THE

LEGAL, LITERARY, AND POLITICAL

LIFE

OF THE

LATE THE RIGHT HONOURABLE

JOHN PHILPOT CURRAN,

ONCE MASTER OF THE ROLLS IN IRELAND:

COMPRISING COPIOUS

ANECDOTES OF HIS WIT AND HUMOUR;

AND

A SELECTION OF HIS POETRY.

INTERSPERSED WITH OCCASIONAL

There are a small number of monographs on political activity in the county, again the emphasis very much on the physical force tradition.[628] Some older books are of value.[629] Electoral politics were not without interest, not least the lengths to which candidates were prepared to go.[630] Evidence from Cashel is illustrative.[631] Tipperary Studies has a number of biographical and autobiographical studies of individuals variously involved in politics.[632] (Also see **Part Three, TL/A/40** for a list of those from Tipperary who provided statements to the Bureau of Military History.)

[625] J.G. Hodges (ed.), *Report of the Trial of William Smith O'Brien for High Treason at the Special Commission for County Tipperary held at Clonmel Sept & Oct 1848* (Dublin, 1849); W.G. Chamney (ed.), *'The Fenian Conspiracy': Report of the trials of Thomas F. Burke and others... Special Commission Dublin* (Dublin, 1869).

[626] *The Royal Commission on the rebellion in Ireland: minutes of evidence and documents* [Cd. 8311], 1916.

[627] *Nationalist* 21 Jan 1950-29 July 1950. See file of cuttings.

[628] W.J. Hayes, *Tipperary in the Year of Rebellion 1798* (Lisheen, Roscrea, 1998); *Carraigmoclear 1798: Rising on Slievenamon* (Committee, 1998); P. Haicead, *In Bloody Protest: North Tipperary's IRA roll of honour 1916-1926* (Author, 1996); C. Ó Labhra (Fr Colmcille), *Trodairí na Treas Briogáide* (Nenagh, 1955); J. Augusteijn, *From Public Defiance to Guerrilla Warfare* (Dublin, 1996); E. Gaynor, *Memoirs of a Tipperary Family* (Dublin, n.d.); S. & S. Murphy, *The Comeraghs: Refuge of Rebels – Story of the Deisi Brigade IRA, 1914-24* (Authors, n.d.); M. Brolly, *The Impact of the War of Independence 1919-21 in parts of County Tipperary.* (Submitted towards an MA in Irish Studies, Bath College of Higher Education, 1996); T.P. Power, *Land, Politics and Society in Eighteenth-Century Tipperary* (Clarendon, Oxford, 1993); J. O'Shea, *Priest, Politics and Society in Post-Famine Ireland* (Dublin, 1983); D.A. Murphy, *The Two Tipperarys* (Relay, Nenagh, 1994); D.A. Murphy, *Blazing Tar Barrels and Standing Orders* (Relay, Nenagh, 1999); B. Long (ed.), *Tipperary SR County Council 1899-1999* (Clonmel, 1999).

[629] W.H. Maxwell, *History of the Irish Rebellion in 1798* (3rd. ed. London, 1853); T. MacNevin, *The Lives and Trials of Archibald Hamilton Rowan, the Rev. William Johnson* (Dublin, 1846).

[630] For electoral politics before the Act of Union, see the magisterial E.M. Johnston-Liik, *History of the Irish Parliament, 1692-1800* (Belfast, 2002) 6 volumes. Also W. Hunt, *The Irish Parliament 1775* (Dublin, 1907) and J.H. Whyte, Landlord influence at elections in Ireland, 1760-1885 in *The English Historical Review*, lxx (1965), pp. 740-60.

[631] *Report of the Commissioners etc. Corrupt Practices at the last Election for Cashel* (Dublin, 1869). Even the Catholic Truth Society of Ireland had an opinion on Cashel local government: J.J. Webb, *The Spoilation of Irish Towns* (CTSI, 1925).

[632] D, Breen, *My Fight for Irish Freedom* (1st ed. 1924); J. Ambrose, *The Dan Breen Story* (Dublin, 1981); B. Ryan, *A full private remembers the Troubled Times* (Tipperary, 1969); K. Rafter, *Martin Mansergh: A Biography* (Dublin, 2002); A. Griffith (ed.), *Meagher of the Sword* (Dublin, 1916); R. Mulcahy, *Richard Mulcahy 1886-1971: A Family Memoir* (Dublin, 1999); P.F. O'Brien, *Memoirs of the War of Independence and the Civil War, 1916-23* (Unpublished typescript, 1968); J. O'Leary, *Recollections* (London, 1896) 2 volumes; M. Bourke, *John O'Leary: a Study in Irish Separatism* (Tralee, 1967); also M. Bourke, John O'Leary's place in the Fenian movement in *N. Munster Antiq. Jn.*, x,2 (1967), pp. 148-56; J. O'Shea, *Prince of Swindlers: John Sadleir 1813-1856* (Dublin, 1999); W. Rutherford, *'67 Retrospective* (Tipperary, 1903); D. Ryan, *Sean Treacy and the 3rd Tipperary Brigade* (Tralee, 1945); S. Fitzpatrick, *Recollections of the fight for Irish Freedom* (Tipperary, n.d.); F. O'Donoghue, *No Other Law: the story of Liam Lynch and the Irish Republican Army 1916-1923* (Dublin, 1954); P. Tobin, "Come Weal or Woe" History of the 3rd Tipperary Brigade IRA (published in *Nationalist*, 2 Nov 1957-15 March 1958 and available in folder); L. Healy, *Brigadier-General Denis Lacy His Life and Adventures A Brief Sketch* (Author, 1924); *Reminiscences of M.V. Hamell, Cloughjordan* (1918-25 viewed from 1986, typescript);

Classic texts on eighteenth century Ireland are Froude and Lecky, the latter much more moderate than the former.[633]

JOHN O'MAHONY

Of general interest are copies of the legal proceedings against the United Irishmen in the House of Commons in 1798.[634] Denis (or Denys) Scully of Kilfeacle was a prominent figure in the campaign for civil liberty and issued an anti-French pamphlet to emphasise Irish catholic loyalty to the crown.[635] For Judkin Fitzgerald, High Sheriff in 1798, the assumption was that disloyalty was endemic.[636] Covering much the same period, Fitzpatrick's well-known books provide local colour.[637] The law was used against Daniel O'Connell in Dublin in 1844.[638] Denys Scully who lived at Kilfeacle between Tipperary and Cashel was an important ally of O'Connell.[639] The correspondence of O'Connell has much of Tipperary interest.[640] Thomas Drummond was Under Secretary in Dublin Castle, an official with whom O'Connell was able to work and a man who coined the memorable rejoinder to a Tipperary landlord about property having its duties as well as its rights.[641] Also of general interest is a small collection of monographs covering various aspects of Irish politics.[642]

[633] J.A. Froude, *The English in Ireland in the eighteenth century* (London, 1886 ed.) 3 volumes; W.E.H. Lecky, *History of Ireland in the eighteenth century* (London, 1892) 5 volumes.

[634] *The Report from the Secret Committee of the House of Commons on the United Irishmen* (Dublin, 1798); see generally R.R. Madden, *The United Irishmen: their lives and times* (New York, 1916 ed.) 12 volumes.

[635] Denys Scully, *An Irish Catholic's advice to his brethren how to estimate their present situation and repel French invasion, civil wars and slavery* (London, 1803). Also: Anon, *Ireland's grievances political and statutory to which is added Mr Scully's celebrated statement of the penal laws published first in 1812 by Mr Fitzpatrick* (Dublin, 1824).

[636] *Report of an interesting case wherein Mr Francis Doyle of Carrick-on-Suir, merchant and cloth-manufacturer was plaintiff and Sir Thomas Judkin Fitzgerald was defendant* (Dublin, 1808).

[637] W.J. Fitzpatrick, *'The Sham Squire'* (London, 1866) and *Secret Service under Pitt* (London, 1892). See also W. O'Regan, *Memoirs of the Legal, Literary and Political Life of the late the Right Honorable John Philpot Curran* (London, 1817).

[638] *Shaw's authenticated report of the Irish State Trials, 1844* (Dublin, 1844). Also J.S. Armstrong & E.S. Trevor, *A report of the proceedings on an indictment for a conspiracy in the case of The Queen v. D. O'Connell, J. O'Connell etc., 1843* (Dublin, 1844).

[639] B. MacDermot (ed.), *The Catholic Question in Ireland and England 1798-1822 The Papers of Denys Scully* (Dublin, 1988); B. MacDermot (ed.), *The Diary of Denys Scully The Irish Catholic petition of 1805* (Dublin, 1992). Also, M. Wall, *The penal laws 1691-1760* (1961).

[640] M.R. O'Connell (ed.), *The Correspondence of Daniel O'Connell, 1792- 1847* (IMC, 1972-80) 8 volumes. See also, T. Wyse, *Historical Sketch of the late Catholic Association of Ireland* (London, 1829) 2 volumes.

[641] R. Barry O'Brien, *Thomas Drummond, Under Secretary in Ireland 1835-40: Life and Letters* (London, 1889).

[642] P.S. O Hegarty, *A History of Ireland Under the Union, 1801-1922 (London, 1952);* D. Gwynn, *Young Ireland & 1948* (Cork UP, 1949); J.H. Whyte, *The Tenant League and Irish Politics in the 1850s* (DHA, 1966); J.H. Whyte, *The Independent Irish Party, 1850-59* (Oxford UP, 1958); G.F.H. Berkeley, *The Irish Battalion in the Papal Army of 1860* (Dublin, 1929); P. Rose, *The Manchester Martyrs: The Story of a Fenian Tragedy* (London, 1970); C.C. O'Brien, *Parnell and his Party, 1880-1890* (Oxford, Clarendon, 1957); P. Hart, *The IRA at War 1916-1923* (Oxford UP, 2003); K.T. Hoppen, *Elections, Politics, and Society in Ireland 1832-1885* (Clarendon, Oxford, 1984); D.W. Miller, *Church, State and Nation in Ireland, 1898-1921* (Dublin, 1973); F.X. Martin OSA (ed.), *The Irish Volunteers 1913-1915* (Dublin, 1963); P. Ó Cathasaigh [Sean O'Casey], *The Story of the Irish Citizen Army* (London, 1919); J. Sheehy, *The Rediscovery of Ireland's past: the Celtic Revival 1830-1930* (London, 1980); R. Sinnott, *Irish Voters Decide: voting behaviour in elections and referendums since 1918* (Manchester, 1995); Also P.J. Tynan, *The Irish National Invincibles and their Times* (London, 1894).

Irish politics of the early 20th century would have been very different without the influence of the cultural revival. Tipperary Studies holds a copy of a thesis about W.P. Ryan from Templemore, one of the promoters of the Irish-Ireland movement.[643] A book by an English journalist with a chapter headed "Miracle and Madness in Tipperary" which describes Templemore during the Troubles, deserves some attention.[644] Few people have written more about the county during this period than Fr Colmcille, and his article in the *Capuchin Annual* should not be overlooked.[645] The view from the Castle (and of the Bagwells) may be seen in Maurice Headlam's book.[646] Also a reminder that many Irishmen saw their duty fighting Germany is a memoir of Charles Dalton (Ballygriffin near Golden) who was killed in 1914.[647] Two books by Desmond Ryan (Sean Treacy's biographer) deal with republicanism.[648] When, during the War of Independence, an American Commission gathered evidence on conditions in Ireland, one of the witnesses was Denis Morgan, chairman of Thurles UDC.[649] When the war was over, it was celebrated for decades in a very gung-ho style.[650] The reality may be seen in the executions of Russell, Burke and Shea in Nenagh in January 1923.[651] What was done with this hard-won freedom is discussed in a study aptly called *A Rocky Road*.[652] Another aspect of this freedom was the desire to control how history was written.[653]

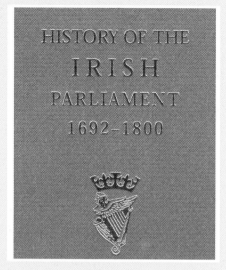

Nicholas Mansergh (1910-91) was Tipperary's most distinguished historian, an expert on Anglo-Irish relations and Commonwealth history.[654]

---

[643] M.J. Waters, *W.P. Ryan and the Irish Ireland Movement* (Unpublished Ph.D. thesis, University of Connecticut, 1970). For a different view of Ireland, H. Plunkett, *Ireland in the New Century* (London, 1904).

[644] *Ireland in Insurrection: an Englishman's record of fact by Hugh Martin* (London, 1921). He was a *Daily News* journalist.

[645] Fr Colmcille, Tipperary's Fight in 1920 in *Capuchin Annual* (1970), pp. 255-75.

[646] M. Headlam, *Irish Reminiscences* (London, 1947). See also "I.O.", *The Administration of Ireland, 1920* (London, 1921). For an earlier Castle perspective see M. MacDonagh, *The Viceroy's Post-Bag* (London, 1904).

[647] *A Memoir of the late Lt Col Charles Dalton RAMC* (Privately published, 1915). With regard to the Irish in the First World War see S. Moore, *The Irish on the Somme – a battlefield guide to the Irish Regiments in the Great War and the monuments to their memory* (Belfast, 2005).

[648] D. Ryan, *The Phoenix Flame: a study of Fenianism and John Devoy* (London, 1937); D. Ryan, *The Rising* (Dublin, 1949). Tipperary Studies has a copy of the *Sinn Fein Rebellion Handbook*. Also F. O'Donoghue (ed.), *Diarmuid Lynch. The IRB and the 1916 Insurrection* (Cork, 1957).

[649] A. Coyle (ed.), *Evidence on conditions in Ireland before The American Commission* (Washington, 1921). See also *Report of the Irish White Cross to 31 August 1922* (Dublin, 1922).

[650] For example; *With the IRA in the Fight for Freedom, 1919 to the Truce. The Red Path to Glory* (Tralee, n.d.).

[651] A. Heffernan, *Story of Russell, Burke and Shea* (Typescript with related documents, 1995).

[652] C. Ó Grada, *A Rocky Road: the irish economy since the 1920s* (Manchester UP, 1997).

[653] G. O'Brien, *Irish Governments and the Guardianship of Historical Records, 1922-72* (Dublin, 2004).

[654] N. Mansergh, *The Irish Free State, its government and politics* (London, 1934); *The Government of Northern Ireland: a study in devolution* (London, 1936); *The Commonwealth Experience* (London, 1969); *Nationalism and Independence*, edited by Diana Mansergh (Cork UP, 1997); *Independence Years: Selected Indian and Commonwealth Papers* (Oxford, 1999). See also M. Mansergh, *The Legacy of History* (Cork, 2003).

The Founders.

St Alberic
Second Abbot of
Citeaux.

St Robert.
First Abbot of Citeaux
St Benedict
Patriarch of Monks.

St Stephen.
Third Abbot of
Citeaux.

E: Religion and Education
(See **Section Four**)

The most significant works relating to religion in the modern county, both institutional and biographical, can be briefly stated: Murphy's History of Killaloe Diocese,[655] O'Shea's study of the role of priests in Tipperary during the second half of the nineteenth-century,[656] biographies of two archbishops,[657] Skehan's reference work on parish priests,[658] two collections of essays[659] and a unique nineteenth century clerical perspective.[660] Of some Tipperary interest are the very many biographies of Father Theobald Mathew.[661] A small number of Tipperary priests have received biographical attention.[662] Two Tipperary-born bishops had influence in Nigeria and Korea.[663] Clonmel-born Edward Clancy (1888-1969) was superior-general of the Irish Christian Brothers.[664]

Some other works, especially biographies, while not dealing with Tipperary, are of great value, especially the study of Bishop O'Dwyer of Limerick.[665] Perhaps St Patrick never came to Tipperary, but two studies, especially Carney, are of value.[666] The *Tipperary Historical Journal* has published

[655] Rev. I. Murphy, *The Diocese of Killaloe in the Eighteenth Century* (Dublin, 1991); *The Diocese of Killaloe 1800-1850* (Dublin, 1992); *The Diocese of Killaloe 1850-1904* (Dublin, 1995).

[656] J. O'Shea, *Priest, Politics and Society in Post-famine Ireland: a study of County Tipperary 1850-1891* (Dublin, 1983). Tipperary Studies holds a copy of the Ph.D thesis (2 volumes) on which this book was based.

[657] M. Tierney, *Croke of Cashel: the life of Archbishop Thomas William Croke 1832-1902* (Dublin, 1976); A.P.W. Malcomson, *Archbishop Charles Agar: Churchmanship and Politics in Ireland, 1760-1810* (Dublin, 2002).

[658] W.G. Skehan, *Cashel & Emly Heritage* (Abbey Books, 1993). Tipperary Studies has a typescript copy of Skehan's work on all priests of the diocese.

[659] W. Corbett & W. Nolan (eds.), *Thurles The Cathedral Town: Essays in honour of Archbishop Thomas Morris* (Dublin, 1989); B. Moloney (ed.), *Times to Cherish: Cashel and Rosegreen Parish History 1795-1995* (Cashel, 1994).

[660] Rev. J. Feehan (ed.), *The O'Carroll Diaries, [1846 & 1862-64]* (Typescript, Editor, 1997).

[661] J.F. Maguire, *Father Mathew: a biography* (London, 1863); K. Tynan, *Father Mathew* (London, 1908); P. Rogers, *Fr Theobald Mathew, apostle of temperance* (London, 1945); C. Kerrigan, *Fr Mathew and the Irish Temperance Movement 1838-49* (Cork, 1992); P.A. Townsend, *Father Mathew, Temperance and Irish Identity* (Dublin, 2002).

[662] J. Feehan, Forgotten by History: the life and times of John Lanigan DD, DCL, DSS, Priest, Professor and Historian in *THJ* (2005), pp. 43-60; Rev. M. Kennedy, *Fr Robert Bradshaw: Priest and Legionary* (Tipperary, 2003); J.A. Feehan, *An Hourglass on the Run: the story of a preacher* (Dublin, 2000); S. Rynne, *Father John Hayes* (Dublin, 1960); L. Maher, *I Remember Neil Kevin (1903-53): an assessment of his life and writings* (Roscrea, 1990); J.A. Feehan, *A Fool for Christ: the priest with the trailer* [Fr James Meehan] (Dublin, 1993).

[663] J.P. Gordon CSSP, *Bishop Shanahan of Southern Nigeria* (Dublin, 1949); C. McHale, *Patron of Partition: Bishop Thomas Quinlan 1896-1970* (Dublin, 1995).

[664] Obit. of Brother E.F. Clancy in *Christian Brothers' Educational Record*, 1970, 114 pp.

[665] J.H. Whyte, *Church and State in Modern Ireland, 1923-1970* (Dublin, 1974); T.J. Morrissey SJ, *William J. Walsh Archbishop of Dublin, 1841-1921* (Dublin, 2000), also the earlier P.J. Walsh, *William J. Walsh Archbishop of Dublin* (Dublin, 1928); T.J. Morrissey SJ, *Bishop Edward Thomas O'Dwyer of Limerick, 1842-1917* (Dublin, 2003); A. Macauley, *The Holy See, British Policy and the Plan of Campaign in Ireland, 1885-93* (Dublin, 2002). Also P Mac Suibhne, *Paul Cullen and his Contemporaries* (Naas, 1961-65) 3 volumes.

[666] J. Carney, *The problem of St Patrick* (Dublin, 1961); R.P.C. Hanson, *St Patrick: his origins and career* (Oxford, 1968).

relevant articles covering both religion and education.[667]

Persecution of catholics during the period of the 'Penal Laws' was the subject of the second book for which Canon Burke of Clonmel is remembered.[668] In this context the 1731 *Report on the state of Popery in Ireland* is an important source.[669] Among the more arcane items in the Library are a few eighteenth-century pamphlets.[670] Payment of tithes was very contentious in the early 19th century.[671] The history of the Church of Ireland was re-examined during the centenary of Disestablishment.[672] A nineteenth-century Fethard rector is the subject of an interesting article.[673] There was interdenominational co-operation occasionally.[674] From the early twentieth-century some catholic

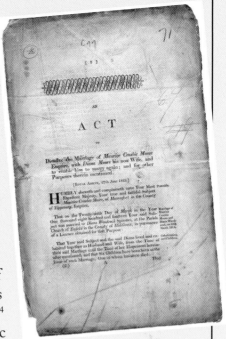

---

667 Rev. C. O'Dwyer, Archbishop Leahy and Faction Fighting (1861-74) in *THJ* (1989), pp. 20-26; C. Ó Laoi, How Cashel and Emly were united in *THJ* (1990), pp. 149-52; J.F. Quinn, Temperance in Tipperary: Father Mathew and Archbishop Slattery, 1839-54 in *THJ* (1995), pp. 133-39; Fr P. Gaynor, The Dean of Cashel and the 1918 general election in *THJ* (1999), pp. 52-58; D. Butler, Presbyterianism in the Fethard area (1690-1919) in *THJ* (2000), pp. 64-72; A.M. Chadwick, Alice O'Sullivan, Colonel missionary and martyr (1836-1870) in *THJ* 2001), pp. 83-88; D. Butler, Presbyterianism in the Fethard area (1690-1919) in *THJ* (2001), pp. 129-38; S. O Cadhla, Captaen na bhFear mBan: Father Nicholas Sheehy in history/folklore in *THJ* (2002), pp. 69-90; D. Butler, Beyond Roman Catholicism: other aspects of Christianity in Carrick-on-Suir since the Reformation in *THJ* (2002), pp. 131-48; D. Butler, Presbyterianism in Clonmel, 1650-1977 in *THJ* (2003), pp. 81-102; M. Ó Drisceoil, Commemorating Croke, ethnic nationalism as spectacle in *THJ* (2004), pp. 161-68; M. Bourke, Erasmus Smith and Tipperary Grammar School in *THJ* (1989), pp. 82-99; M. Ahern, The Quaker Schools in Clonmel in *THJ* (1990), pp. 128-32; M. Ahern, Clonmel Mechanics Institute in *THJ* (1991), pp. 159-62; M. Luddy, Presentation Convents in County Tipperary, 1806-1900 in *THJ* (1992), pp. 84-95; S.M. Parkes, Sources for the history of education in Co Tipperary: a case-study from Fethard in *THJ* (1992), pp. 116-21; M. Ahern, Clonmel Charter School in *THJ* (1992), pp. 148-52; M. Ahern, Clonmel Grammar School in *THJ* (1993), pp. 128-34; M. Ahern, Clonmel Model School in *THJ* (1996), pp. 110-16; M. Ahern, Clonmel's pay schools- "urban hedge schools" in *THJ* (2000), pp. 132-35.

668 W.P. Burke, *The Irish Priests in the Penal Times (1660-1760)* (Waterford, 1914); with references to Clonmel: Cardinal Moran, *Historical Sketch of the persecutions suffered by the Catholics of Ireland under the rule of Cromwell and the Puritans* (Dublin, n.d.)

669 Report on the state of Popery in Ireland, 1731 (dioceses of Cashel & Emly, Killaloe, Waterford & Lismore in *Arch. Hib.*, 2 (1913), pp. 108-55.

670 *To the Rev. Doctor James Butler, a titular archbishop. From a Friend* (Dublin, 1787) 15pp.; A *letter from the Most Rev. Doctor Butler Titular Archbishop of Cashel to the Right Hon. Lord Viscount Kenmare* (Kilkenny, 1787) Printed by J.C. Finn. 8 pp. Also Dr James Butler, *Remarks on the justification of the tenets of the Papists etc* (Dublin, 1787) and Dr James Butler, *A justification of the tenets of the Roman Catholic religion and a refutation of the charges brought against its clergy by the Rt Rev The Lord Bishop of Cloyne* (Dublin, 1787).

671 J. Dalton, *The History of Tithes, Church Lands and other Ecclesiastical Benefices* (Dublin, 1832) and a modern treatment of the topic in Tipperary: N. Higgins, Tipperary's Tithe War 1830-1838 (St Helen's Press, 2002). Also N. Higgins, The 1832 Clergy Relief Fund for Co Tipperary in *THJ* (2004), pp. 207-222.

672 M. Hurley SJ, *Irish Anglicanism, 1869-1969: essays on the role of Anglicanism on Irish Life* (Dublin, 1970); R.B. McDowell, *The Church of Ireland, 1869-1969* (London, 1975). Of interest: *Diocesan Council of Cashel & Emly: Reports 1870-75, Bishop Robert Daly* (1875).

673 K. Homfray, The Rev. Henry Woodward, Rector of Fethard, 1812-1863 in *THJ* (2005), pp. 87-95.

674 E. Farrell, Interdenominational co-operation in a Tipperary parish during the "Tithe War" in *THJ* (2005), pp. 97-104.

propaganda is of interest.[675] Fr David Humphreys, a Tipperary priest fought for catholic rights in education.[676] Something perhaps more heard about than actually seen is *Butler's Catechism*.[677] A key event in Irish catholicism and in the history of Thurles was the 1850 synod.[678] Kevin Whelan's article on the catholic chapel discussed its geographical context.[679]

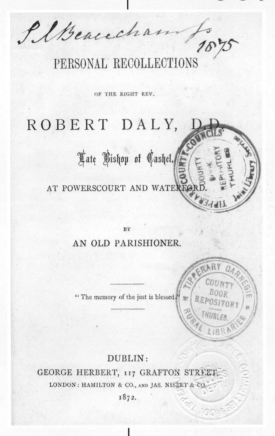

For many decades the professor of education in UCD was Fr Timothy Corcoran SJ, a native of North Tipperary. His *Selected Texts* was widely used.[680] From the nineteenth-century, there are some government inquiries touching on education and related matters.[681]

There is also a 1906 report on industrial schools.[682] A modern study of charter schools has material relevant to Tipperary.[683] Three works discuss different aspects of hedge schools.[684]

A History of Irish Catholicism under the general editorship of the Rev. P.J. Corish was an ambitious multi-volume undertaking. Tipperary Studies has some of these volumes.[685]

Kilcooly Sunday School
1862 Bible

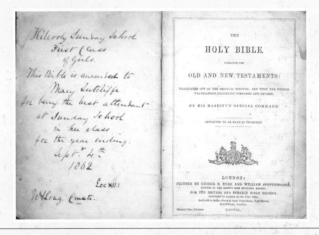

---

[675] *Catholic Emancipation, Celebrations Dublin, June 16-23 1929* (Dublin, 1929); *23rd annual Catholic Truth Conference, Souvenir and Programme, Mansion House Dublin 5-9 Oct 1925; A Roll of Honour: Irish Prelates and priests of the Last Century* (CTS, Dublin, 1905);

[676] D. Humphreys, *Evidence submitted to the Commissioners of the Educational Endowments (Ireland) Act* (Dublin, 1889).

[677] *Butler's Catechism* (Dublin, 1944).

[678] Rev. J. Ahern, The Plenary Synod of Thurles in *IER*, lxxv (1951), pp. 385-403 and lxxviii (1952), pp. 1-20. Also a file of related material.

[679] K. Whelan, The Catholic Parish, the Catholic Chapel and Village Development in Ireland in *Irish Geography*, xvi (1983), pp. 1-15.

[680] Fr T. Corcoran SJ, *Selected texts on educational systems in Ireland from the close of the middle ages* (UCD, 1928).

[681] 1st *Report of the commissioners on Education in Ireland, with appendices, May 1825; Educational Endowments (Ireland) Commission, annual report 1887-88, with minutes of evidence* [C-5546] (Refers to Rockwell, Cashel schools, Clonmel schools and Abbey Grammar School Tipperary).

[682] *44th Report of the Inspector appointed to visit the Reformatory and Industrial Schools of Ireland, 1906* [Cd. 3146].

[683] K. Milne, *The Irish Charter Schools, 1730-1830* (Dublin, 1997).

[684] P.J. Dowling, *The Hedge Schools of Ireland* (London, 1935); A. McManus, *The Irish Hedge School and its Books, 1695-1831* (Dublin, 2002); T. Corcoran SJ, *Some Lists of Catholic lay Teachers and their Illegal Schools in the Late Penal Times* (Dublin, 1932).

[685] Fr P.J. Corish (ed.), *A History of Irish Catholicism*, vol 2, no. 1; vol 3, nos. 7&8; vol 4, nos. 2&3; vol 5, nos. 7-10; vol 6, nos. 1, 3-5, 8.

ANNO UNDECIMO & DUODECIMO

VICTORIÆ REGINÆ.

****

Cap. 22.

An Act for the Relief of the Right Honourable *Richard* Earl of *Glengall* in respect of his Estates in the Counties of *Waterford* and *Tipperary* in *Ireland*, and for vesting the same Estates in Trustees for effecting such Relief. [4th *September* 1848.]

WHEREAS James Baron *Cahir* deceased was in and previous to the Year One thousand seven hundred and eighty-four seised or entitled in Fee Simple of or to all that and those the Manor of *Cahir*, the Manor of *Castlegrace*, the Manor of *Knockgraffon*, the several Towns and Lands of *Bunrora*, *Ballybynona*, *Ballinagiery* otherwise *Ballingeary*, *Ballyknockane*, *Bohernagore East*, *Bohernagore West*, *Ballygeary*, *Ballylegan*, *Ballyhurrow*, *Brokarts*, *Bonly Kennedy*, *Ballytrehy* otherwise *Ballytrihy*, *Cahir Castle*, *Castle-grace*, *Carrigeen*, *Upper Clonmore*, *Lower* or *Under Clonmore*, *Close-calane* otherwise *Clonscullane*, *Clostany*, *Clonmel*, *Clocuty*, *Croghta*, *Carraganroe* otherwise *Carraganeroe*, *Curraghclony* otherwise *Cur-raghaghley*, *Clogkeenfishoge* otherwise *Clogheensisoge*, *Curraghtown*, *Coolelomper*, *Carraganerese*, *Cloniley Dromleman* otherwise *Dromolan*, *Doughill* otherwise *Duhill*, *Ervaghta*, *Farranagark*, *Farrowvelly*, *Farronshonokee*, *Garronavilly* otherwise *Garranvelly* otherwise *Gar-navilla*, *Garrownelly*, *Garrycloher*, *Old Graige*, *New Graige*, *Garry-duffe*,

[*Private.*]　　　7 n

Section Fourteen: Legal Sources

In terms of shelf space, nothing in Tipperary Studies comes close to its collection of statutes: intention, endeavour and not infrequently failure, gathered between covers and spanning the entire nineteenth century.[686] More in keeping with today, the acts of the Oireachtas between 1923 and 2002 are also available, but in CD Rom.[687] Some indices are useful.[688] Sources are available covering statutes prior to the Act of Union.[689]

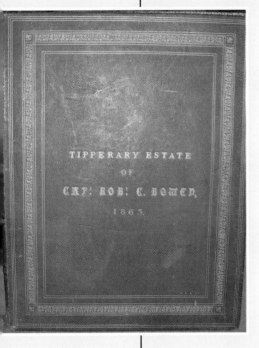

Of much more local interest is the Library's small collection of private acts of parliament. An individual (always wealthy, influential and of course male) who for example wanted a divorce or who wanted to undo some family arrangement about property, had to finance a private act of parliament to achieve his desired end. When in the late 18th century Humphrey Minchin of Busherstown, Dunkerrin near Roscrea wanted to sell up and emigrate to England, such an act had to be obtained to allow the sale of family land. When Richard Fitzgibbon (in 1851 succeeding to the earldom of Clare) fell for Diana Moore, she had the inconvenience of a husband, Maurice Crosbie Moore of Mooresfort near Tipperary town. That marriage was dissolved by act of parliament in 1825. When the earl of Glengall was in financial difficulty, his father-in-law's money bailed him out.

One consequence of the struggle over New Tipperary was that leases were broken and settlement necessitated a private act of parliament.

---

[686] *The Public General Acts* passed between 1801 and 1920. (1816 is missing).

[687] *Acts of the Oireachtas, 1923-2002* (CD Rom).

[688] *An Index to the Statutes, Public and private, 1801-1859* (London, 1860); *Index to the Statutes 1922-1958 with chronological tables* (Government Publications).

[689] E. Bullingbrooke & F. Vesey (eds.), *An Abridgement of the Public Statutes of Ireland [from 1215 to 1781]* (Dublin, 1786) 2 volumes; *The Irish Statutes: Revised Edition – 3 Edward II to The Union AD 1310-1800* (London, 1885).

*An Act concerning fines in the County Palatine of Tipperary (Dublin, 1695).

*An Act on repairing the Road leading from the city of Kilkenny to the town of Clonmel in the County of Tipperary (Dublin, 1731).

*An Act for sale of part of the estate of Thomas Lord Baron of Cahir, towards discharging the debts and encumbrances affecting the same, 17 Geo II c. 25(1744).

*An Act for vesting the settled estates of Humphrey Minchin in Trustees ... (to sell and use the money to purchase property in England), 11 Geo III c. 106 (1772).

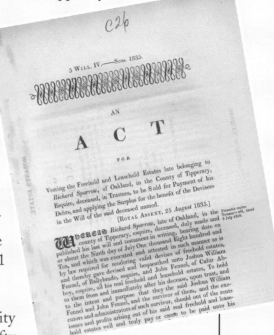

*An Act for settling and securing a certain annuity on Lord Hutchinson of Alexandria and Knocklofty, 42 Geo III c. 113 (1802).

*An Act for the sale of part of the estates of the Right Honourable Robert Earl of Roden, 43 Geo III c. 73 (1803).

*An Act ... agreement Stephen Earl of Mount Cashel and John Power of Affane, County Waterford for the surrender of a lease ... to the earl ... lands of Kilcarroon called Doon County Tipperary ... in the marriage settlement of said John Power and Ann his late wife, 55 Geo III c. 83 (1814-15).

*An Act allowing property in County Kilkenny of Cornwallis Viscount Hawarden be sold and pay his charges on his Tipperary estates and use the surplus to purchase more land in Tipperary, 1 Geo IV c. 47 (1820).

*An Act to dissolve the marriage of Maurice Crosbie Moore and Diana Moore, 6 Geo IV c. 77 (1825).

*An Act for vesting the freehold and leasehold estates late belonging to Richard Sparrow of Oakland [Clonmel] deceased, in trustees and to be sold for payment of his debts, 5 & 6 Will IV c. 26 (1835).

*An Act for completing a railway communication between Clonmel and the Great Southern & Western Railway at or near Thurles, 9 & 10 Vict c. 198 (1846).

*An Act for the relief of the Right Honourable Richard Earl of Glengall in respect of his estates in the counties of Waterford and Tipperary in Ireland, and for vesting the same estates in Trustees for effecting such relief, 11 & 12 Vict c. 22 (1848).

*An Act to authorize the Trustees of the will of William Mellish Esq., deceased, to invest a portion of the funds subject to the trusts of the will of the said William

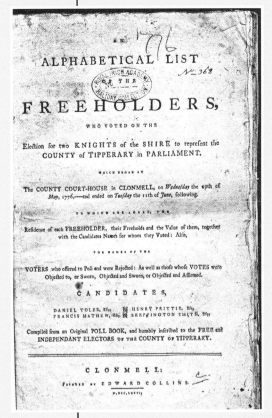

ALPHABETICAL LIST
OF THE
FREEHOLDERS,
WHO VOTED ON THE
Election for two KNIGHTS of the SHIRE to represent the
COUNTY of TIPPERARY in PARLIAMENT.
WHICH BEGAN AT
The COUNTY COURT-HOUSE in CLONMELL, on *Wednesday* the 29th of
May, 1776,——and ended on *Tuesday* the 11th of *June*, following.
TO WHICH ARE ADDED, THE
Residence of each FREEHOLDER, their Freeholds and the Value of them, together
with the Candidates Names for whom they Voted; Also,
THE NAMES OF THE
VOTERS who offered to Poll and were Rejected: As well as those whose VOTES were
Objected to, or Sworn, Objected and Sworn, or Objected and Affirmed.
CANDIDATES,
DANIEL TOLER, Esq;   HENRY PRITTIE, Esq;
FRANCIS MATHEW, Esq;   SKEFFINGTON SMITH, Esq;
Compiled from an Original POLL BOOK, and humbly inscribed to the FREE and
INDEPENDANT ELECTORS of the COUNTY of TIPPERARY.
CLONMELL:
PRINTED BY EDWARD COLLINS.
M,DCC,LXXVI;

Mellish in the purchase of the family estates in Ireland of the Right Honourable Richard Earl of Glengall, 13 & 14 Vict c. 17 (1850).

*An Act to enable the Great Southern & Western Railway to make a railway from Roscrea to Birdhill, 24 & 25 Vict c. 197 (1861).

*An Act to enable the Kilkenny Junction Railway Company to abandon part of their line between Abbeyleix and Mountrath and extend new lines to the Maryborough Station and to the Roscrea Junction on the Great Southern & Western Railway, 24 & 25 Vict c. 232 (1861).

*An Act to authorize the construction of railways from the Waterford & Limerick Railway at Clonmel to Lismore and Dungarvan, 28 & 29 Vict c. 264 (1865).

*An Act to authorize trustees of the settlement of property of Dame Florence Ann Maria Power, wife of Sir Richard Crompton Power Bart, 37 & 38 Vict c. 1 (1874).

*Southern Railway (Cashel Extension Abandonment) Act, 43 & 44 Vict c. 56 (1880).

*An Act to confirm certain provisional orders of the Local Government Board … burial ground .. town of Thurles, 47 & 48 Vict c. 105 (1884).

*An Act to confirm certain orders under the Labourers (Ireland) Act, 1883 … Unions of Cashel, Clogheen … Tipperary, 47 & 48 Vict c. 110 (1884).

*An Act to enable the Baron Barrymore to restore certain forfeited leases in the town of Tipperary and for other purposes, 5 Edw VII c. 1 (1905).

Clonmel PLU Minute Book 1849

Extract from Punishment Book

Edmond Baldwin, Frank Mara, Andy Russell & Thomas Sheehan, for burning a table trussell the property of the Union, when on Guard – 24 hours Confinement and Milk Stopped

Catherine Kennedy, for Refusing to Work,   like punishment

Bridget McGrath, for tearing an Apron the property of the Union 24 hours Confinement and Milk Stopped

MANUSCRIPT SOURCES for the HISTORY of IRISH CIVILISATION — Edited by Richard J. Hayes — Vol. 11 LISTS OF MANUSCRIPTS — G. K. HALL & CO.

MANUSCRIPT SOURCES for the HISTORY of IRISH CIVILISATION — Edited by Richard J. Hayes — Vol. 10 DATES 1700-1900 — G. K. HALL & CO.

MANUSCRIPT SOURCES for the HISTORY of IRISH CIVILISATION — Edited by Richard J. Hayes — Vol. 9 DATES TO 1699 — G. K. HALL & CO.

MANUSCRIPT SOURCES for the HISTORY of IRISH CIVILISATION — Edited by Richard J. Hayes — Vol. 8 PLACES I - Z — G. K. HALL & CO.

MANUSCRIPT SOURCES for the HISTORY of IRISH CIVILISATION — Edited by Richard J. Hayes — Vol. 7 PLACES A - K — G. K. HALL & CO.

MANUSCRIPT SOURCES for the HISTORY of IRISH CIVILISATION — Edited by Richard J. Hayes — Vol. 6 SUBJECTS — G. K. HALL & CO.

MANUSCRIPT SOURCES for the HISTORY of IRISH CIVILISATION — Edited by Richard J. Hayes — Vol. 5 SUBJECTS — G. K. HALL & CO.

MANUSCRIPT SOURCES for the HISTORY of IRISH CIVILISATION — Edited by Richard J. Hayes — Vol. 4 PERSONS P - Z — G. K. HALL & CO.

MANUSCRIPT SOURCES for the HISTORY of IRISH CIVILISATION — Edited by Richard J. Hayes — Vol. 3 PERSONS L - O — G. K. HALL & CO.

MANUSCRIPT SOURCES for the HISTORY of IRISH CIVILISATION — Edited by Richard J. Hayes — Vol. 2 PERSONS E - K — G. K. HALL & CO.

MANUSCRIPT SOURCES for the HISTORY of IRISH CIVILISATION — Edited by Richard J. Hayes — Vol. 1 PERSONS A - D — G. K. HALL & CO.

Section Fifteen: Reference Material

The most important reference work in Tipperary Studies is *Sources for the History of Irish Civilization*.[690] Compiled by former Director of the National Library Richard Hayes, these two sets of volumes respectively list manuscript sources for Irish history found in libraries all over the world and articles in the most important Irish periodicals. Entries are organized under the headings: Persons, Subjects, Places, and Dates. An obvious limitation is that these works do not cover the past thirty to forty years. The same company published a catalogue of Cashel Diocesan Library (now Bolton-GPA), listing the ten thousand plus rare early books and pamphlets.[691] There is also a listing of Irish Archives, an invaluable reference, now in its 4th edition.[692]

Tipperary Historical Journal published two very useful guides: one to Tipperary newspapers and the other to articles of Tipperary interest published in the century-old *Journal of the Cork Historical and Archaeological Society*.[693] A guide to Irish periodicals is of value (See **Part Two** of Finding Tipperary).[694]

As part of the RIA New *History of Ireland*, a number of reference volumes were published dealing respectively with 19th and 20th century Parliamentary Election

---

[690] R. Hayes, (ed.), *Sources for the History of Irish Civilization: Manuscripts* (Boston, 1965) 11 volumes, also 3 supplementary volumes 1965-75; *Sources for the History of Irish Civilization: articles in Irish periodicals* (Boston, 1970) 9 volumes.

[691] *Catalogue of the Cashel Diocesan Library, Co Tipperary, republic of Ireland* (Boston, 1973). See also R.S. Matteson, *A Large Private Park: the collection of Archbishop William King, 1650-1729* (Cambridge, 2003) 2 volumes.

[692] S. Helferty & R. Refausse (eds.), *Directory of Irish Archives* (4th ed. Dublin 2003).

[693] J.C. Hayes & M. Bourke, Guide to Tipperary Newspapers, 1770-1989 in *THJ* (1989), pp. 17-19; M. Bourke, Journal of Cork Historical and Archaeological Society: an Index to Tipperary material, 1892-1991 in *THJ* (1992), pp. 57-62. For newspapers, see also M-L Legg, *Newspapers and Nationalism: the Irish provincial press, 1850-1892* (Dublin, 1999); also of interest S.J. Potter (ed.), *Newspapers and Empire in Ireland and Britain: reporting the British Empire, c.1857-1921* (Dublin, 2004).

[694] B. Hayley & E. McKay, *300 Years of Irish Periodicals* (Mullingar, 1987).

results; Population Statistics 1821-1971; a Chronology of Irish History and a compilation of maps, genealogies and lists.[695]

Under British rule, a census was conducted at the beginning of each decade. Because of the Great Famine, the returns for 1841 and 1851 are of particular importance and interest. (See **Section Thirteen B**) Tipperary Studies has census information for the county from other years, general statistical data, not the actual household returns which are only available for 1901 and 1911.[696] (See **Section Three**) For the diocese of Cashel & Emly, *Pobal Ailbe* gives a townland by townland return of houses and persons for each census between 1841 and 1971.[697]

NEWPORT NEWS
DECEMBER 1995
Price £3.00
Published by Newport Newsletter Committee
The Famine

Maynooth University has a long established local history programme and publishes comprehensive guides to sources relating to various topics: Landed Estates, the Church of Ireland, the Catholic Church, Medieval Records, Pre-Census Sources, Irish Censuses, Maps, Military History, Crime and Material Culture.[698] Because of their connections with South Tipperary, a guide to Quaker records is of interest.[699] There is also a guide to sources for Irish medieval history in the UK.[700] As part of the Famine commemoration, two guides to sources were published.[701] A useful if biased guide to Ireland in the 1920s is the 'official handbook' of the Free State.[702]

Tipperary Studies has three related sources with respect to Irish landownership in the 1870s when landlordism was at its optimum before the impact of land purchase legislation.[703]

Fiction can be an interesting source for social history and a guide to the large number of Irish novels from the 19th and early 20th centuries is Stephen Brown.[704] (See **Section Sixteen**)

---

[695] B.M. Walker, *Parliamentary Election results in Ireland 1801-1922* (RIA, 1978); B.M. Walker, *Parliamentary Election Results in Ireland 1918-92* (RIA, 1992); W.E. Vaughan, A.J. Fitzpatrick (eds.), *Irish Historical Statistics Population 1821-1971* (RIA, 1978); Moody, Martin, Byrne (eds.), *A New History of Ireland VIII A Chronology of Irish History to 1976* (Clarendon, Oxford, 1992); Moody, Martin, Byrne (eds.), *A New History of Ireland IX Maps, Genealogies, Lists* (Clarendon, Oxford, 1984).

[696] Tipperary returns for 1831, 1841, 1851, 1861, 1891, 1901, 1911. Also 1991, 1996 and 2002.

[697] *Pobal Ailbe, Cashel & Emly Census of Population, 1841-1971* (Thurles, 1975).

[698] T.A.M. Dooley, *Sources for the history of landed estates in Ireland* (Dublin, 2000); R. Refaussé, *Church of Ireland records* (Dublin, 2000); P.J. Corish & D.C. Sheehy, *Records of the Irish Catholic Church* (Dublin, 2001); P. Connolly, *Medieval record sources* (Dublin, 2002); B. Gurrin, *Pre-census sources for Irish demography* (Dublin, 2002); E.M. Crawford, *Counting the people: a survey of the Irish censuses, 1813-1911* (Dublin, 2003); J. Prunty, *Maps and map-making in local history* (Dublin, 2004); B. Hanley, *A guide to Irish military history* (Dublin, 2004); B. Griffin, *Sources for the study of crime in Ireland, 1801-1921* (Dublin, 2005); T. Barnard, *A guide to the sources for Irish material culture, 1500-2000* (Dublin, 2005).

[699] O.C. Goodbody, *Guide to Irish Quaker Records 1654-1860* (IMC, 1967).

[700] P. Dryburgh & B. Smith (eds.), *Handbook and Select Calendar of Sources for Medieval Ireland in the National Archives of the UK* (Dublin, 2005).

[701] D. Lindsay & D. Fitzpatrick, *Records of the Irish Famine a guide to local archives, 1840-1855* (Dublin, 1993); A. Eiriksson & C. Ó Grada, *Estate Records of the Irish Famine* (Dublin, 1995).

[702] B. Hobson (ed.), *Saorstat Eireann Irish Free State: Official Handbook* (Dublin, 1932).

[703] *Return of owners of land of an acre and upwards*, [C 1492], HC 1876, lxxx; J. Bateman, *The Great landowners of Great Britain and Ireland* (4th ed. Reprint, New York, 1970); U.H. Hussey de Burgh, *The Landowners of Ireland* (Dublin, 1878).

[704] S.J. Brown SJ, *Ireland in Fiction* (Dublin, 1919); S.J. Brown SJ, *Novels and Tales by Catholic Writers: A Catalogue* (8th ed., Dublin, 1946).

Irish place names resonate with attachment and history. The standard reference is Joyce.[705] The most comprehensive listing of Irish townlands, civil parishes and baronies is based on the 1851 census.[706] There are also guides to both ancient and 17th century place names.[707] Some sources provide information with respect to Tipperary.[708] A variety of guides provide information with respect to aspects of man's impact on the landscape, from prehistoric tombs to Victorian villas.[709]

The Central Statistics Office published a very useful and interesting compilation of information about Ireland in the second half of the 20th century.[710]

The most comprehensive biographical source is the *Dictionary of National Biography* and while Tipperary Studies does not have the 2004 edition, the earlier edition is an entertaining source of information on the lives of the famous.[711] Tipperary Studies has a small collection of biographical guides, some quite specialized. For example, the history of the Irish parliament before the Act of Union has biographical information on all those who represented Tipperary.[712] A useful reference work is a listing of Irish statutes between the reigns of Edward II and George II.[713]

A good deal of biographical information is available regarding catholic clergy in Cashel & Emly and Tipperary generally.[714] There is also a dictionary of biography for Tipperary. [715]

---

705 P.W. Joyce, *The Origin and History of Irish Names of Places* (Dublin, 1995 ed.) 3 volumes. See M. Seoighe, *The Joyce Brothers of Glenosheen* (Author, 1987); also P.J. O'Connor, *Atlas of Irish Place-Names* (Newcastle West, 2001).

706 *General Alphabetical Index to the townlands and towns, parishes and baronies of Ireland* (Baltimore, 1984).

707 E. Hogan SJ, *Onomasticon Goedelicum: an index with identifications to the Gaelic names of places and tribes* (Dublin, 1910); M. Goblet, *A Topographical Index to the Parishes and Townlands of Ireland in Sir William Petty's MSS Barony Maps (c.1655-9) and Hiberniae Delineatio (c.1672)* (IMC, 1932).

708 P. Ó Cearbhaill (ed.), *Liostaí Logainmneacha Contae Thiobraid Arann* (Dublin, 2004); *Placenames of Townlands in Tipperary North* (North Tipperary Federation ICA, n.d.); Rev. P. Power, *The Place-Names of Decies* (London, 1907); Rev. M. O'Flanagan, *O.S. Name Books, Co Tipperary*, 9 volumes.

709 A. Weir, *Early Ireland: A Field Guide* (Belfast, 1980); Lord Killanin & M.V. Duigan, *Shell Guide to Ireland* (London, 1962); P. Harbison, *Guide to National and Historic Monuments of Ireland* (Dublin, 1992 ed.); H.G. Leask, *Irish Churches and Monastic Buildings* (1st ed., 1955, Dundalk, 1996) 3 volumes; H.G. Leask, *Irish Castles and Castellated Houses* (Dundalk, 1941); P.M. Kerrigan, *Castles and Fortifications in Ireland, 1485-1945* (Collins Press, 1995); A. Thomas, *The Walled Towns of Ireland* (Dublin, 1992) 2 volumes; S. Rothery, *A Field Guide to the Buildings of Ireland* (Dublin, 1997); J. Williams, *A Companion Guide to Architecture in Ireland, 1837-1921* (Dublin, 1994); F.H.A. Aalen, K. Whelan & M. Stout (eds.), *Atlas of the Irish Rural landscape* (Cork UP, 1997).

710 A. Redmond (ed.), *That Was Then, This Is Now: Change in Ireland 1949-1999* (Dublin, 2000).

711 Sir. L. Stephen & Sir S. Lee (eds.), *The Dictionary of National Biography* (Oxford UP, 1973) 22 volumes.

712 J.S. Crone, *A Concise Dictionary of Irish Biography* (Dublin, 1928); T. Snoddy, *Dictionary of Irish Artists 20th Century* (2nd ed., Dublin, 2002); M. McNamara & P. Mooney (eds.), *Women in Parliament: Ireland 1918-2000* (Dublin, 2000); S.J. Brown SJ, *An International Index of Catholic Biographies* (2nd ed., London, 1935); J.J. Burke (ed.), *The Last Resting Places of Notable Irishmen* (London, n.d.); R. Hayes, *Biographical Dictionary of Irishmen in France* (Dublin, 1949); R.S. Harrison, *A Biographical Dictionary of Irish Quakers* (Dublin, 1997); E.M. Johnston-Liik, *History of the Irish Parliament, 1692-1800* (Belfast, 2002) 6 volumes.

713 *Abridgement of all the Irish Statutes from 3rd year Edward II and 8th year George II* (Dublin, 1736).

714 W.G. Skehan, *Cashel & Emly Heritage* (Abbey Books, 1993); see also Skehan's full unpublished data in Tipperary Studies. J. O'Shea, *Priest, Politics and Society in Post-famine Ireland: a study of County Tipperary 1850-1891* (Dublin, 1983).

715 M. O'Dwyer, *A Biographical Dictionary of Tipperary* (Cashel, 1999).

C. J. KICKHAM
Charcoal/conte/paper,/40x31, Paul M.O'Reilly

Section Sixteen: Prose and Verse

Looking back on his early life, David Copperfield acknowledges the huge debt he owed to his father's small collection of novels, which were his escape from the misery imposed by the dreadful Murdstones and provided sustenance for his imagination. Reading Fielding's *Tom Jones*, our hero tells us, allowed him become Tom Jones for a week. As Charles Dickens knew, fiction is just a different kind of truth. For generations of Tipperary people, their understanding of the county in the mid-nineteenth century comes not from any works of scholarship but from a novel, the Tipperary novel, Kickham's *Knocknagow* or the *Homes of Tipperary*, first published in 1873. Kickham's fiction holds prime position in Tipperary Studies small collection of novels and stories, works either about Tipperary or written by Tipperary authors.[716]

Probably the earliest 'Tipperary novel' was published in 1693, a story with Clonmel references.[717] Also with a Clonmel connection is Laurence Sterne (1713-68), one of the great 18th century novelists, creator of *Tristram Shandy*. Sterne was born in that town where his father was stationed as a soldier.[718] Clonmel has associations with two of the most unusual books in English, each difficult to classify and certainly each without peer. *Tristram Shandy* is one, the other is *Lavengro*, written by George Borrow (1803-81), who though born in England was educated in Clonmel in 1815-16 when his father was with the army in that town. *Lavengro The Scholar The Gypsy The Priest*, published in 1851, purports to be based on the author's own early life and refers generously to Clonmel.[719]

---

[716] C.J. Kickham, *The Eagle of Garryroe and Tales of Tipperary* (Dublin, 1963 ed.); C.J. Kickham, *For the Old Land* (Dublin, 1908 ed.); C.J. Kickham, *Knocknagow* (Dublin, 1962 ed.); C.J. Kickham, *Sally Cavanagh* (Dublin, 1948 ed.); C.J. Kickham, *Tales of Tipperary* (Dublin, n.d.).

[717] H. McDermott (ed.), *Vertue Rewarded or the Irish Princess* (Colin Smyth, 1992).

[718] L. Sterne, *The Life and Opinions of Tristram Shandy, Gentleman* (London, 1970 ed.); also his collected works (Edinburgh, 1803) 8 volumes.

[719] G. Borrow, *Lavengro* (London, n.d.)

DEDICATION

——o——

I Dedicate this Book

ABOUT THE HOMES OF TIPPERARY

TO

MY LITTLE NIECES, ANNIE AND JOSIE,

WITH MANY REGRETS AND APOLOGIES

THAT IN SPITE OF ALL THEIR ENTREATIES I WAS OBLIGED TO

"LET POOR NORAH LAHY DIE."

C.J.K.

The Rev. W.G. Dowsley (1871-1947) was born and educated in Clonmel. After taking Anglican orders, he spent many years in South Africa. His novel *Travelling Men* is set around Clonmel in the early 19th century and features George Borrow as one of its characters. Another of his novels *Long Horns* deals with 1848 and is partly set in South Africa.[720]

Mrs James Sadlier (1820-1903), a native of Cavan emigrated to Canada in 1844 and was a prolific writer of material that was both catholic and nationalist. Two of her stories have Tipperary settings.[721]

Julia Kavanagh (1824-77) was born in Thurles but, as a child, was brought to France by her parents and after their separation, moved to London with her mother. She was the author of over twenty novels, of which Tipperary Studies holds a small selection.[722]

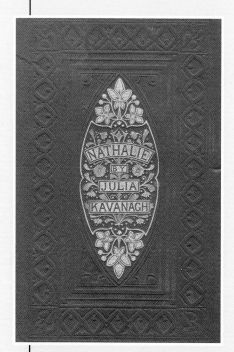

A novel with autobiographical elements is *Innisfail, or Distant Days in Tipperary* by Father Patrick Hickey. Written in New South Wales, the story traces the fortunes of a young priest from Tipperary to Australia. Published in 1906, by the following year the novel was in its 4th edition.[723] Also written from a nationalist perspective is a novel by Templemore-born journalist, W.P. Ryan (father of Sean Treacy's biographer).[724]

Temple Lane (1899-1982) was the pseudonym of Mary Isabel Leslie, who was the daughter of a Church of Ireland clergyman and was brought up in Tipperary. She wrote fifteen novels, of which Tipperary Studies holds five.[725]

In the 1930s, Austin Clarke (1896-1974) began a trinity of novels with medieval settings, one of which *The Singing-Men at Cashel* includes King Cormac Mac Cuileanain as a character. It had the distinction of being banned.[726]

---

[720] W.G. Dowsley, *Travelling Men* (Dublin, 1925); W.G. Dowsley, *Long Horns, the O'Briens of the Glen's Story* (London, 1937 ed.)

[721] Mrs J. Sadlier, *The Hermit of the Rock* (New York, 1863); Mrs J. Sadlier, *The Fate of Father Sheehy* (New York, 1863).

[722] J. Kavanagh, *Adele* (London, 1858); J. Kavanagh, *Daisy Burns* (London, 1853) 3 volumes; J. Kavanagh, *Nathalie* (London, 1859); J. Kavanagh, *Queen Mab* (New York, 1889 ed.). See E. Fauset, The politics of writing: Julia Kavanagh (1824-77) in *Irish Feminist Studies*, pp. 58-68 (copy). Also on Kavanagh's father: R.J. Kavanagh, The Mysterious Irishman, Morgan Peter Kavanagh (Typescript, 2001).

[723] Rev. P. Hickey, *Innisfail or Distant days in Tipperary* (Dublin, 1907 ed.).

[724] W.P. Ryan, *The Heart of Tipperary* (London, 1893).

[725] T. Lane, *No Just Cause* (London, 1925); T. Lane, *House of Pilgrimage* (Dublin, 1941); T. Lane, *Friday's Well* (Dublin, 1943); T. Lane, *Come Back* (Dublin, 1945); T. Lane, *My Bonny's Away* (Dublin, 1947).

[726] A. Clarke, *The Singing-Men at Cashel* (London, 1936).

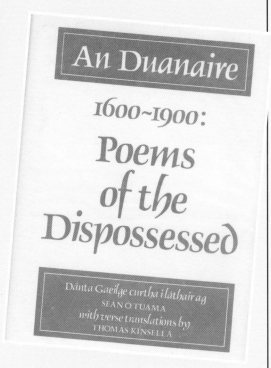

Two
well-written   volumes   of   thinly
disguised autobiography tell something of the story of the remarkable
Browne family of Grangemockler.[727] Laurence Power entertainingly described rural
life in the 1930s and '40s and T.D. Griffin delivered a portrait of Thurles.[728]

In modern Tipperary two creative writers, Michael Coady from Carrick-on-Suir
and Dennis O'Driscoll from Thurles, are especially important and Tipperary
Studies has full collections of their works.[729]

In recent years, fiction with a Tipperary setting and/or a Tipperary author has been
more comprehensively collected than in the past.[730] There has also been something

[727] J. Brady, *The Big Sycamore* (Dublin, 1958) and *In Monavalla* (Dublin, 1963).

[728] L. Power, *Half the Battle: a memoir of a Tipperary boyhood* (Naas, 2000); T.D. Griffin, *A Drawerful of Memories* (Thurles, 2000); *Words that Made a Difference* (Thurles, 2002); *Searching for New Horizons* (Thurles, 2004).

[729] M. Coady, *Two for a Woman Three for a Man* (Dublin, 1980); *Oven Lane* (Dublin, 1987); *All Souls* (Oldcastle, 1997); *Full Tide* (Nenagh, 1999); *One Another* (Oldcastle, 2003). D. O'Driscoll, *Kist* (Mountrath, 1982); *Hidden Extras* (London, 1987); *Long Short Story* (Dublin, 1993); *The Bottom Line* (Dublin, 1994); *Weather Permitting* (London, 1999); *Troubled Thoughts, Majestic Dreams: selected prose writings* (Oldcastle, 2001); *Exemplary Damages* (London, 2002)

[730] A. Atcheson, *Scrouthea* (Clonmel, 2001); M. Armitage, *A Long Way to Go: an Anglo-Irish near tragedy* (London, 1989); A. Broomfield, *When the Dust Settles* (Ballyfin, 1993); J. Brady, *The Big Sycamore* (Dublin, 1958); B. Coogan, *The Big Wind* (London, 1969); L. Cullen, *Let's Twist Again* (Belfast, 2001); F. Delaney, *At Ruby's* (London, 2001); F. Delaney, *The Sins of the Mothers* (London, 1992); K. Fitzgerald, *Snapdragons* (Dingle, 1999); B. Graham, *The White Flower* (London, 1999); G. Greene, *Hound* (London, 2003); A. Haverty, *One Day as a Tiger* (London, 1997); A. Haverty, *The Far Side of a Kiss* (London, 2000); M. Ryan Hayes, *The Flight of Other Days* (Tipperary, n.d.); M. Hill, *Something You Should Know* (Dublin, 2003); M. Hill, *Not What You Think* (Dublin, 2004); M. Hill, *Never Say Never* (Dublin, 2005); J.M. Meagher, *A Bluebell in a Quarry* (Canada, 1999); O. Murray, *Mikey* (Roscrea, n.d); M. O'Sullivan, *Wash Basin Blues* (Dublin, 1995); M. O'Sullivan *Melody for Nora* (Dublin, 1995); M. O'Sullivan *More than a match* (Dublin, 1997); M. O'Sullivan *Angels without wings* (Dublin, 1997); M. O'Sullivan *White Lies* (Dublin, 1997); M. O'Sullivan *Enright* (Belfast, 2005); L. Power, *The Bright Boys* (Dun Laoghaire, 1984); M. Quarton, *One Dog and His Trials* (Belfast, 1986); M. Quarton, *Corporal Jack* (London, 1987); M. Quarton, *No Harp Like My Own* (London, 1990); M. Quarton, *Renegade* (London, 1991); M. Quarton, *Saturday's Child* (London, 1993); M. Quigley, *Drifting With the River Gods* (Cork, 2003); J.C. Ryan, *The Broken Plate* (Manchester, 2000); R.G. Walshe, *Knocknagow* (Dublin, 1919).

of a renaissance in poetry publications.[731] Tipperary Studies is committed to filling the gaps in its collection.

Collections of verse of great historical interest include *Poems on the Butlers of Ormond, Cahir and Dunboyne (A.D. 1400-1650)* and *Poems on Marcher Lords from a sixteenth-century Tipperary manuscript*.[732] Dermot Gleeson edited a collection of *Songs of Ormond*.[733] James Maher is particularly associated with the works of Charles Kickham.[734] Darby Ryan and J.J. Finnan ('Myles') were well-known writers of popular verse, each of whom had a collection of songs and poems published.[735] *The Spirit of Tipperary* was a collection of poems and ballads in Irish and English prepared for school-children.[736] Tipperary Studies has copies of a number of ballad collections published

Triumphalia Chronologica (Murphy)

---

[731] S. Baker, *Petals in the Wind* (Roscrea, 2000); B. Barry Kerley, *Soliloquy of Life* (ca. 1979); D. Brennan, *I Reilig na mBan Rialta* (Dublin, 1984); P. De Brún, *1916* (Dublin, n.d); S. De Burca, *Knocknagow* (Dublin, 1945); S. De Burca, *Phil Lahy* (Dublin, n.d); John Cantwell, *Anner's Bright Stream*; Joan Pollard Carew *Moll Strings and others* (Roscrea, n.d); P. Carter & N. Adams, *So Close* (Towson, 1996); Cashel Writers Circle, *The Gathering* (Thurles, 1997); E. Clancy, *Poems*; Clonmel Writers Circle, *Collectively Speaking* (Clonmel, 1992); Cluain Meala Writers, *A Flight of Writers* (Portlaw, 2003); B. Conti, *From Words to Infinity* (Clonmel, 2003); Ú. Crowe, *Waiting for the Beasts* (Roscrea, 1999); C. Cullen, *Under the Eye of the Moon* (Cork, 2001); E. Cullen, *No vague Utopia* (Kinvara, 2003); P. Dwyer, *From Thurles to Cuba with Love* (2001); G. Fone, *Midnight Oil* (2001); T. W. Greene, *Scars* (Roscrea, 1988); S. Hogan, *Interweavings* (Paris, 1988); P. Kearney, *Poems of Time and Space* (Cahir, 1994); D. MacDonagh, *Veterans and Other Poems* (Dublin, 1941); T. MacDonagh, *Songs of myself* (Dublin, 1910); T. MacDonagh, *Lyrical Poems* (Dublin, 1913); T. MacDonagh, *The Poetical Works* (Dublin, 1919); T. MacDonagh, *Pagans* (Dublin, 1920); P. Moran, *Stubble Fields* (Dublin, 2001); O. Murray, *The Welcome Rain* (Nenagh, 1991); Nenagh Writers Group, *A Treasury of Story and Verse* (Nenagh, n.d); F. Neville, *Horns on the Wind*; M. Ní Cheallacháin, *Filíocht Phádraigín Haicead* (Baile Átha Cliath, 1962); M. Noonan, *Thoughts and Echoes* (Cashel, 1999); M. Noonan, *Yours and Mine* (Cashel, 2003); B. O'Connor, *Because I am the Best* (1990); B. O'Connor, *Come with Me a Hunting* (1990); B. O'Connor, *Why Pick on Me* (1990); Y. O'Connor, *Happy Endings* (Cork, n.d); Y. O'Connor, *Poems of the Golden Years* (1993); M. O'Gorman, *Barking at Blackbirds* (Cork, 2001); M. Roper, *The Hen Ark* (Galway, 1990); D. Ryan, *The Blind Seanachie* (Tipperary , 2003); E. Ryan, *Angels in the Dark* (Piltown, 2000); G. Ryan, *Treasures to Share* (1997); P. Ryan, *Ballad and Balance* (Dublin, 1998); Shinrone Tidy Towns Committee, *Poems for Lughnasa*; South Tipperary Adult Learning Scheme, *We got there* (Clonmel, 2002); M. Toppin, *African Violets and Other Poems* (1995); D. Walsh, *Windgap Miscellany*; P.J. Whelan, *Tales in Songs and Story, Heroes of Great Renown* (Roscrea, 2004); A. White, *Amandlea*, (Carrick-on-Suir, n.d); R.D. Williams, *The Poems of R.D. Williams* (Dublin, 1882); T. Wood & M. Noonan, *My Favourite Haunt: the Collected Poetry of Michael Luke Phillips* (Cashel, 2003).

[732] J. Carney (ed.), *Poems on the Butlers* (Dublin, 1945); A. O'Sullivan (ed.), *Poems on Marcher Lords* (Irish Texts Society, 1987).

[733] D. Gleeson, *Songs of Ormond* (Nenagh, n.d.).

[734] J. Maher, *The Valley Near Slievenamon* (Mullinahone, 1942) and *Romantic Slievenamon* (Mullinahone, 1954). For a modern anthology, see S. Nugent (ed.), *Slievenamon in Song & Story* (Author, n.d.).

[735] (Darby Ryan), *The Tipperary Minstrel: being a collection of the songs written by the late Mr Jer. O'Ryan of Ashgrove, Bansha County Tipperary commonly known as Darby Ryan The Poet* (Dublin, 1861); Darby O'Ryan, *Poems: Original and Translated* (Dublin, 1871); Darby Ryan, *The Peeler and the Goat and other songs* (Dublin, 1965); J.J. Finnan ("Myles"), *The Patriotic Songs and Poems 1865-1912* (Limerick, 1913). Also two collections by a Tipperary town poet: J.P. MacCarthy Reagh, *A Friend in Need and other verse* (Tipperary, 1952) and *A Visit from a Friend and other verse* (Tipperary, 1953).

[736] T. Mac Domhnaill & P. Ó Meadhra (eds.), *The Spirit of Tipperary* (Nenagh, n.d.)

in the local press.[737] Ballads inspired by the GAA have been collected and published.[738]

A modern anthology relating to the Galtees region contains a deal of interesting prose and verse, especially William O'Brien's famous "Christmas on the Galtees".[739] The well crafted entertaining essay, as a literary form was the forte of two Tipperary writers, one a priest, the other a schoolmaster.[740]

John Davis White, nineteenth-century Cashel antiquarian and publisher was an avid collector of ballads, nearly one thousand of which are now in the Early Printed Books Department of Trinity College Dublin. Tipperary Studies has a typescript index to this material.[741]

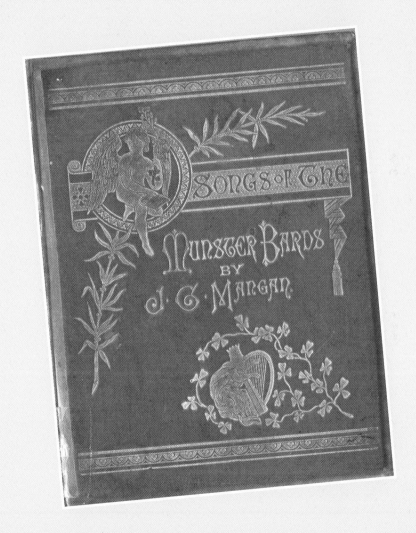

---

[737] Poems, *Songs and Ballads of Tipperary: A Selection* (published as a supplement to the Tipperary Star, 18 Dec 1954); J.J. Hassett, *Tipperary Ballad Roundabout* (published in the Tipperary Star, 13 Jan – 5 May 1990).

[738] S.J. King, L. Ó Donnchu, J. Smyth (eds.), *Tipperary's GAA Ballads* (Thurles, 2000).

[739] J. Gallahue (ed.), *The Galtees Anthology* (Author, 2002). See also his *By Old Paradise Vale* (Author, 2004).

[740] N. Kevin, *I Remember Karrigeen* (London, 1944); N. Kevin, *No Applause in Church* (Dublin, 1947); N. Kevin, *I Remember Maynooth* (London, 1937); E.J. Delaney, *Listen Here, Lads!* (Tralee, 1945); E.J. Delaney, *Tales Out of School* (Tralee, 1966).

[741] *An Index to the Ballad Collection of John Davis White of Cashel held in the Early Printed Books Department, Trinity College Dublin.* Compiled by Denis G. Marnane. See also The Ballad Collection of John Davis White in *THJ* (2005), pp. 61-85.

PART TWO

Periodicals

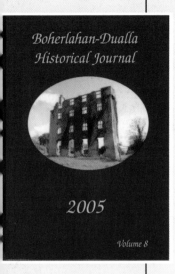

Boherlahan-Dualla Historical Journal

2005

Volume 8

Tipperary Studies has a large collection of learned journals or periodicals. Subjects covered include history, archaeology, philosophy, politics, local studies, sociology and theology. While the collection is extensive, there are very few complete sets of any periodical.

Periodicals are listed alphabetically. All numbers held are noted and in some instances articles of particular interest are indicated.

Analecta Hibernica
This is the official publication of the Irish Manuscripts Commission (IMC), which was established in 1928, and its purpose is to publish Irish historical manuscripts.

1 (March 1930) Obit. of W.F. Butler, 2 (Jan. 1931),
3 (Sept. 1931), 4 (Oct. 1932),
5 (May 1934) Index to 1-4,
6 (Nov. 1934), 7 (n.d),
8 (March 1938), 10 (July 1941), 11 (July 1942),
12 (Jan. 1943) MSS at Kilboy Co. Tipperary; The Annals of Nenagh,
13 (Nov. 1944) Index to 10 and 12,
14 (Dec. 1944),
15 (Nov. 1945?) Report on Vere Hunt Diary; Report on MSS in private keeping,
16 (March 1946) Obit. of Dr T. Corcoran SJ,
19 (1957) Index to 16 and 17,
20 (1958) Report on MSS in private keeping and in NLI,
21 (1959),
23 (1966) Legal proceedings against earl of Desmond; Guide to Registry of Deeds; Report on Ordnance Survey MSS; Report on MSS in private keeping,

Castle and Boathouse, Lough Derg, Nenagh

24 (1967),
25 (1967) Report on MSS in private keeping,
26 (1970) Guide to records in Genealogical Office, Dublin, Index,
27 (1972) Report on Sir William Betham's MSS [wills], with Index of persons,
28 (1978), **29** (1980), **30** (1982).

Archaeology Ireland

The primary contemporary general interest periodical on Irish archaeology. Vol. 1 Number 1 was published in September 1987. Tipperary Studies has an almost complete set. (Missing **1:2, 3:1, 5:2 & 3, 6:2 & 4, 7:1 & 3, 16:1**.)

Archivium Hibernicum

Began publication in 1912 by the Catholic Record Society of Ireland, Maynooth. Publishes MSS relating to the history of the Roman Catholic church in Ireland and on the continent.

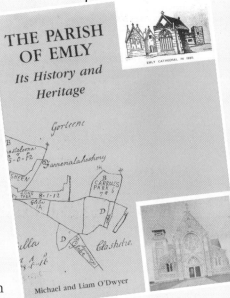

THE PARISH OF EMLY
Its History and Heritage

Michael and Liam O'Dwyer

1 (1912) List of ecclesiastics who took the oath of allegiance, 1774; The correspondence of Dr Bray Archbishop of Cashel & Emly 1792-1820; Royal visitations of Cashel & Emly, 17th century,
2 (1913),
3 (1914) Synod of Rathbreasail; Royal visitation of Killaloe, 17th century,
4 (1915), **5** (1916),
6 (1917) A letter about the massacre in Cashel Cathedral, 17th century,
7 (1918-22) Documents about the appointments of the Archbishop of Cashel in 1791 and of a coadjutor to Waterford in 1801,
8 (1941), **9** (1942), **10** (1943),
12 (1946) Obligationes pro annatis diocese of Waterford,
14 (1949), **15** (1950), **16** (1951),
17 (1953) Catholics and catholicism in the 18th century press,
18 (1955), **19** (1956),
20 (1957) The Tirry documents in Paris and in the Augustinian archives,
21 (1958) Documents from State Papers concerning Miler Magrath,
22 (1959), **23** (1960), **24** (1961), **25** (1962), **26** (1963), **27** (1964) **28** (1966),
29 (1970), **31** (1973), **32** (1974),
33 (1975) Archbishop Butler's visitation section only,
34 (1977) Archbishop Butler's visitation section only,
35 (1980), **36** (1981), **37** (1982), **38** (1983),
39 (1984) Archbishop Slattery and the Episcopal controversy on Irish National Education, 1838-1841,
40 (1985), **41** (1986), **42** (1987), **43** (1988), **44** (1989), **45** (1990), **46** (1991-2),
47 (1993), **48** (1994), **49** (1995), **50** (1996), **51** (1997), **52** (1998), **53** (1999),
54 (2000), **55** (2001), **56** (2002), **57** (2003), **58** (2004).

Banba

Tipperary Studies holds just a few issues of this journal whose Managing Director was Eamon O'Duibhir of Ballagh.

Vol. 111. Nos. 1-4, May–Sept 1922.

Bealoideas
In 1927 the Folklore of Ireland Society was founded and the first issue of their journal *Bealoideas* appeared in 1927-28. This first issue had an article by Rev St. J. Seymour, (author of a history of the diocese of Emly) on seasonal customs and beliefs from Limerick and Tipperary.

Tipperary Studies holds some odd numbers of this journal.
Vol. 1 (1927-28), **Vol. 2** (1929-30), **Vol. 3 No. 1** (1931), **Vol. 3 Nos. 3 & 4** (1932), **Vol. 4 Nos. 1 & 2** (1933), **Vol. 17 Nos. 1 & 2** (1947), **Vol. 18 Nos. 1 & 2** (1948), **Vol. 19 Nos. 1 & 2** (1949), **Vol. 20 Nos. 1 & 2** (1950), **Vol. 21 Nos. 1 & 2** (1951-52), **Vol. 29** (1961), **Vol. 30** (1962), **Vol. 31** (1963), **Vol. 32** (1964), **Vol. 33** (1965), **Vol. 34** (1966), **Vol. 70** (2002).

Boherlahan-Dualla Historical Journal
Published annually from 1998.

Cahir Heritage Newsletter
Nos. 21-30 (1988) and **Nos. 31-40** (1989).

Capuchin Annual
Began in the early 1930s but no longer published. There are gaps in the Tipperary Studies collection.

(1936), (1937),
(1939) Centenary of Fr Theobald Mathew,
(1940) Portrait gallery of Irish leaders 1798-1939,
(1942) Photographs of 1916 and War of Independence (1944), (1945-6), (1946-7), (1948), (1949), (1950-51), (1952), (1953-4), (1955),
(1956-7) Article on the Mathew family,
(1958) Feature on Rock of Cashel,
(1959),
(1960) Features on GAA and St Patrick's College Thurles,
(1961), (1962), (1963), (1964), (1965),
(1966) Feature on 1916,
(1967) Feature on 1917,
(1968) Feature on 1918 including General Election,
(1969) Feature on First Dail,
(1970) Feature on War of Independence by Fr Colmcille,
(1971) Feature on the Treaty,
(1972) Feature on Holy Cross Abbey,
(1973), (1974),
(1975) Article on John Hughes RHA, sculptor of Kickham statue in Tipperary town,
(1976), (1977).

Clonmel Historical and Archaeological Society Journal
Vol. 1 No. 1 1952, Vol. 1 No. 2 1953-54, Vol. 1 No. 3 1954-55, Vol. 1 No. 4 1955-56.

Cloughjordan Heritage
Vol. **1** (1985), **2** (1987), **3** (1992), **4** (1996), **5** (2001).

Collectanea Hibernica
The Franciscans produce this journal, which publishes sources for Irish history, the first issue appearing in 1958. There are large gaps in the Tipperary Studies holding.

3   (1960),

12   (1969) Correspondence with Archbishop Leahy about disestablishment of the Church of Ireland, 1862-9,

18 & 19 (1976-7) 4 letters of Fr James White of Clonmel, 1668-79; Calendar of MSS of Archbishop James Butler II Cashel, 1773-86, Part 1,

20   (1978) Butler Calendar, 1787-91, Part 2,

27 & 28 (1986),

29   (1988) Fabian Ryan OP, possible candidate for Cashel, 1652; List of Dominicans in Ireland, 1832,

30   (1989) Calendar of MSS of Archbishop Slattery, 1822-39, Part 1,

31 & 32 (1989-90) Slattery Calendar, 1840-45, Part 2,

33   (1991) Slattery Calendar, 1846, Part 3,

34 & 35 (1992-93) Maurice MacBrien, Bishop of Emly and the confiscation of his baggage, March 1578, Slattery Calendar, 1847, Part 4,

36 & 37 (1994-95) Slattery Calendar, 1848, Part 5,

38   (1996) Death of Terence Albert O'Brien, Bishop of Emly, 1651,

39 & 40 (1997-98) Jesuit parish missions, 1863-76, Part 1,

41   (1999) Typhus epidemic Ireland, 1817-19; Jesuit parish missions, 1863-76, Part 2,

42   (2000) Jesuit parish missions, 1873-6, Part 3; Supplement to 1731 Report on State of Popery; Biographical register of Irish Dominicans at Lisbon before 1700,

43   (2001),

44 & 45 (2002-3) Slattery Calendar 1849-52, Part 6,

46 & 47 (2004-5).

Decies: Journal of the Waterford Archaeological & Historical Society
Tipperary Studies has this journal from

51 (1995) to **60** (2004),
56 (2000) The Grubbs of Tipperary; The original subscription list of the
Waterford & Limerick Railway Company, 1845.

Dublin Penny Journal
Vol. 1 No. 1, 30 June 1832, Tipperary Studies holds vols. 1-4,
Vol. 1 No. 1, 5 April 1902 (New Series), Tipperary Studies holds **Vols. 1-3** (1902-3).

Éile
This Journal of the Roscrea Heritage Society was edited by George Cunningham.

The Library has **No. 1** (1982) and **No. 2** (1983). These were the only two numbers published.

Ériu
Founded in 1904 as the Journal of the School of Irish Learning, Dublin, it is a very specialised and scholarly journal. Tipperary Studies holds the first eleven volumes (1904-32). Vol. 3 part 1 (1907) has an article on the Rule of St Ailbe of Emly.

Foundations
The magazine published by the archdiocese of Cashel and Emly. Tipperary Studies has a complete set of this journal.

History Ireland
Described as Ireland's only history magazine, Tipperary Studies has a complete run of this journal, which was first published in 1993. Normally, published four times yearly, the issues due in Autumn and Winter 2002 were never produced. It is now being produced six times yearly.

The Irish Ancestor
Tipperary Studies has a very incomplete set of this genealogical journal. However it has the complete set (1969-86) on the Eneclann published CD.

Vol. 3: No. 1 (1971), **3:2** (1971), **8:1** (1976), **8:2** (1976), **9:2** (1977),
10:1 (1978), **10:2** (1978), **11:1** (1979), **11:2** (1979), **12:1 & 2** (1980),
13:1 (1981), **13:2** (1981), **14:1** (1982), **14:2** (1982), **15:1 & 2** (1983),

16:1 (1984),
16:2 (1984) Census of protestants in Shanrahan & Tullaghorton, 1864-70,
17:1 (1985) Emigration from the workhouses of Nenagh Union, 1849-60; Census of Protestants in Clogheen Union, 1873, 1877, 1880; The Rev. Edward Bacon's Register, Clonmel 1785,
17:2 (1985) The Rev Edward Bacon's Register, Clonmel 1785,
18:1 (1986) Don Jorge Rian of Inch Co. Tipperary, 1748-1805.

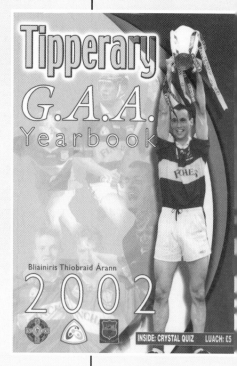

Irish Archives Bulletin

An incomplete collection:

Vol. 1 No. 2 (Oct 1971), **2:1** (May 1972), **2:2** (Oct 1972),
Vol. 4 (1974) An article by R.D. Edwards on County Libraries and their policy towards local archives,
6 (1976) Local historical studies of rural areas: methods and sources,
7 (1977), **8** (1978).

This bulletin became
Irish Archives

Vol. 1 (1989), **Vol. 2. No. 1** (Summer 1992),
(Autumn 1994) Two useful articles: The Registered Papers of the Chief Secretaries Office and The Archives of the OPW,
2:2 (1995) The Relief Commission Papers in the National Archives,
3:2 (1996) The Development of Local Government in Ireland,
4:2 (1997) Introduction to the archives of RC Congregations of Women,
5:1 (1998), **5:2** (1998), **6:1** (1999),
6:2 (1999) An article by Tipperary town native John Heuston on the use of oral history,
7 (2000), **8** (2001-2), **9** (2003-4), **10** (2004-5), **11** (2005).

The Irish at Home and Abroad

'A Newsletter of Irish Genealogy and Heritage' published in Salt Lake City, a major centre for genealogy because of the Church of Jesus Christ of Latter Day Saints (Mormons).

Vol. 1, Numbers **1-4** (1993-4),
Vol. 2, Numbers **1-4** (1994-5),
Vol. 3, Numbers **1-4** (1995-6), In **3:4** an article on Tipperary County by the editor,
Vol. 4, Numbers **1-4** (1997),
Vol. 5, Numbers **1-3** (1998),
Vol. 6, Numbers **1-4** (1999), **6:4** appears to be the final issue.

The Irish Book Lover

The first number of this appeared in August 1909 edited by John S. Crone. As the title suggests, it explored all aspects of Irish writing and writers. The earliest issue in Tipperary Studies is 1928, at which time the editor was Seamus O Casaide who died in April 1943. His particular interest was the history of printing in Ireland. Generally, this periodical appeared bi-monthly.

Vol. 16:1 (Jan-Feb 1928), 2 (March-April 1928), 4, 5, 6 (July-Dec 1928),
Vol. 17:5 (Sept-Oct 1929),
      6 (Nov-Dec 1929),
Vol. 18, 6 numbers (1930),
      with Index to 1930,
Vol. 19, 6 numbers (1931),
Vol. 20, 6 numbers (1932),
Vol. 21, 6 numbers (1933),
Vol. 22, missing 3
      (May-June 1934),
Vol. 23, missing 2
      (March-April 1935),
Vol. 24:2 (March-April 1936),
Vol. 27, 6 numbers (1940-41),
Vol. 28, 6 numbers (1941-42),
Vol. 29, 6 numbers (1943-45),
Vol. 31:1 (March 1949).

Irish Ecclesiastical Record
(Presumably left to the Library from some clerical shelf.)

Vol. 2 (1881) to Vol. 16 (1895) but missing 9 (1888) and 13 (1892).

Irish Family History
This 'Journal of the Irish Family History Society' began publication in 1985. The Tipperary Studies holding is almost complete.

3 (1987), 4 (1988), 5 (1989), 6 (1990),
7 (1991) Has a useful article on the Registry of Deeds,
8 (1992), 9 (1993),
10 (1994) Has a useful article on Encumbered Estates Court rentals, also
    Gravestone inscriptions for St. Mary's churchyard, Thurles,
11 (1995) Has a useful article on urban history records,
12 (1996),
13 (1997) Also for 1997 a Directory of Parish Registers indexed in Ireland,
14 (1998), 15 (1999), 16 (2000), 17 (2001), 18 (2002), 19 (2003).

Irish Forestry
Tipperary Studies holds a small number of issues of this periodical, the Journal of the Society of Irish Foresters. Two issues appear to have been published annually.

Vol. 43. No. 2 (1986) to Vol. 54. No. 2 (1997),
Of particular interest is 49:1 & 2 (1992) An article on 50 years of Irish forestry.

The Irish Genealogist
No holding except Index of Persons 1956-67 and 1968-1973.

Tipperary Studies has copies of the following items of Tipperary interest:

Vol. 3:11 (Oct. 1966) Irish Provincial Directories, 1788 which covers the following places in Tipperary: Borrisoleigh, Carrick-on-Suir, Cashel, Clonmel, Thurles and Tipperary.

Vol. 10:2 (1999) Two articles – History of the Sall(e) Family of Cashel and the Scully tombstones on the Rock of Cashel.

Irish Geography
This began publication in 1944 and is the primary academic geography periodical.

The Library's holding is very sparse.

Vol. 8 (1975) An article on John Wesley in Ireland,
19 (1986), 2 parts, **20** (1987) 2 parts,
21 (1988) part 1 An article on the classification of medieval Irish towns,
23 (1990) 2 parts, **24** (1991) part 2, **25** (1992) part 1, **26** (1993) part 2,
27 (1994) part 2,
29 (1996) part 2 An article on manorial organization in 13th century Tipperary,
30 (1997) part 1.

Irish Historical Studies
The first number appeared in March 1938 edited by its founders, R Dudley Edwards and T.W. Moody. Generally two issues appear each year.

Vol. 2. No. 5 (March 1940),
Vol. 2. No. 6 (Sept 1940),
Tipperary Studies has a complete run from **Vol. 22. No. 85** (March 1980)
to **Vol. 32. No. 126** (Nov 2000), also available **Vol. 33. No. 132** (Nov 2003),
Vol. 34. No. 133 (May 2004) and **Vol. 34. No. 134** (Nov 2005).

Articles of interest include:
23:90 (Nov 1982) The establishment of Poor Law Unions in Ireland, 1838-43,
24:94 (Nov 1984) The Chief Secretary's Office, 1853-1914,
25:98 (Nov 1986) Geoffrey Keating and 17th century interpretations of the past,
25:99 (May 1987) Women and poultry in Ireland, 1891-1914,
28:112 (Nov 1993) A critical bibliography of the Church of Ireland, 1536-1992.

Irish Link
An Australian published family history magazine. The complete run from 1992-1999 is available in Tipperary Studies.

Irish Roots
1992-2004.

The Irish Sword
The Journal of the Military History Society of Ireland first appeared in 1949.
Tipperary Studies has **Vol. 1.4** (1952-3) and a complete run from
Vol. 4. No. 15 (1959) to **Vol.19. No. 77** (1995).

Articles of interest include:
5:18 (1961) Black Tom of Ormond,
8:32 (1968) Thomas MacDonagh's role in the 1916 Rising,
12:47 (1975) A contemporary plan of the siege of Cahir Castle, 1599,
13:52 (1978-9) Special Issue on The Volunteers of 1778,
14:56 (1981) Assistant Surgeon William Bradshaw V.C., born Thurles,
15:58 (1982) The overthrow of the Plantation of Munster in Oct 1598,
16:63 (1985) Guns and Castles in Tipperary (Conrad Cairns),
17:67 (1987-8) Michael Doheny,
18:70 (1990) Special Issue: The War of the Kings, 1689-91,
18:74 (1992) Index: vols. 1-18 (1949-1992),
19:75 & 76 (1993-4) Special Issue: The Emergency, 1939-45.

Journal of the Butler Society
Volume One had eight issues, published between Dec 1968 and 1979. Tipperary Studies also holds **Volume Two**, three issues between 1980-81 and 1984.
And **Volume Three**, four issues, 1986-94. Also **Volume Four**, 2 issues.

Many of the articles refer to Tipperary.

Journal of the Cork Historical and Archaeological Society

This journal was first published in January 1892. Tipperary Studies has very few issues. To mark the journal's centenary, *Tipperary Historical Journal* in 1992 published an index to Tipperary material 1892-1991 published in the Cork journal.

Vol. 33:No. 135 (1927), **33:136** (1927), **33:137** (1928), **33:138** (1928),
35:142 (1930) Index Volume 1892-1940,
45:161 (1940), **46:164** (1941), **52:175** (1947), **53:178** (1948),
54:180 (1949), **55:181** (1950), **56:183** (1951), **57:186** (1952),
58:188 (1953), **59:190** (1954),
82:236 (1977), **83:237** (1978), **83:238** (1978), **84:239** (1979),
84:240 (1979), **90:249** (1985).

Journal of the Historical and Archaeological Association of Ireland

See *Journal of the Royal Society of Antiquaries.*

Journal of the Kilkenny and South East of Ireland Archaeological Society

See *Journal of the Royal Society of Antiquaries.*

Journal of the Limerick Field Club

Founded in 1892, this journal is the ancestor, as it were, of the *North Munster Antiquarian Journal.* Tipperary Studies has just six issues:

Vol. **1:3** (1899), **1:4, 2:8, 3:10, 3:11, 3:12.**

Journal of the North Munster Archaeological Society

Vol. 1, No. 1 (1909), The Library holds three bound volumes:
1 (1909-11), **2** (1911-13), **3** (1913-15), Unbound: **Vol. 4:1** (1916).

Journal of the Old Limerick Society

Vol. 1 No. 1 (1946).

Journal of the Royal Society of Antiquaries of Ireland

This journal now published as the Journal of the Royal Society of Antiquaries has undergone several name changes in its long history. Originally called

Transactions of the Kilkenny Archaeological Society.
Vol. 1 (1849-51), **Vol. 2** (1852-3), **Vol. 3** (1854-5).

Journal of the Kilkenny & South East of Ireland Archaeological Society
Six bound volumes
Vol. 1 (1856-7), **Vol. 2** (1858-9), **Vol. 3** (1860-61),
Vol. 4 (1862-3), **Vol. 5** (1864-6), **Vol. 6** (1867).

Journal of the Historical and Archaeological Association of Ireland
Vol 1 (3rd series) 1868-9, **Vol.1** (4th series) 1870-71, **2** 1872-73, **3** 1874-75, **4** 1876-78, **5** 1879-82, **6** 1883-84, **8** 1887-88, **9** 1889, **Vol. 1** (5th series) 1890-91.

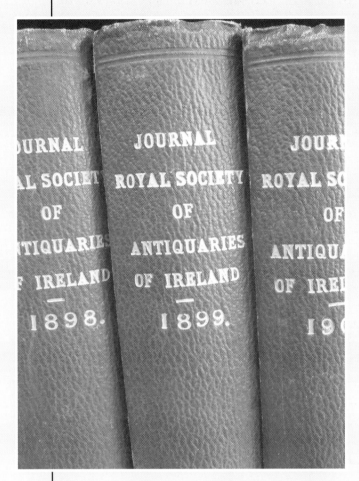

Journal of the Royal Society of Antiquaries of Ireland
Dating from 1892, Tipperary Studies holds a substantial number of volumes. The following issues are missing 1895 part 2, 1900 parts 2 & 3, 1926 part 2 and 1946 part 1.

The run consists of a mixture of bound volumes and unbound numbers. The holdings finish at **No. 133** (2003). There are two Index volumes 1849-89 and 1891-1910.

Luceat
This was produced by the students of St Patrick's College Thurles, from 1952.

The Library holds issues from 1955, 1958, 1960, 1961, 1962, 1963, 1964, 1965, 1987 and 1995.

Memorials of the Dead, Ireland
Published by the Association for the Preservation of the Memorials of the Dead in Ireland. Of obvious genealogical interest.

(1890), (1897) part 3, (1900) parts 1 & 2, (1901) parts 1 & 2, (1902) parts 1 & 2, (1903) Part 1, (1904) parts 1 & 2, (1905) parts 1 & 2, (1906) parts 1 & 2, (1907) parts 1 & 2, (1908) part 2, (1909) part 2, (1910) parts 1 & 2, (1911) parts 3 & 4, (1912) parts 5 & 6, (1913) part 1, (1914) part 2, (1915) part 3, (1916) parts 5 & 6 (1917), (1918) parts 3 & 4 (1919) part 5, (1919-20) parts 5 & 6, (1921) parts 1 & 2, (1922) part 3, (1923) parts 4 & 5, (1925) part 6, (1929) part 4, (1930) part 5, (1933-4) part 1.
Index (1888-1908) 'An index of the churchyards and buildings from which inscriptions on tombs and mural slabs have appeared in the *Journal of the Association for the Preservation of the Memorials of the Dead in Ireland.*' Vol. XIII is an *Index to the parish register section of the journal of the Irish Memorials Association.*

Molua
Annual periodical of the diocese of Killaloe, 1933-59. Complete run is available in Tipperary Studies.

Muintir na Tire Publications

Muintir na Tire Catalogue for Thurles Show
1960–1964, 1966-1968.

Muintir na Tire Handbook
1941, 1943, 1944, 1945, 1946.

Muintir na Tire 31st National Rural Week, St. Munchin's, College, August 11-17, 1968.

Rural Ireland
1949, 1950, 1951, 1952-3, 1953, 1955, 1956, 1957, 1958, 1959, 1960, 1961, 1962, 1963, 1964, 1965, 1966, 1967, 1968, 1969, 1971-72.

North Munster Antiquarian Journal
While Tipperary Studies has many issues, its run is far from complete.
Vol. 1 No. 1 (1936), **1:2** (1937), **1:3** (1938), **1:4** (1939),
2:1 (1940), **2:2** (1940), **2:4** (1941), **3:1** (1942), **3:3** (1943),
4:1 (1944), **4:2** (1944), **4:3** (1945), **5:2 & 3** (1946), **5:4** (1948),
7:2 (1955).

There is an almost complete run from **Vol. 11** (1968) to the present.
Missing is **15** (1972).

Old Kilkenny Review
1948, 1950, 1954, 1956–7, 1960, 1963–65, 1973, 1978, 1980–2005.

Rockwell College Annual
1953–1997, 1998-99 & 1999–2000 (1 issue), 2000-01, 2001-02, 2002-03.

Stair: Journal of the History Teachers Association of Ireland
1980 to 1985.

The Stag Trippant: Official Journal of the Clan Mac Carthy
No. **1** (1994), **2** (1995), **3** (1996), **4** (1997), **5** (1998), No. **2:1** (1999).

Studies: an Irish quarterly review
First published in 1912. Tipperary Studies has a large though very incomplete collection of this periodical.

The run begins with **Vol. 19, No. 73** (March 1930). The following list refers to the numbers in the collection.

73, 74, 77, 78, 79, 81, 83, 84, 87, 88, 89, 90, 91, 92, 93, 96, 101, 111, 112, 113, 116, 118, 119, 120, 121, 122, 125, 126, 127, 128, 129, 131, 132, 133, 134, 135, 136, 137,

138, 139, 140, 142, 143, 144, 145, 146, 148, 149, 150, 151, 152, 153, 154, 155, 156, 157, 158, 159, 160, 161, 162, 163-4, 165, 166, 167, 168, 169, 170, 171, 172, 174, 175, 176, 178, 179, 180, 181, 182, 184, 185, 186, 187, 188, 192, 193, 194, 195, 196, 197, 198, 200, 201-42, 246, 251, 256, 284, 285, 287, 288, 289, 290, 292, 293, 294, 295, 296, 297, 298, 299, 300, 304-75.

Tipperary's Annual
Edited by B.J. Long and D. O'Connor and published in Clonmel, this appeared between 1909 and 1913. Edited by W.C. Darmody, there was an even shorter revival in 1955. Tipperary Studies only holds photocopies.

Tipperary Historical Journal
Published annually by the County Tipperary Historical Society since 1988.

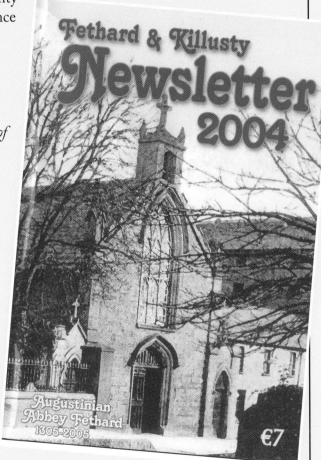

Transactions of the Kilkenny Archaeological Society
See *Journal of the Royal Society of Antiquaries.*

Waterford & South East Ireland Archaeological Society
1906-1911 bound, July 1895, 1912, 1914 and 1915 unbound, Jan 1920 unbound. Typescript index Vol. 1 (1894) to Vol. 18 (1915).

Writings on Irish History
Produced by the Irish Committee of Historical Sciences and Irish Historical Studies

1973-83, 1985, 1986, 1987, 1988, 1989-90, 1991-92, 1993-94.

Parish Magazines
Some Tipperary parishes produce annual magazines, usually at Christmas. There are many gaps in the Tipperary Studies collection.

Anacarty-Donohill
1997, 1998, 1999, 2000, 2002, 2003.

Ballingarry
1997, 1998, 2000, 2001, 2002, 2003, 2004, 2005.

Ballyporeen
1991, 1992, 1993, 1994, 1997, 1999.

Borrisokane
2001.

Cois Deirge
1977 to 1990.

Echoes of the Hills [Kilcommon, Rearcross, Hollyford]
1981-84, 1988 to 2003, originally known as

Kilcommon Calling
1966, 71, 73, 76-80, typescript.

Emly
1990, 1993.

Fethard & Killusty
1966-72 some photocopies, 1973 to 2004.

Gortnahoe & Glengoole
1987 to 2005.

Holycross
1971-74, 1995, 1996, 1998, 1999, 2000, 2002.

Killenaule-Moyglass
1993, 1994, 2004, 2005.

Kilsheelan/Kilcash
2002.

Lattin-Cullen
1988, 1992.

Lorrha
2003.

Loughmore
1968-1994, 1996, 2000-2005.

Moycarkey Borris
1975, 1976, 1980-82, 1986-88, 1990-1999, 2001-2003.

Moyne Templetuohy
This parish had newsletters published by various local groups at different times.

Lisheen News Vol.1 March 1997.
Moyne Templetuohy a Life of Its Own 2004, 2005.
Moyne Templetuohy Parish Newsletter Jan 1973, Oct 1974, April 1992.
Templetuohy Moyne Millennium Newsletter 2000.

Mullinahone
1984, 1987-2005.

Newport
1983-85, 1987-2005.

Slieveardagh News (Killenaule)
Vol. 1 Dec 1995, **Vol. 2** Feb. 1996.

Slievenamon Echoes (Drangan)
1993.

Roscrea Castle, County Tipperary

136

"While Evening, veil'd in shadows brown,
Puts her matron-mantle on."

PART THREE

Unpublished Sources

Introduction

Tipperary Studies has an eclectic collection of unpublished source material. This is a polite way of saying that much of the collection came together more by accident than design. The upside is that the researcher never knows what may be found. Many of these sources are original documents but Tipperary Studies also has copies of material in private hands or in other collections. In volume, local government records account for much of the collection and of this, material relating to the operation of workhouses in the county, especially during the Famine, is of the greatest interest. Tipperary Studies has the most important collection of this material in the county.

Land: getting it, exploiting it and using it, generated a deal of material. Managing estates meant keeping records such as rentals and Tipperary Studies has a selection of such records, though no more than a fraction of what has been destroyed. The greatest volumes of sources are for the Mathew (Thurles & Thomastown), Cole Bowen (Ballymackey, Upper Ormond) and the Bagwell (Marlfield, Clonmel) estates. These records are also very useful in the context of genealogy. After the Famine, many estates were sold and the records generated by such transfers of ownership are especially informative and user-friendly because they were printed.

Before the Famine it was difficult to sell estates because of doubts and complications due to debts and ownership. In 1849 the Encumbered Estates Court was established by act of parliament. ("Encumbered" meaning laden with debt.) This made selling estates easier and gave purchasers clear title backed by law. Part of the preparation for selling an estate was the printing of a sales brochure, giving details about the history of the property, its tenants and their holdings and tenure. Maps were included and for bigger estates, illustrations. In 1858, the Encumbered Estates Court was replaced by the Landed Estates Court, which in turn was replaced by the

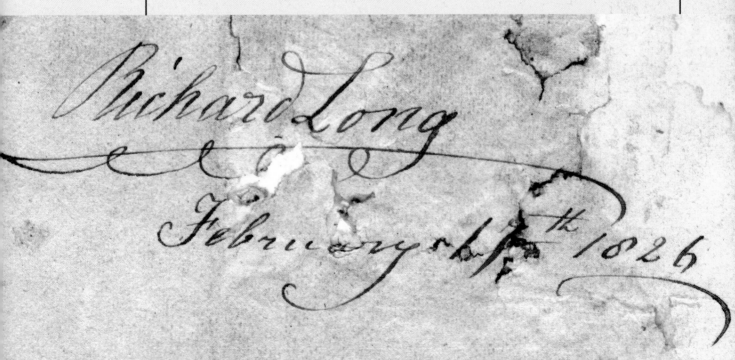

Land Judges Court in 1877. Tipperary Studies has a small but expanding collection of these brochures, those for the estates of the earl of Portarlington (Dawson-Damer) being the most useful because they deal with the greatest amount of land.

Scully Papers (Mantlehill, Golden) TL/F/1

(A very successful catholic family of middlemen in the 18th century. Originated in Dualla but moved to Kilfeacle, which was rented, and later to Mantlehill, which was owned. James Scully (1737-1816) established a bank in Tipperary that eventually was linked to John Sadleir. James's son Denys (1773-1830) was associated with the campaign for catholic emancipation. Denys's son William (1821-1906) was the landlord of Ballycohey. Vincent Scully died in 1927).

THOMASTOWN CASTLE.
THE SEAT OF THE EARL OF LANDAFF, CO. OF TIPPERARY.

1   Vincent Scully's copy of the famous book by his grandfather Denys Scully: *A Statement of the Penal Laws* (1812) Noted by Vincent Scully on the fly and dated 23 Sept 1884: "This copy of the Penal Laws is unique, part of Sir Robert Peel's 'Select Irish Library'."

2   "Denys Scully of Kilfeacle (1773-1830) Accounts, 1810-1815".
    Small notebook. Household accounts, indexed. Examples: "Wearing Apparel"; "Hay, Oats and Straw"; "Gifts, Charities Etc."

3   Large notebook compiled by Vincent Scully's aunt Maryanne Scully (d.1898) dealing with family history. Photographs of family members identified on back, inserted.

Wall Papers (Holycross) TL/F/2

(In 1834, William Henry Armstrong sold this estate of around fifteen hundred acres to the Rev. Charles William Wall, later Vice Provost of Trinity College).

1   Bundle of correspondence, 1924-27, including some earlier legal documents. Estate business.
2   Bundle of maps and conveyances, late 19th and early 20th centuries. Includes sale of Holycross House and land in 1922 and purchased by Fr M. Ryan PP for £2450.
3   Bundle of legal documents, 19th and 20th centuries. Includes 1848 lease to Fr W. Laffan PP.
4   Correspondence, early 20th century, disposal of the estate.
5   Envelope with 4 photographs, Holycross.
6   Plan of Holycross Abbey.

Lalor Cambie Papers (Killoran) TL/F/3

(The founder of this family in Ireland was Solomon Cambie, a Cromwellian grantee in North Tipperary. In 1798 Thomas Cambie married a daughter of Thomas Lalor of Killoran. In the 1870s the Killoran estate was around seventeen hundred acres).

Copies (originals property of Edward Cambie), 1 box.
Estate documents, marriage settlements, wills, genealogical information including tomb inscriptions and photographs of family members. Also information from Registry of Deeds. Late 18th to 20th centuries.

Lismore (O'Callaghan) Papers (Clogheen) TL/F/4

(One of the largest land-owning families in the county, c. 35,000 acres. Cornelius O'Callaghan, was created Baron Lismore of Shanbally Co Tipperary in 1785).

1 box. Parchment deeds, 18th and 19th centuries. Example, Lismore to Frederick Grubb, lease 1854 lands of Coole. Also appointment as Lord Lieutenant of the county, mid-19th century.

O'Rourke Papers (Tipperary) TL/F/5

(The O'Rourke family originally from Ardpatrick, Kilfinnan).

Copies of 22 letters, (originals property of Tom Blackburn, Tipperary.)
19 letters from Garret O'Rourke in St Louis USA to his brother Denis in Tipperary (1862-79). References to American civil war ("the North will never be able to conquer the South" – 11 Oct 1862) and Fenian activity (he disapproved).
1 letter from Garret O'Rourke to his parents.
2 letters from Thomas McDonnell to Garret O'Rourke.

Cole Bowen Papers (Bowen's Court, Co Cork) TL/F/6

(While this family was based in Co Cork, the bulk of their land was in Tipperary, around 5,000 acres. This came through the 1716 marriage of Henry Bowen to Jane, only child and heiress of Robert Cole of Ballymackey Co Tipperary).

This is a large collection of mainly 19th century estate material: rentals and maps. Sixteen townlands in the parish of Ballymackey in Upper Ormond.
1   Large volume of Tipperary estate maps.
2   Rental 1788-96.
3   Rental 1797-1805.
4   Rental 1838-1843.
5   Rental 1848-1853.
6   Rental 1854-1863.
7   Rental 1863-1869.
8   Rental 1869-1876.
9   Rental 1877-1883.
10 Estate record 1852-1862.
11 File of correspondence, estate matters, late 19th century.

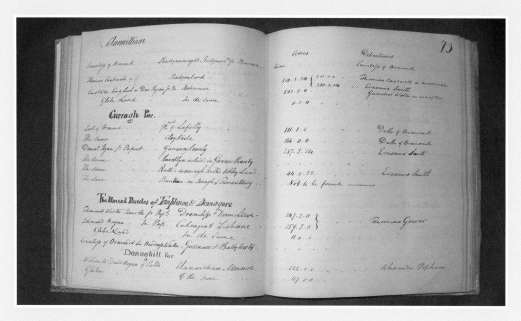

Walsh Papers (Walsh Park, Borrisokane) TL/F/7

1   Copies of Walsh family material gathered by Ms Josephine Carter, (good example of exhaustive genealogical research) – copies of records from Registry of Deeds.
2   Encumbered Estates Court rental, John Adams Walsh of Walsh Park, sale 24 April 1857, 5 lots: 2,143 statute acres, Lower Ormond.

Chadwick Papers (Shronell) TL/F/8

(John Craven Chadwick (1768-1851) held a small estate on perpetual lease from the Damer/Portarlington estate. Elizabeth Cooper died in 1831).

1   Marriage settlement, John Craven Chadwick of Ballynard Shronell and Elizabeth Cooper of Killenure, 24 Sept 1799.
2   Map July 1808, lands in Ballynard, Shronell. Estate John Craven Chadwick, 526 plantation acres. Six tenants named.

Cooper Papers (Killenure, Dundrum) TL/F/9

(The first of the family in Killenure was William George who purchased the property in 1746. He came to the area with Archbishop Price of Cashel. Samuel (below) was William's son. Regarding the diaries, see D.G. Marnane, Samuel Cooper of Killenure: a Tipperary land Agent and his Diaries in *THJ* (1993), pp. 102-27).

1   Copies of the diaries of Samuel Cooper of Killenure Castle (1750-1831).
    for 1782, 1785, 1786, 1795, 1802, 1804, 1806, 1807, 1809, 1811, 1814, 1823.
    (Originals property of R. Austin-Cooper).
2   House Keeper's book, Killenure, 1846-49.
    Includes references to Cooper family members ("Master Alfred died the 7th of Aug 1846").
3   Copies of estate papers regarding Mocklershill, Ardmayle, Ballysheehan, Coleraine (late 19th century).

Also estate papers regarding Rathordan, early 19th century and Moanmore and Gortenerig, mid 19th century.
Family records: Cooper of Killenure.
(4 folders: 37 items. See Tipperary Studies List).

Birch Papers (Roscrea) TL/F/10
(See TL/F/18)

1 Schedule of debts and assets of Richard Birch, Roscrea, June 1823, who was then in debtor's prison in Dublin.
2 Family settlement, Birch's sister and her husband, 1807. Also five ancillary documents.

Lenigan Papers (Castle Fogarty) TL/F/11
(Originally the property of the fogerty (sic) family. James died unmarried in 1788, his sister Elizabeth Lenigan being his heir. James (below) was her grandson).

Copies of 17 photographs of Castle Fogarty "The property of James Lenigan Esq. 1868" (Originals property of Molloy Family, Crossoges).

Mathew Papers (Thurles & Thomastown) TL/F/12
(This family's fortune established in the 17th century because of their relationship with Butlers of Ormond. Thomas Mathew eventually inherited their three estates, Thomastown, Thurles and Annefield. Two generations, Francis and Francis James enjoyed a peerage (1782-1833). The property was inherited by the latter's sister Eliza (or Elizabeth) who died unmarried in 1841. The estates then passed to cousins: two generations of a French family. When the last of these died in 1875, the heir was a cousin Denis St George Daly, 2nd baron Dunsandle (1810-93).

A large collection of estate material, divided between Tipperary Studies and St Patrick's College Thurles. Tipperary Studies holds some of the St Patrick's material on microfilm.

Clogheen PLU
Minute Book

Locations in the following list are indicated as follows:
TS (Tipperary Studies)
P (St Patrick's College)
MF (Microfilm)

1 Map of Thurles estate – a 1930 copy of an 1827 copy of the 1819 original (P, MF).
2 Printed rental of Thurles estate, prepared for proposed sale in 1819 – 7578 statute acres, annual rental £8809 (P, MF and photocopy).
3 Rental Thurles & Thomastown, 1826-27 (TS, MF).
4 Estate accounts book, 1827-28 (TS).
5 Rent ledger Thurles, 1829 (TS).
6 Rent ledger Thurles & Thomastown, 1831-32 and Thomastown expenditure account, 1832-33 (TS).
7 Rent ledger Thurles & Thomastown, 1839-43 (TS).
8 Rental Thurles, 1842 (TS, MF).
9 Rental Thurles, 1843 (TS, MF).
10 Rental Thurles, 1847-48 (P, MF).
11 Rental Thurles, 1848-49 (P, MF).
12 Rental Thurles & Thomastown, 1851/52 (P, MF).
13 Rental Thurles & Thomastown, c.1858 (TS).
14 Rental Thurles & Thomastown, c.1859 (P, MF).
15 Encumbered Estates Court rental, Viscount de Chabot, sale 3 June 1859. parts of Thurles & Thomastown, 1713 and 2378 acres respectively (TS, P, MF).
16 Rental Thurles & Thomastown, c.1863 (TS, MF).
 * Loose folios: Thurles, 1868; "Mrs Maher's Rental"; Thomastown, 1868-69 (P).
17 Rental Thurles, 1867-68, 1875 incomplete (TS).
18 Rental Thurles & Thomastown, c.1870, includes references to 1893 (TS, MF).
19 Rental Thurles & Thomastown, 1872 (P, MF).
20 Rental Thurles & Thomastown, 1876 (P, MF).
21 Landed Estates Court, final notices to tenants Thurles estate, 1876 (TS, MF).
 * Rental Thurles & Thomastown, 1877 (P).
22 Rental Thurles & Thomastown, 1879 (P, MF).
 * Daily receipt book, Thurles, 1880 (P).
23 Rental Thurles & Thomastown, 1882 (P, MF).
24 Rental Thurles & Thomastown, 1884 (P, MF).
25 Rental Thurles & Thomastown, 1885 (P, MF).
26 Rental Thurles & Thomastown, 1886 (P, MF).
 * Daily rent receipts Thurles, 1885-87 (P).
 * Daily rent receipts Thurles, 1892 (P).
 * Daily rent receipts Thurles, 1899 (P).
27 Rental Thurles, 1899 (P, MF).
 * Daily rent receipts Thurles, 1900-06 – "late N.V. Maher section" (P).
 * Daily rent receipts Thurles, 1902 (P).
 * Daily rent receipts Thurles, 1903 (P).

Additional Mathew material
28 Unbound rental Thurles estate, 1744 (TS).
29 Map "Watercourse to Thomastown Demesne, the estate of Lord Dunsandle" no date, late 19th century.
30 Thurles Estate: John Dullany's Accounts, 1744-45 (Originals in Glenstal Abbey).

Beere Papers (Thurles) TL/F/13

Rental estate of Usher Beere Esq, 1839-43.
Eleven townlands c. Thurles.

Donoughmore Papers (Knocklofty, Clonmel) TL/F/14

(In 1751, an ambitious lawyer John Hely married the heiress of Richard Hutchinson of Knocklofty. The Donoughmore peerage was created in 1783, not for Hely Hutchinson but for his wife, an example of his influence. The family held some 4,700 acres in Tipperary, nearly 3,000 acres in Waterford and some 2,000 acres in Cork.)

Six volumes of typescripts prepared by the PRONI of papers now in TCD
Includes material relating to:
Provost Hely Hutchinson (1668-1758),
1st earl (1779-1825),
2nd earl (1793-1832),
Hon. Francis Hely Hutchinson (1730-1827),
3rd earl (1808-32),
Also wills and family settlements 19th century and estate matters 17th to 20th centuries.

Armitage Papers (Noan) TL/F/15

(In 1860 Thomas Armitage married the heiress of the Noan estate. Their son Frederick (1867-1952) kept these accounts (below)).

A copy of estate accounts ledger, 1926-27.

Poe Papers (Solsborough, Nenagh) TL/F/16

Estate map, William Poe, June 1810
Donnybrook and Ballymackey.

Walsh Papers (Ballynevin, Carrick-on-Suir) TL/F/17

Copy of farm accounts book, John Walsh of Ballynevin, 1850s.

Milton (Damer) Papers TL/F/18

(See TL/F/25)
(The enormous fortune in Irish land created by Joseph Damer (1630-1720) was inherited eventually by another Joseph Damer (1717-98) who was created Baron Milton of Shronell and 1st earl of Dorchester. His sister married William Henry Dawson in 1737 and their descendants (Dawson-Damer) inherited in time. John Dawson-Damer was created earl of Portarlington in 1785).

1 "Rent roll of the estates of Lord Milton Tipperary County", 1787-98.
2 "Rent roll of the lordship, manor, town and lands of Roscrea", 1769-70.
  Unbound and very fragile, includes map of Roscrea, 1811 showing Mr Birch's
  holding.
3 Abstract title of Lord Dorchester to the Cloneen estate, Eliogarty, 824
  plantation acres, 1787.

Carrick-on-Suir Estates TL/F/19

Ledger with records from a number of Carrick-on-Suir properties, 1880s.
References to Despard, Power, O'Donnell, Briscoe, Nicholson and Walsh.

Bagwell Papers (Marlfield, Clonmel) TL/F/20
(Through skill in business and local politics, this family emerged as a force in
Clonmel during the 18th century. In the 19th century, the family had an estate of
about 3,500 acres in Tipperary. Richard Bagwell (1840-1918) was a noted historian
and public figure).

The largest collection in Tipperary Studies. Recently acquired and consequently
what follows is a tentative listing.

1 One box with "MSS pre-1700". Two bundles of legal documents; with 8 items
  (1670-97) and 34 items respectively. Concerns the duke of Ormonde's
  proprietorship. Families named include Woods, Foley, Dennison, Draper, Ellis,
  Davin, Slaterie, Hoare, Russell, Nicholson, Craddock and Ladyman.

Bagwell Papers

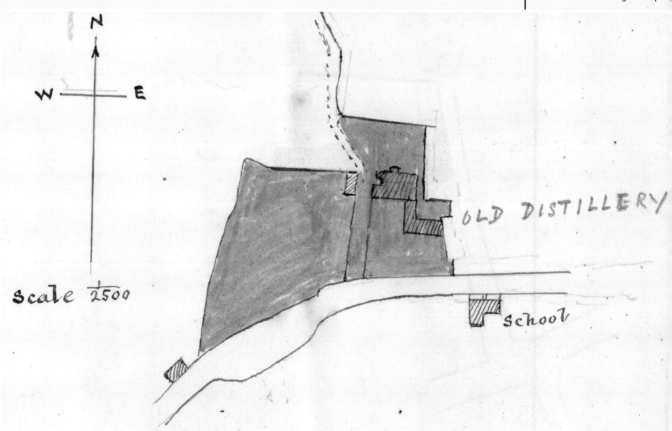

2   One box with "MSS 1700-1750". Two bundles of legal documents; with 23 items and 24 items respectively. Includes references to families of Mathew, Moore and Cleare. Documents about Quaker Meeting House Clonmel.
3   One box with large parchment document. Ormonde and Hamerton.
4   One Box with "MSS 1750-1800". Two bundles of legal documents; with 14 and 18 items respectively. References to Phineas Riall, Richard Sparrow, Stephen Moore. Lease of Burgagery lands, 1774.
5   One box with "MSS 1801-1849".
6   One box with "MSS 1850-1899".
7   Boxes of unsorted 20th century papers and accounts.
8   File of papers dealing with Clonmel Model School.
9   Collection of maps, 20th century.

Ryan Papers (Inch, Thurles) TL/F/21
(An important Tipperary catholic family who managed to hold their land through the 18th century, not least because of their connection with the Mathew family).

Unsorted collection of copies of originals in the Boole Library, UCC (BL/EP/R).

Ponsonby Barker Papers (Kilcooley) TL/F/22
(In 1818, on the death of Sir William Barker, Kilcooley was inherited by his nephew Chambre Brabazon Ponsonby who took his uncle's surname).

Collection of estate papers, 19th century. 28 items.
Includes 24 leases from Chambre Brabazon Barker to various tenants, all dated 1828.

Brereton Papers TL/F/23

Rathurles (Kilruane, Nenagh) stock book and labourers' accounts, 1889-97.

Lawder Papers TL/F/24

Encumbered Estates Court rental, Christopher Hume Lawder
(For William Pennefather)
Sale 20 June 1851, c.900 acres in Clonegoose, Poulecopple and Ballylanigan in the parish of Kilvemnon, Slieveardagh.

Portarlington Papers TL/F/25
(See TL/F/18)

1   Encumbered Estates Court rental, earl of Portarlington
     Sale 23 Nov 1858, 9th Division Roscrea, 1601 acres in 89 lots, (Original).
2   Encumbered Estates Court rental, earl of Portarlington
     Sale 16 Jan 1855, 4th Division "Golden Vein Estate", 15,363 acres in 51 lots.

Also Borrisoleigh estate, 7,783 acres in 26 lots. (Copy)

Hunt Papers TL/F/26
(Had been purchased in the Encumbered Estates Court in 1855 from Sir Vere-Edmond de Vere).

Land Judges sale of estate of Robert Langley Hunt
Sale 15 June 1883, Part of Glengoole in Kilcooley, Slieveardagh.

Sausse Papers TL/F/27

Landed Estates Court rental, Richard Sausse & Mathew Richard Sausse
Sale 12 Jan 1860, Property in Carrick-on-Suir.

Watson Papers TL/F/28

Encumbered Estates Court, Mrs Watson
Sale 1857, Garrykennedy, Owney & Arra, (Damaged)

Rowley Papers TL/F/29
(An estate of nearly 1,400 acres).

Landed Estates Court, Frederick Pelham Rowley.
Consolidated final notice, 1873 Moheraneragh c.1,300 acres, Upper & Lower Ormond.

THREATENED EVICTION IN TIPPERARY.
A MONSTER INDIGNATION MEETING
WILL BE HELD IN
THE TOWN OF TIPPERARY
AT 2 O'CLOCK.
On SUNDAY, 15th JUNE,
For the purpose of censuring the conduct of Mr. SMITH BARRY'S Agent, for his Wanton Threats to the Sisters of Mercy, and Christian Brothers at Tipperary,
For his Threatened Evictions of Solvent and Respectable Householders in that Town,
And also to ask Mr. SMITH BARRY to reinstate the Butchers of Tipperary to their old Shambles.
Several Distinguished National Speakers will attend.
Come in your Strength Legally and Constitutionally and
DENOUNCE OPPRESSION.

Smith Papers TL/F/30

Encumbered Estates Court rental, Richard Flood Smith
Sale 31 March 1857, Milford House & Demesne, Cooga, etc. 871 statute acres, Lower Ormond & Kilnamanagh.

Carden Papers TL/F/31

Landed Estates Court, Dame Mary Carden
Sale 16 June 1868, Cooleeshill/Mount Butler and Upper Clashagad, (Roscrea) 550 statute acres.

Head Papers TL/F/32

Landed Estates Court rental, William Henry Head
Sale 29 June 1869, Modreeny (Part), 387 statute acres, Lower Ormond.

LOUGH DERG ON RIVER SHANNON FROM PORTROE

Egan Papers TL/F/33

Encumbered Estates Court rental, Howard N. Egan & Terence C. J. Egan
Sale 13 May 1853, Rathnaganana, c. 1,400 statute acres, Lower Ormond.

Cosby Papers TL/F/34

(Based at Stradbally Hall in Laois. Robert A.G. Cosby succeeded his uncle in 1851).

Landed Estates Court rental, Robert A Godolphin Cosby
Sale 9 July 1869, 10 lots "near Nenagh" & 2 lots "near Thurles" 1,602 statute acres, Owney & Arra and Kilnamanagh Upper.

Steele Papers TL/F/35

Encumbered Estates Court rental, Mary Steele
Sale 22 Feb 1853, Slevoir & Terryglass, 406 statute acres, Lower Ormond.

Falkiner Papers TL/F/36

Landed Estates Court rental, John Falkiner
Sale 18 June 1872, Derrylusky and Terryglass, 164 statute acres, Lower Ormond.

Pennefather Papers TL/F/37

Marriage settlement, Richard Pennefather of Lakefield and Emma Elizabeth Vaughton of Warwick in England, 1857. (He died in 1876).

Diary of Nicholas Kenny, Carrick-on-Suir TL/F/38

Nicholas Kenny, Woolen merchant, The Quay, Carrick-on-Suir
Scrap book, memoir and diary, 1870s, (Copy)
"There are not six people in this town at present who know or care to know anything of the place they live in; beyond what is passing around them."
"I have often spent hours in the libraries of Trinity College and the Royal Dublin Society endeavouring to unearth scraps relating to Carrick."
"The writer can vouch his personal authority for anything subsequent to 1860."

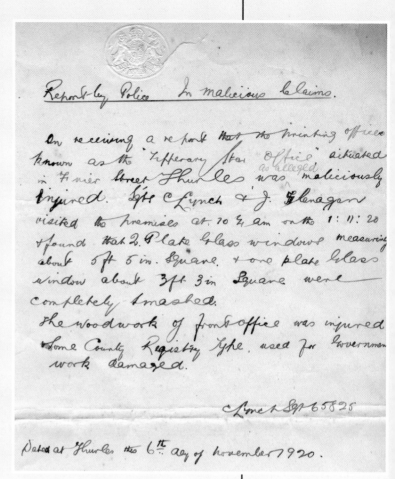

Pedigree of Power TL/F/39

Privately printed pedigrees of Power and associated families.
Compiled by Edmund de la Poer, Gurteen le Poer, April 1881, (Copy).

Modreeny Farm Accounts TL/F/40

Bound volume, 1898, Family unknown.

Sadleir Papers (Butler-Cahir) TL/F/41

Encumbered Estates Court rental, The late John Sadleir
Kilcommon Demesne, Cahir Castle and other portions of the estates of the late John Sadleir MP, Sale 17 Nov 1857, 5,625 statute acres,
(Purchased by Sadleir after the sale by Glengall in 1853).

Will of Nicholas Sadleir (Tipperary) TL/F/42

Copy of will of Nicholas Sadlier Henry St Tipperary. He died in 1858.

Will of Valentine Maher, Turtulla, 1844 TL/F/43

Valentine Maher (1780-1844), MP Tipperary County, 1841-44.

Memo by John Trant (1819-87), Dovea, Thurles TL/F/44

"Two years skirmish with the Land League, 1880-82"
("Ex PC 24, NLI").

"Autographs of Visitors to The Rock of Cashel" 1857-60 TL/A/1

"Presented to the County Library Committee by Austin Cooper of Killenure Castle, 27 July 1963" (Ornate bound volume) Includes visitor's "Observations" Signatures of Viscount Hawarden and Sir Leopold Cust (Smith-Barry estate agent).

Irish Tourist Association Report, 1943 County Tipperary TL/A/2

In the early 1940s the ITA commissioned researchers to compile files of information at town and parish level of interest to visitors. Much of the historical material was compiled from secondary sources but the files include some original photographs of antiquities.
In 1983, Bord Failte distributed these files to the relevant county libraries.
There are four folders.
1 Thirteen parishes South Tipperary: Anacarty to Clogheen.
2 Eighteen parishes South Tipperary: Clonmel to Oola.
3 Sixteen parishes North Tipperary: Ballinahinch to Loughmoe.
4 Ten parishes North Tipperary: Littleton to Upperchurch.
The file on each parish includes information on archaeology, antiquities, history, recreation and accommodation.

Alphabetical List of Freeholders, Tipperary County Election 1776 TL/A/3

Gives the residence of each freeholder, their freeholds and their value.
Also a record of their votes.
Candidates: Daniel Toler, Francis Mathew, Henry Prittie, Skeffington Smith.
(Copy of original in RIA [RIA MS 12 D 36]).

The Book of Survey and Distribution, County Tipperary TL/A/4

"A copy of the Down Survey of the County of Tipperary made by Sir William Petty in the year 1654."
A history of this manuscript is given: it was copied in 1832-33 from an 1805 copy of a 1718 copy. This was in possession of Archbishop Leahy and was copied by Fr

James O'Carroll of Clonoulty and in turn copied by Maurice Lenihan (*Limerick Reporter and Tipperary Vindicator*) and well-known historian of Limerick.

This source, which supplements the Civil Survey, has never been published for Tipperary.

Tithe Arrears, 1831 TL/A/5

Thurles, Crohane, Modeshil, Lismolin, Mowney
(Copy).

Religious Census, 1766 Diocese Cashel & Emly TL/A/6

Carried out by Church of Ireland parochial clergy by order of Parliament in order to quantify religious persuasions. Gives heads of households. The original returns were destroyed in 1922.

Cormack Brothers TL/A/7

File relating to the exhumation and re-burial of the remains of William and Daniel Cormack in 1910. They had been executed in 1858 for the murder of John Ellis. Contains newscuttings and copies of photographs and copies of documents.

Davin Postcards TL/A/8

Copies of 8 postcards to Maurice Davin.

Assisted Passage to Australia, 1849-61 TL/A/9

Computer printout for County Tipperary
(Donated by Richard Reid, 1988).

Clonmel Incumbent Book, 1703 TL/A/10

Fees etc relating to Clonmel parish
(Copy of original in Clonmel Museum).

Thurles Folder TL/A/11

23 misc. items including maps.

Thurles Savings Bank TL/A/12

Large collection of bound volumes and assorted papers: audit books, cash books, depositors' books, ledgers, minutes and treasurers' books. 1829-74.
Index to clients.

Account Book, Clonmel Area, Early 18th Century TL/A/13

Contains recipes for folk-cures.
(Provenance unknown).

Tithe Applotment TL/A/14

Parishes of Ardmayle and Ballysheehan, 1790-99.

Co Tipperary Schools Folklore Collection, 1937-38 TL/A/15

Scheme of the Irish Folklore Commission (established 1935) enlisting teachers and senior students in primary schools to collect folklore.
(Originals in Irish Folklore Dept. UCD. Tipperary Studies has copies of the Tipperary material on eleven microfilm reels).

Clonmel Corporation Minute Book, 1608-49 TL/A/16

(Microfilm of original in Cork Library).

Transportation Registers, 1830s & 1840s TL/A/17

Penal transportation to Australia, Co Tipperary convicts.
Gives name, age, crime, sentence and date of assizes.
(Microfilm of original documents in National Archives).

Fr Kenyon Letters TL/A/18
(Fr John Kenyon (1812-69) PP Templederry, Young Irelander)
Copies of two letters from Fr Kenyon,
To Charles G. Duffy, 16 Sept 1847 and G.H. Moore MP, 23 Feb 1863.

Dr Martin Callanan Papers TL/A/19
(Callanan (1866-1941) a Thurles MD is best remembered for his book *Records of Four Tipperary Septs* (1938). His papers were donated to the National Library in 1948). Tipperary Studies has a small part of the collection on microfilm.

Microfilm of part of the Callanan Papers in NLI (MS 1661-73). His research notes on aspects of Tipperary history.
(See also copy of *Collection List No. 94 Callanan Papers*, which outlines the full holding of his papers in the NLI).

Carrick-on-Suir Census, 1799 TL/A/20

"Among the most detailed of all unofficial censuses taken in the British Isles." (Clarkson) Compiled by three individuals: a local gentleman, a militia officer and a schoolmaster. Gives information on the occupational and family structures in the town.
(Microfilm).

Thurles Swimming Club TL/A/21

Subscription Book; Petty Cash Book; Cash Receipts; Carnival Ledger, 1948-52, 4 volumes.

"Tintown" Hunger Strike Autograph Book, TL/A/22

Richard Purcell, Bawndonnell, Nine-Mile-House, Carrick-on-Suir.
"Tintown" Camp No. 3, The Curragh
Date on page 1: 27 Oct 1923.

Thurles Christian Brothers School Registers TL/A/23

Copies of registers, 1856-1899, 6 volumes.

Thurles Historical Society TL/A/24

Bank Book; Cash Book 1958-71; Minute Book 1953-66; folder of correspondence including list of members.

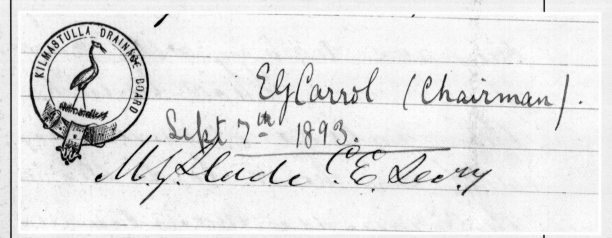

County Tipperary Historical Society TL/A/25

Founded in 1987: Minutes and correspondence. **Closed.**

Tithe Applotment TL/A/26

Copy of tithe applotment records for Clonoulty, 1824.

Carrick-on-Suir Hospital TL/A/27

Copy of volume from collection of Hugh Ryan. Minutes and financial information Carrick-on-Suir (Fever?) Hospital, 1823-28.

Tithe Defaulters, 1831 TL/A/28

Typescript of Tipperary records. Also (CD Rom) Records for several Irish counties. (Originals in the NA.). An important census substitute.

Cashel Tolls TL/A/29

Correspondence between Major Pennefather, New Romney, Kent and Cashel UDC, 1926-36, with ref. to purchase by the UDC of the tolls.

GAA Convention Thurles 1887 TL/A/30

Copies of letters and documents from Croke and Dublin Castle regarding the attempt by the IRB to take control of the GAA.

Letter of Major A.J. Wilson, 1798 TL/A/31

Letter from Wilson to Lord William Bentinck, Lt Col 22 Dragoons Armagh, 4 July 1798. Contains Wilson's reflections on Clonmel.
(Copy of original in Portland MSS, University of Nottingham MSS Dept – PW JA 424).

Catholic Inhabitants of Ikerrin, 1750 TL/A/32

List of Catholic inhabitants of the half barony of Ikerrin Co Tipperary, returned by James Hutchinson, High Constable, 1750. Also a related valuation for cess (taxation) purposes.
(Copies of originals in NLI, MSS 8913, 8914).

Lalor Shiel Letters TL/A/33

Copies of eleven letters, 1840s.

Borlase MSS, 1641 Rebellion TL/A/34

"An attestation by His Majesty's Commissioners how and in what manner Henry Peisley held his own castle of Archerstown against the rebels, 11 Nov 1642. (Copy of Sloane MS 1008, fo 75B-88).

Will of W.P. Ryan, 17 March 1942 TL/A/35
(Native of Templemore, journalist and novelist and father of Desmond Ryan).

Kyle Park Female National School TL/A/37

Copy of register, 1866-1917.

Thurles Town Commissioners, Collector's Rate Book, 1877 TL/A/38

Tipperary PLU, Workhouse National School, (Male) TL/A/39

1   Daily report book 1911-14.
2   District Inspector's observation book 1856-1914.
3   Register 1868-1914.
4   Roll book 1906-14.

The Bureau of Military History TL/A/40

The Bureau was established in 1947 "to assemble and co-ordinate material to form the basis for the compilation of the history of the movement for Independence from the formation of the Irish Volunteers on 25 November 1913 to The Truce on 11 July 1921."

The following witness statements are available in Tipperary Studies:
Seamus Babington, Carrick on Suir, (W.S 1595)
Dan Breen, Dublin, (W.S 1739, W.S 1763)
Patrick Cash, Moneygall, (W.S 1372)
Edmund Crowe, Oola, (W.S 599)
Maurice Crowe, Rathkea, (W.S 517)
Tadhg Crowe, Solohead, (W.S 1658)
Richard Dalton, Clonmel, (W.S 1116)
Michael Davern, Cashel, (W.S 1348)
Jerome Davin, Fethard, (W.S 1350)
Frank Drohan, Clonmel, (W.S 702)
James Duggan, Templemore, (W.S 1510)

Tadhg Dwyer, Dundrum, (W.S 1356)
Phil Fitzgerald, Dublin, (W.S 1262)
Michael Fitzpatrick, Tipperary, (W.S 1433)
Sean Fitzpatrick, Dublin, (W.S 1259)
Padraig Ua Floinn, Fethard, (W.S 1221)
Jeremiah Frewen, Waterford, (W.S 930)
Sean Gaynor, Nenagh, (W.S 1389)
Edward Glendon, Clonmel, (W.S 1127)
Martin Grace, Nenagh, (W.S 1463)
Edmond Grogan, Cashel, (W.S 1281)
John Hackett, Toomevara, (W.S 1388)
Thomas Halpin, Cork, (W.S 742)
James Hewitt, Birdhill, (W.S 1465)
William Hanly, Kilcommon, (W.S 1368)
Liam Hoolan, Glasnevin, (W.S 1553)
Patrick Keane, Cashel, (W.S 1300)
James Keating, Fethard, (W.S 1220)
Andrew Kennedy, Tipperary, (W.S 963)
James Kilmartin, Monard, (W.S 881)
Patrick Kinnane, Upperchurch, (W.S 1475)
James Leahy, Nenagh, (W.S 1454)
Edmond McGrath, Cahir, (W.S 1393)
Edward McGrath, Templemore, (W.S 1522)
Frank McGrath, Nenagh, (W.S 1558)
Mrs M.A McGrath, Clogheen, (W.S 1704)
Maurice A. McGrath, Clogheen, (W.S 1701)
Thomas F. Meagher, Templemore, (W.S 1541)
William Meagher, Nenagh, (W.S 1391)
Paul Merrigan, Shronell, (W.S 1667)
Paul Mulcahy, Cashel, (W.S 1434)
Philip Murphy, Carrick on Suir, (W.S 1197)
William Myles, Thurles, (W.S 795)
John Nagle, New Inn, (W.S 1394)
Martin Needham, Lorrha, (W.S 1323)
Sean O'Carroll, Cahir, (W.S 1702)
Thomas O'Carroll, Drangan, (W.S 1243)
William O'Donnell, Cashel, (W.S 1304)
Denis J. O'Driscoll, Carrick on Suir, (W.S 1159)
Eamon O'Duibhir, Ballagh, (W.S 1403, W.S 1474)
Patrick H. O'Dwyer, Golden, (W.S 1432)
James O'Flynn, Fethard, (W.S 1249)
William O'Flynn, Fethard, (W.S 1235)
John O'Keeffe, Carrick on Suir, (W.S 1168)
Edward O'Leary, Dublin, (W.S 1459)
Seamus Ó'Néill, Cashel, (W.S 1557)
Bridget Ryan, Ballynonty, (W.S 1488)
Edward John Ryan, Nenagh, (W.S 1392)
Jerry Ryan, Ballynonty, (W.S 1487)
John C. Ryan, Dundrum, (W.S 1450)
Patrick Ryan, Fethard, (W.S 1380)
Thomas Ryan, Dublin, (W.S 783)

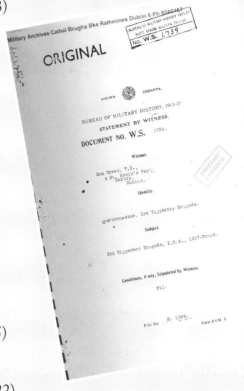

Sean Scott, Templemore, (W.S 1486)
John Sharkey, Clonmel, (W.S 1100)
Thomas Sheehan, Carrick on Suir, (W.S 1177)
Con Spain, Thurles, (W.S 1464)
Timothy Tierney, Fethard, (W.S 1227)
Peter Tobin, Carrick on Suir, (W.S 1223)
Sean E. Walshe, Fethard, (W.S 1363).

Duggan Business Records Carrick on Suir TL/A/41

1   Day Books 1936-71, (16 volumes).
2   Ledgers 1916-1972, (28 volumes).

Collection includes various other records such as a small number of Stock records, Sales, Debtors Ledgers, Customer Accounts, and Bank Statements.

Meanys Shoe Shop Records Carrick 0n Suir TL/A/42

1   Ledgers 1920-25, 1936-45, 1944-52, 1952-59 (4 volumes)
2   Bad Debtors Ledger 1927-30
3   Miscellaneous Accounts 1919-39
4   Sales Ledger 1956-60.

Murnane TL/A/43

Murnanes, carpenters and wheelwrights of Kilmoyler, Cahir
1   Account book 1858-1919.
2   Indenture 1869.
3   Typed abstracts from the original account book 1858-1919.

Brady's Mill, Ballynonty TL/A/44

Account Books 1884-1918, (4 volumes).

Carrick on Suir Irish Union of Distributive Workers and Clerks TL/A/45

Membership 1977-82.

St Patrick's College Thurles Archive TL/A/46

Over its long history St. Patrick's accumulated a large body of papers, some generated internally, others the work of various priests of the diocese of Cashel and Emly. Under this latter heading, the research papers of Fr Michael Maher, Fr Walter Skehan (1905-71) and Fr Philip Fogarty (1889-1976) are especially valuable.

Mount St. Joseph Abbey, Roscrea, Co. Tipperary.

1   The Census of the United Parishes of Newport and Birdhill, January 1835. Compiled by Rev Edward (Edmund) O'Shaughnessy (1793-1835).
2   St Patrick's College Deeds (1828-87) including building specifications.
3   Articles on St Patrick's College (Ryan, O'Neill, Fogarty).
4   Notes on Fr Richard Devane (1890-1959).
5   Notes by Fr William Fitzgerald (1875-1951) on diocesan history
6   Papers on Fr Philip Fogarty on diocesan history. 6 volumes. See separate list.
7   Notes and articles by Fr Christy O'Dwyer (former president of the college) on college and diocesan history. See separate list.
8   Papers of Fr Michael Maher (1872-1937) on diocesan history. See separate list.
9   Chronological list of Students who matriculated into Maynooth for the Archdiocese of Cashel. (Compiled from various sources).
10 Minutes of St Patrick's College Literary and Debating Society, 1916-46.
11 Rules and Regulations of St Patrick's College, Thurles, 1928.
12 Papers of Fr Walter Skehan on diocesan history. 92 volumes. See separate list.
13 Register of the Students of St Patrick's College, Thurles.
14 Notes on Thurles (3 pp. n.d).
15 Rentals of Thurles and Thomastown Estate (Mathew Family).
    8 volumes 1848-77. See **TL/F/12**.

O'Grady Papers TL/A/47

A comprehensive collection of research material dealing with the "Battle of Ballycohey" in 1868 and the 1870 Land Act. The collection, put together by Peter O'Grady (Shronell), contains extracts from a wide range of contemporary newspapers; Larcom Papers, Gladstone Papers, Scully Papers, police reports: Ballycohey land valuation and census records; official inquiries into land and tenure and some secondary published sources on these topics. A detailed list is available.

Birr Rural District Council TL/LG/1

1   RDC No. 1 Labourers Cottage Repair Ledger 1925.
2   RDC No.2 Ledger 1919-20.
3   Register of Mortgages 1887-1917.

Borrisokane Poor Law Union TL/LG/BG/46

1   **Minute Books June 1850-October 1923**
    missing Oct 1853-Sept 1854, Nov 1855–Jan 1862, Aug 1863–Oct 1868,
    Apr-Oct 1869, May–Dec 1870, Jan–Aug 1872, Feb–Sept 1873,
    Mar 1875–Dec 1876, Dec 1877–Apr 1880, Dec 1881–Aug 1882,
    Feb 1883–Mar 1884, Sept 1886–Apr 1887, Oct 1887–June 1889,
    Nov 1889-Dec 1890, June 1891-Jan 1894, July 1895–Sept 1898,
    Mar 1899–Apr 1900, May–Dec 1901, June 1902–Aug 1903,
    Feb 1905–Oct 1906, Apr–Nov 1911, (61 volumes).
2   Indoor Relief Registers 1894–98, 1912-13, 1923-24, (3 volumes).
3   Register of Births 1850–1906, (1 volume).
4   Awards re: Labourers Acts 1887–1908.
5   Treasurer's Accounts Book, 1899–1925.
6   Union Ledgers, 1909–11, 1913-15, 1921-23, (3 volumes).

Borrisokane Rural District Council TL/LG/2

1   Minute Books 1899–1925, (19 volumes).
2   Treasurers Receipt and Payment Book 1899–1931.
3   Treasurers Receipt and Payment Book 1899–1925, Loans Account.
4   Rate Books 1913-14, 1918-19, 1922-23, 1923-24, (4 volumes).
5   Register of Mortgages 1885-1936.
6   Finance Committee Minute Book 1911-13, 1923-25, (3 volumes).
7   Ledger 1921-23.

Carrick on Suir Town Commissioners TL/LG/3

Minute Book 1896-1902.

Carrick on Suir Urban District Council TL/LG/ 4

1   Valuation of Carrick on Suir UDC, Feb 1907, 1913-16, (2 volumes).
2   Carrick on Suir UDC Minute Book 1922-33, (1 volume).

Carrick on Suir, St Vincent's Home TL/LG/5

1   Day Book 1926-81.
2   Bundle of miscellaneous accounts.

Cashel Corporation Book 1826-1843 TL/LG/6

Appointments, includes hand drawn map of Cashel (ca. 1840)

Old Church, Nenagh

Cashel Poor Law Union TL/LG/BG/54

1 **Minute books March 1844-December 1923**
missing Nov 1845-July 1846, Oct 1851-June 1852,
Dec 1852-July 1853, (128 volumes).
2 Rough Minute Books Jan 1855-Mar 1869.
missing July 1855-Dec 1858, (18 volumes).
3 Contagious Diseases (Animals) Minutes Jan 1879-Nov 1892.
4 Burial Board Minutes Mar- Nov 1873.
5 Cottage Expenses July 1886-Jan 1925.

Cashel, County Infirmary TL/LG/7

Housekeepers Account and Expenditure Book Sept 1831-May 1840.

Cashel Rural District Council TL/LG/8

Minute Books 1899-1924, (12 volumes).

Clogheen Poor Law Union TL/LG/BG/64

1 **Minute Books, Mar 1839-Jan 1924**
missing Jan- July 1863, Oct 1878-April 1879, April-Oct 1889, Mar-July
1900, (140 volumes).
2 Dispensary Committee Book, Cahir district 1852-1899.

159

Clogheen Rural District Council TL/LG/9

Minute Books April 1899-Jan 1925 collection includes a mixture of general and financial minutes, (20 Volumes).

Clonmel Poor Law Union TL/LG/BG/67

1   **Minute Books May 1839-Jan 1924**
    missing Feb 1844-Jan 1845, Jan 1854-Jan 1855, Jan-July 1857, Jan-July 1858, Jan-July 1859, Aug 1860-Feb 1861, Sept 1867-Mar 1868, Apr-Oct 1869, Apr-Nov 1871, Oct 1898-Apr 1899, (142 volumes).
2   Rough Minute Books, May 1839-Jan 1903, (incomplete, 11 volumes).
3   Dispensary Committee Minutes
    Clonmel District Feb 1852-Feb 1886.
    Clonmel and St. Mary's Feb 1886-Aug 1898.
    Kilsheelan Sept 1852-Mar 1899.

Clonmel Rural District Council TL/LG/10

1   Minute Books May 1899-Jan 1925, (18 volumes).
2   Minute Book, Labourers' Cottages Repairs Account 1915-1927.

County Asylum, Clonmel Tl/LG/11

Minute Books for Clonmel Lunatic Asylum later Clonmel District Mental Hospital 1834-1971 (43 volumes).

Nenagh Library Commissioners TL/LG/12

Minute Book 1895-1905.

Nenagh Poor Law Union TL/LG/BG/129

1   **Minute Books May 1839-Jan 1924**
    early volumes badly damaged, (101 Volumes).

2   **Rate Books**
    Abington 1852-1854, (5 volumes)
    Annameadle 1846-1856, (15 volumes)
    Ardcroney 1842-1867, (17 volumes)
    Ballina 1850-1867, (17 volumes)
    Ballygibbon 1850-1856, (9 volumes)
    Ballymackey 1842-1853, (19 volumes
    Ballynaclogh 1850-1867, (8 volumes))
    Birdhill 1850-1854, (6 volumes)
    Borrisokane 1842-1850, (12 volumes)

Norman Doorway, Roscrea. Co. Tipperary.

Burgessbeg 1845-1853, (17 volumes)
Carrigatoher 1846-1853, (6 Volumes)
Castletown 1843-1853, (11 volumes)
Cloghprior 1842-1850, (10 volumes)
Cloughjordan 1843-1859, (3 volumes)
Derrycastle 1850-1853, (5 volumes)
Dolla 1845-1853, (10 volumes)
Greenhall 1850-1854, (7 volumes)
Kilbarron 1842-1850, (9 volumes)
Kilcomenty 1843-1853, (14 volumes)
Kilkeary 1850-1857, (8 volumes)
Killoscully 1843-1854, (17 volumes)
Kilmastulla 1843-1850, (8 volumes)
Kilmore 1842-1867, (13 volumes)
Kilnaneave 1850-1867, (8 volumes)
Kilnarath 1847-1867, (9 volumes)
Kilruane 1843-1850, (10 volumes)
Knigh 1845-1853, (10 volumes)
Lackagh 1851-1854, (7 volumes)
Latteragh 1850-1857, (7 volumes)
Lisboney 1843-1850, (7 volumes)
Monsea 1851-1853, (4 volumes)
Nenagh 1852-1853, (6 volumes)
Newport 1843-1867, (19 volumes)
Templederry 1840-1853, (16 volumes)
Templekelly 1842-1850, (10 volumes)
Terryglass, 1842-1850, (11 volumes)
Youghalarra 1843-1853, (15 volumes)

Unfortunately some of the above volumes are badly damaged and consequently too fragile to handle.

3   **District Rate Books**
No.3 District. Ballina, Burgessbeg, Derrycastle, Aug 1855.
No.4 District. Abington, Kilnerath, Newport, Birdhill, Kilcomenty, Killoscully, Aug 1855.
No. 6 District. Greenhall, Kilmore, Lackagh, Carrigatoher, Aug 1855.
No.7 District. Ballygibbon, Ballymackey, Aug 1854, Aug 1855, (2 volumes).
No. 8 District. Annameadle, Latteragh, Aug 1855.

4   Dispensary Committee Minute Book.
Newport Apr 1852-Oct 1898.

5   Labourers' Acts Minute Books, Jan 1886-Mar 1887, Apr 1894-Mar 1895, (2 volumes).

6   Misc. Papers re: Labourers Acts 1885-1905.

7   Nenagh Union Ledgers, 1905-07, 1921-1923, (2 volumes).

8   **Poor Law Union Correspondence**
Local Government Board correspondence to Nenagh Union, 1894-98, 1915-20, 1917-19.
Local Government orders to Nenagh Union 1897-99.
General Register Office correspondence to Nenagh Union, 1897-1901.
Poor Law Commission Office correspondence to Nenagh Union 1853-55.
Vouchers for building schemes, 1896-99, 1913-14.
Copies of outward correspondence 1919-23.

Correspondence from Veterinary Department, Dublin Castle to Nenagh Union 1878-83.
9   Receipt Book 1909-14.

Nenagh Rural District Council TL/LG/13

1   **Minute Books 1899-1925**, (14 volumes)
2   Bank Pass Book, 1910-24.
3   Correspondence from Labourers Department, Local Government Board 1908.
4   Labourers Cottage Rent Collection Book, Silvermines, 1922-29.

Roscrea Poor Law Union TL/LG/BG/141

1   **Minute Books 1839-1923**, (90 volumes).
2   Rough Minute Book, 1839-41.
3   Indoor Relief Registers, 1906-08, 1910-11, 1918-24, (3 volumes).
4   Outdoor Relief Register, 1899-1917.
5   Dispensary Committee Minute Book
    Bourney 1852-92.
6   Letters from Poor Law Commissioners and Local Government Board, 1839-1863, 1873, 1875, 1893, (24 volumes).
7   Orders from Poor Law Commissioners and Local Government Board, 1886-1902, (1 bundle).
8   Outward Letter Books 1909-15, 1923-24, (2 volumes).
9   Union Ledgers, 1905-09, 1911-15, (3 volumes).

Roscrea Rural District Council TL/LG/14

1   Minute Books, 1899-1918, 1929-24, (8 volumes).
2   Rate Book 1924-25.
3   General Valuation Books. Divisions of Bourney East, Bourney West, Killavinogue, Killea, Rathnavogue (3), Timoney, (8 volumes, n.d).
4   Register of Mortgages 1893-1940.
5   Roscrea Water Supply Minute Book 1926-33.
6   Roscrea Water Supply water rents 1901-33.
7   Box of miscellaneous papers.
8   Correspondences 1900, 1921-23, 1920-24.

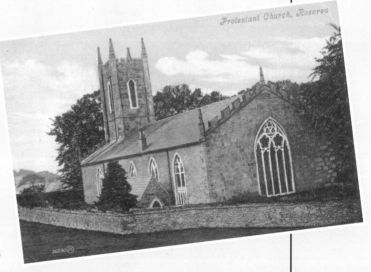

Slieveardagh Rural District Council TL/LG/15

1   Minute book, 1902-1925, (10 volumes).
2   Tenants Agreements, 1909-1924, (1 volume).

Templemore Urban District Council TL/LG/16

Rate Book 1910.

Thurles and Rahealty Famine Relief Committee TL/LG/17

Minute Book 1846-47, (p/copy).

Thurles Petty Sessions TL/LG/18

'Order book, as approved of by the Lord Lieutenant with the advice and consent of the Privy Council'. Details of the various crimes committed by the defendants and the resulting particulars of order or dismissal 1855-1856.

Thurles Poor Law Union TL/LG/BG/151

1   **Minute Books 1839-1924**
    missing Sept 1847-Jan 1848, Feb–Aug 1882, (145 volumes).
2   **Rate Books**
    Ballycahill 1842-98, (32 volumes)
    Ballymurreen 1842-94, (24 volumes)
    Buolick 1842-49, (8 volumes)
    Borrisoleigh 1846-92, (26 volumes)
    Drom 1842-94, (23 volumes)
    Fennor 1842-49, (6 volumes)
    Foilnamon 1850-98, (20 volumes)
    Glenkeen 1850-95, (20 volumes)
    Gortkelly 1850-95, (22 volumes)
    Holycross 1842-98, (30 volumes)
    Inch 1842-94, (33 volumes)
    Kilcooley 1842-49, (8 volumes
    Kilrush 1850-98, (20 volumes)
    Littleton 1850-92, (17 volumes)
    Longfordpass 1850-98, (23 volumes)
    Loughmore 1842-98, (31 volumes)
    Moyaliff 1843- 85, (28 volumes)
    Moycarkey 1846-98, (27 volumes)
    Moyne 1843-98, (36 volumes)
    Rahealty 1842-93, (23 volumes)
    Templebeg 1845-48, (6 volumes)
    Templemore 1842-95, (32 volumes)
    Templeree 1842-49, (7 volumes)

Templetuohy 1842-97, (29 volumes)
Thurles 1845-94, (28 volumes)
Twomileborris 1842-96, (30 volumes)
Upperchurch 1851-95, (16 volumes).

3 **Indoor Relief Registers**
1866-72, 1872-80, 1885-87, 1887-90, 1892-94, 1894-96, 1902-04, 1909-13, 1916-21, (9 volumes).
The workhouses were abolished in 1924; later indoor registers for the Hospital of the Assumption survive as follows:
1930-33, 1937-39, 1941-42, 1942-44, 1945-46, 1946-47, 1948, 1948, 1949-51, (10 volumes).

4 Outward Letter Books 1902-06, 1910-12, (2 volumes).
5 Letters from Local Government Board 1878-1923, (13 volumes).
6 Register of Deaths in Workhouse 1869-1900.
7 Union Ledgers 1907-21, (3 volumes).
8 Bank Pass Book 1899-1908, (includes RDC).
9 Financial Statements, Expenditure 1903-07.
10 Thurles Board of Guardians acting as rural Sanitary Authority Minute Books 1886-92, (2 volumes).
11 Thurles Dispensary District Medical Relief Registers 1916-21, (2 volumes).
12 Porters Books 1860, 1862-63, 1881, 1882-83, 1892, 1908, (6 volumes).
13 'Personal Ledger'. Details of Suppliers 1890-91.
14 Thurles Fever Hospital Account Book 1841-47.
15 Persons returned for Gratuitous Relief 1847, (p/copy).

Thurles Rural District Council TL/LG/19

1 Minute Books 1899-1925, (20 volumes).
2 Quarterly Minute Books, Oct 1900-July 1910, Feb 1911-Jan 1924, (2 volumes).
3 Box of documents relating to Labourers Act includes Plan for cottage.
4 Rate Books 1919-20, 1924, 1924-25, (3 volumes).
5 Registers of Mortgages 1888-1910, 1881-1913, (2 volumes).
6 Correspondence Files, Local Government Board to Thurles RDC 1911-19, (3 volumes).
7 Ledger 1913-15.

Thurles Urban District Council TL/LG/20

Barony of Eliogarty Rate book 1876.

Tipperary Joint Libraries Committee TL/LG/21

Founded in 1927 to replace Tipperary Carnegie Libraries, which had been responsible for the administration of the county's library service since 1925.
1 Minute Books 1927-to date, (9 volumes).
2 Annual Reports 1927-41, (1 volume).

3   Book Selection Minutes 1947-57, 1958-59, 1960-62, 1970-84,
     (3 volumes and 1 box).
4   Correspondence File 1928-34.
5   Carnegie Trust Correspondence File 1925-26.
6   Building File 1928-35.
7   Manager's Orders 1927- to date, (10 volumes).
8   Financial Statements, (9 volumes).
9   Financial Statements Receipts 1949-71, 1983-97, (5 volumes).
10   Salary Registers 1949-93, (7 volumes).
     Collection of other financial and staff material.

Tipperary North Riding Board of Health and Public Assistance TL/LG/22

Minutes for the meetings of this board in two separate collections
1   Public Health Minutes July 1925-June 1941, (40 volumes).
2   Public Assistance Minutes Jan 1924-Jan 1942, (42 volumes).
     Thurles Office Outward Correspondence 1939-41.
     Public Assistance Advertisements, 1931-36, 1938-41, 1942-44, (3 files).
     Ledgers 1932-1940, (3 volumes).

Tipperary North Riding County Committee of Agriculture TL/LG/23

1   Minute Books 1910-87, (13 volumes).
2   Financial Statement Books, Expenditure 1948-80, (8 volumes).
3   Members Attendance Register 1958-86.
4   Register of Cheques 1947-55.
5   1 Volume with miscellaneous payments, e.g. Suppliers 1949-50,
     Premiums to Bull Owners 1960s, Attendances at Training Courses 1970s.
6   Register of Dairymen ??-1988.
7   Register of Slaughterhouses 1952-73.
8   Register of Slaughterhouses and Abattoirs 1947-63.
9   Register of Dealers Licences 1952-77.
10   Animal Diseases Committee Minute Book 1900-17.

Tipperary North Riding County Council TL/LG/24

1   Barony of Eliogarty Rate Book 1874.
2   Thurles District Rate Book 1925.
3   Receipt Books 1899-1916, 2 volumes.
4   Expenditure Book 1910-17.
5   Loan Account Book (Water and Sewerage) 1950-54.
6   Abstract of Liabilities for half year ending Sept 1911.
7   File of Circular letters from Local Government Board to Tipperary NR
     County Council and Nenagh UDC 1902-1919.
9   Members Attendance Register 1926-28.

10 Machinery Yard Expenditure and Receipts 1960-61, 1962-63, 1968-69, 1973-74, (4 volumes).
11 Correspondence between Tipperary NR County Council and the Ministry of Local Government 1904-34, (2 bundles).
12 File relating to Damer House Roscrea.
13 Correspondence relating to Council Meetings, (1 bundle).
14 Building of Cottages ca. 1948, (1 bundle).
15 Suir Drainage Templemore District Assessment Book 1900-20.
16 Finance Committee Minutes 1925-30.
17 Roll of members North Tipperary County Council 1903-26.
18 Scholarship Committee Minute Books, Primary, Secondary and University 1911-36, ??-1942, (2 volumes).
19 Resolutions passed by County Councillors 1899-1908.
20 Register of Documents Sealed 1952-60.
21 Notice of Motion 1899-1930, ??- 1961, 1979-82, (3 volumes).
22 Roads Areas Committee Minute Book Borrisokane, Nenagh, Roscrea, Thurles Dec 1954.
23 **Urban Council Demands**
    Nenagh UDC 1912-15.
    North Tipperary UDCs 1899-1904.
24 Statement of Accounts for half year ending March 1905.
    Unsorted loose-leaf material, relating to finance, meetings and drainage schemes (9 boxes, poor condition).

Tipperary Poor Law Union TL/LG/BG/152

1 **Minute Books 1839-1923**
   missing Mar 1845-Mar 1846, Aug 1868-Aug 1869, Dec 1879-Jan 1881, July 1897-Dec 1898, Sept 1908-Nov 1910, Dec 1915-Jan 1917, (83 volumes).
2 Rough Minute Books 1849-69, (19 volumes).
3 Fine Minute Books 1867-68, 1888-89 (2 volumes).
4 Boarded and Hired Out Children Minute Book 1912-15.
5 Dispensary Committee Minute Books
   Bansha District 1879-98
   Emly 1882-1898.
6 Labourers Acts Rough Minutes 1889-1895.

Tipperary Rural District Council TL/LG/25

1 Minute Books 1899-1925, (16 volumes).
   Assorted collection of monthly, quarterly and financial minute books.
2 Treasurers Receipt and Payment Book 1910-18.

Carrick on Suir Town TL/LG/26

Rent Book 1881-84.

Crown and Peace Material TL/LG/27

Assorted material, some containing extracts from *Dublin Gazette* relating to crime in Co. Tipperary, (2 boxes).

Presentments of the Grand Jury, North Tipperary TL/LG/28

Abstracts of the presentments discharged, undischarged and passed by the Grand Jury of North Tipperary 1842-1910. After the Local Government Act of 1898, the volumes became known as *North Riding of the County of Tipperary. An abstract of County Liabilities and Expenditure.*
Missing 1843-44, 1849-Spring 1851, Spring 1852-Summer 1854, Summer 1855-Spring 1859, Summer 1875-Spring 1876, Mar-Sept 1910. A small number of volumes contain the presentments for South Tipperary in the rear of the volume, (94 volumes).

Presentments of the Grand Jury, South Tipperary TL/LG/29

Abstracts of the presentments discharged, undischarged and passed by the Grand Jury of South Tipperary.
Spring 1855-Summer 1859, Spring 1871, Spring 1891, (3 volumes).

George Street, Templemore.   Co. Tipperary.

Tipperary Star

VOL. 38, No. 35. THURLES, SATURDAY, SEPTEMBER 1, 1945. PRICE—THREEPENCE

Telegrams—"Star," Thurles. Telephone—"Thurles 5." Registered at the G.P.O. as a Newspaper

TY BED CO. HOSPITAL NOT TABLE FOR SOUTH TIPPERARY"

ouncillor's Complaints And Manager's Reply After Investigation

NEED FOR ADEQUATE WATER SUPPLIES

Shortage In Many South Tipperary Areas

Embezzlement And Fraudul Conversion Charges Again Suspended Garda

DECLARES HIS MIND WAS UNBALANCED AND NOT RESPONSIBLE FOR HIS ACTIONS

JOHN J. Broughton, a suspended member of the Garda Siochana, stationed at Ballylooby, Cahir, was, at Cahir District Court, last week, returned for trial to the Circuit Court, on charges of embezzlement, obtaining money under false pretences and fraudulent conversion.

Defendant has been suspended from the Garda since August 4th last.

The Cashel Gazette

Tipperary Reporter,   and Weekly Advertiser,

NO. 797 — VOLUME XVI.   PRICE—TWO PENCE Unstampe

JOURNAL FOR MID-TIPPERARY.

SATURDAY   *The Noblest Motive is the Public Good*   NOV 26, 1881

A CARD.
JOHN DAVIS WHITE,

Encourage

Tipperary

VOL. II—No. 68.   THURLES: SATURDAY, JUNE 10, 1882   PRICE—TWOPENCE

MICHAEL PHELAN,
76, MAIN-STREET, CLONMEL,

"TIPPERARY."

"TIPPERARY,"

THOMAS P. GILL,
THE CENTRAL OFFICE, THURLES.

SEED SEASON, 1882.

TO SEED AND MANURE MERCHANTS
R. GILL AND SONS, NENAGH,

ALL SIZES OF BEST QUALITY ROPE AND HALF ROPE
SEED BAGS.

POSTERS AND HAND-BILLS

PART FOUR

Newspapers

Newspapers are a core resource in Tipperary Studies and an effort has been made to have as complete a holding as possible. Having a copy of every newspaper ever published in the county is an ambitious undertaking and there is still a way to go.

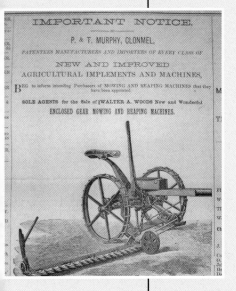

This list gives: the name of the newspaper; the period of its publication; place of publication; the proprietor/s; its political stance; if a full run of the paper exists and finally the Tipperary Studies holding of the newspaper.

Generally unless indicated otherwise, these newspapers are available only on microfilm. Where hardcopy exists, in annual bound volumes, for reasons of conservation, it is preferred that microfilm is used.

For additional information see J.C. Hayes, Guide to Tipperary Newspapers, 1770-1989 in *THJ*, (1989) pp. 1-16; M-L Legg, *Newspapers and Nationalism: the Irish Provincial Press, 1850-1892* (Dublin, 1999); J. O'Toole, *Newsplan: report of the newsplan project in Ireland* (Dublin, 1998) revised edition.

Cashel Sentinel (1885-1914) Cashel
Thomas Walsh proprietor. Nationalist.
No full run. Tipperary Studies holds 1889-1914.

Cashel Gazette (1864-1893 – not published between 14 July 1866 and 27 Sept. 1868) Cashel
John Davis White proprietor. Neutral, emphasis on culture.
Tipperary Studies holds a full run: 8 Oct 1881 to 29 Sept. 1883 hardcopy, otherwise microfilm.

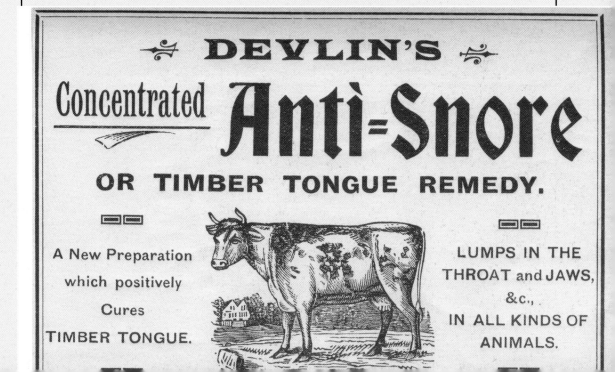

Clonmel Advertiser (1811-1843) Clonmel
William Carson proprietor (1811-32); John Kempston proprietor (1832-38);
John Hackett proprietor (1838-43). Policy varied.
No full run. Tipperary Studies holds 1811-1825, 1828-37.

Clonmel Chronicle (1848-1935) Clonmel
Edmund Woods proprietor (1848-93); Messrs. Clarke, Barrett & Montgomery
proprietors (1893-1935). Originally conservative.
Tipperary Studies holds a full run.

Clonmel Gazette (1775-1804) Clonmel
Edmund Power proprietor (1798-1804). Pro-Donoughmore and anti-Bagwell.
No full run. Tipperary Studies holds 1788-95, 1802-04.

Clonmel Herald (1802-1840) Clonmel
George Grace proprietor (1802-21); William B. Upton proprietor (1821-40).
Pro-government.
No full run. Tipperary Studies holds 1828-1840.

County Tipperary Independent (1880-1892) Clonmel
G. Fisher proprietor. Nationalist.
No full run. Tipperary Studies holds 1882-1891.

Midland Tribune (1881–to date) Birr.
Tipperary Studies holds 1920-1952.

Munster Tribune (1955-1967) Clonmel
Tipperary Studies holds a full run.

Nationalist (1889 – to date) Clonmel
James Long proprietor. Nationalist
Tipperary Studies a full run. Hardcopy from 1970.

Nenagh Guardian (1838 – to date) Nenagh
John Kempston proprietor (1838-57); Prior family (1857-1916).
Pro-government, later nationalist.
Tipperary Studies holds a full run. Hardcopy from 1970.

Nenagh News (1894-1926) Nenagh
John F. Power proprietor. Mildly nationalist.
No full run. Tipperary Studies holds 1898-1924.

Tipperary Advocate (1858- 1889) Nenagh
Peter E. Gill proprietor. Strongly nationalist.
Tipperary Studies holds 1860-1889 (excluding 1888).

Tipperary Champion (1899- 1910) Clonmel
Mildly nationalist. No full run.
Tipperary Studies holds 1904-1910.

Tipperary Constitution (1835-1848) Clonmel

Joseph Going proprietor. Strongly anti-catholic and anti-nationalist.
Tipperary Studies holds a full run.

Tipperary Free Press (1826-1881) Clonmel
James Hackett proprietor. Moderate nationalist.
Tipperary Studies holds a full run.

Tipperary Leader (1855-56) Thurles
William Kenealy proprietor (1855-56). Strongly nationalist.
Tipperary Studies has a full run.

Tipperary Leader (1882-1885) Thurles
Patrick O'Gorman proprietor. Strongly nationalist.
Tipperary Studies has a full run.

Tipperary People & Mercantile and Agricultural Gazette (1865-66) Clonmel
Henry O'Connell Hackett proprietor. Nationalist.
Tipperary Studies holds a full run.

Tipperary People (1876-1921) Tipperary
John McCormack proprietor. Strongly nationalist. No full run.
Tipperary Studies holds 1876-77; 1879-1891; 1893-1904; 1906-1918; 1920-21.

Tipperary Star (1909–to date) Thurles
Edward Long proprietor. Nationalist.
Tipperary Studies holds a full run. Hardcopy from 1970.

Tipperary Vindicator (1844–1849) Nenagh
Maurice Lenihan proprietor. Nationalist.
Tipperary Studies holds 1844-49.
(Lenihan refocused his paper to Limerick. From 1850 it became the *Limerick Reporter and Tipperary Vindicator* and lasted until 1895.)

Tipperaryman (1921-1934) Tipperary
Continued from **Tipperary People**.
Tipperary Studies has a full run.

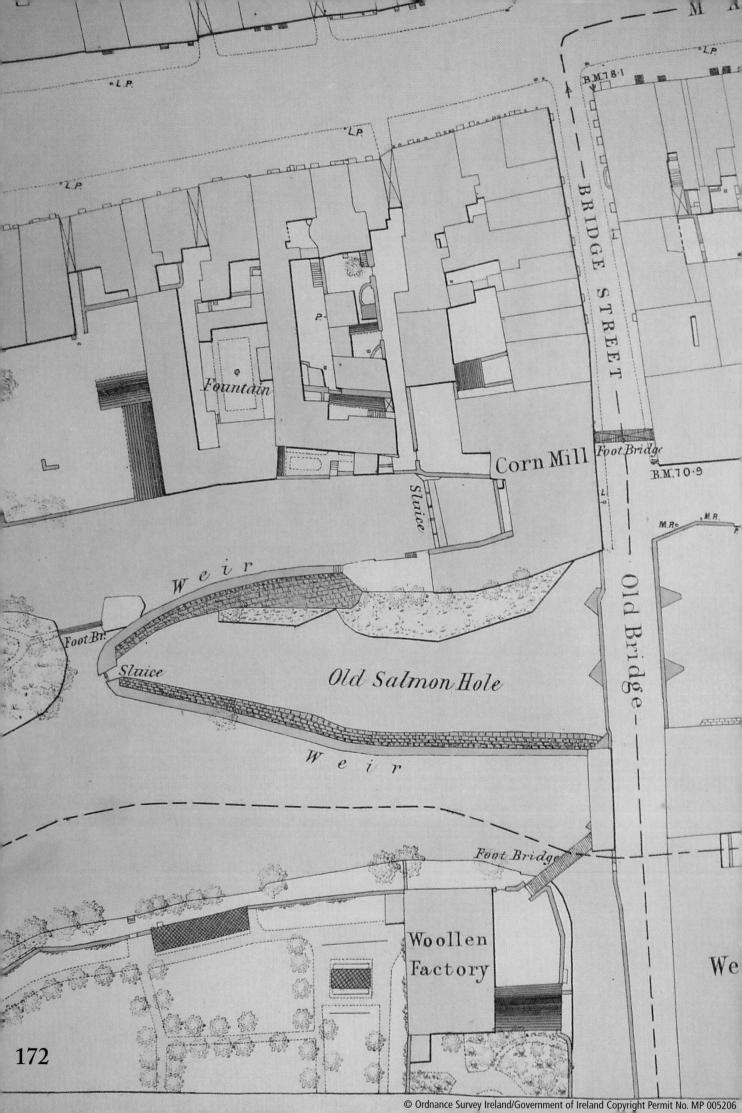

Fountain

Sluice

Corn Mill

BRIDGE STREET

Foot Bridge

B.M.78·1

B.M.70·9

Old Bridge

Weir

Foot Br.

Sluice

Old Salmon Hole

Weir

Foot Bridge

Woollen Factory

We

172

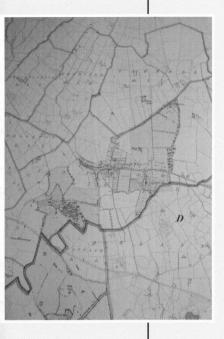

PART FIVE

Maps

1 Down Survey Parish Maps 1650s

Sir William Petty who directed the *Civil Survey*, which was organized on the basis of descriptive evidence from jurors in each parish with respect to land ownership, quality and usage, was also contracted by the government to map forfeited land. (Called the "Down Survey" simply because the information was set down or mapped by trained surveyors). Tipperary Studies has maps for parishes in the following baronies: Upper Ormond, Lower Ormond, Owney & Arra, Kilnamanagh & Kilnelongurty, and Slieveardagh.

2 Down Survey Barony Maps

Available for each barony in the county.

3 Hiberniae Delineatio: Atlas of Ireland by Sir William Petty

This is a bound volume, a 1960s copy of the original, showing Petty's maps for each county in Ireland.

4 Rocques Plan of Camp near Thurles

Plan of military camp located near Thurles, drawn by John Rocque in 1755, on a scale of 320 perches to an Irish mile.

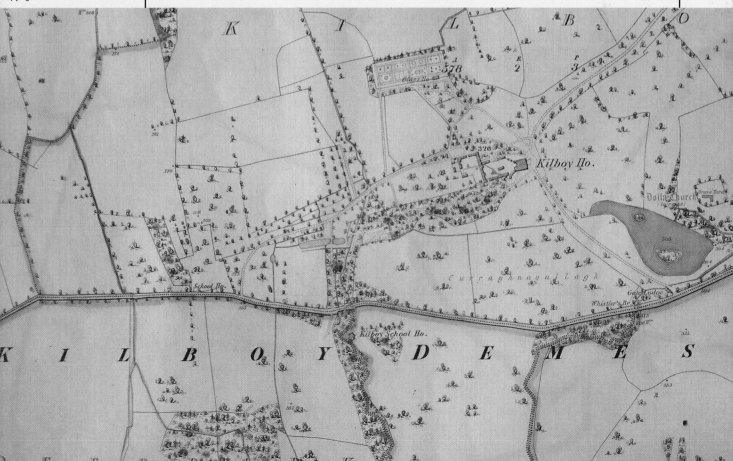

5   Composite Maps

These maps are especially usefully because information from the Down Survey is superimposed on 1st ed. O.S. maps.

Tipperary Studies has these maps for the entire county, in 91 sheets.

6   1st edition Ordnance Survey Maps for County Tipperary

The Ordnance Survey was established in Ireland in 1824 and the entire country was mapped between 1833 and 1846, with Tipperary being mapped 1840-41. Maps for County Tipperary on a scale of six inches to one statute mile are available in two bound volumes. For the North Riding, sheets 1 to 46 and for the South Riding, sheets 47 to 91. (Sheet One covers the very north of the county, while Sheet 91 shows the southeast corner.)

Tipperary Studies has a second set of these maps in which all boundaries of townlands, parishes and baronies, are shown in colour.

The Library also has these maps on microfilm, from which copies may be obtained.

7   Townland Index Maps

Available for North and South Tipperary, with a scale of one inch to one statute mile.

Boundaries are shown but not topographical features. The relevant six-inch sheets are indicated by roman figures. These maps were used in Number **14** below, the *Cashel & Emly Diocesan Atlas*.

8   Tenement (Griffith's) Valuation Maps

These maps from the Valuation Office in Dublin show the ongoing valuation revisions and are available in CD Rom. The printed valuations have map references. These maps are especially interesting for urban centres and can be of varying dates.

9   Recorded Monuments (Duchas)

Shows archaeological features protected under Section 12 of the National Monuments (Amendment) Act, 1994, on the basis of surveys in the 1990s and mapped on 2nd edition O.S. maps (1905). As with 1st edition maps, available for the county in 91 sheets. The archaeological survey is available in separate volumes, with full grid references for each feature of interest. The sheets are unbound.

10   Urban Archaeological Survey (OPW)

A volume of maps to accompany *The Urban Archaeological Survey, Co Tipperary, North Riding* by J. Farrelly & M. Carey (OPW, 1994) – includes Ballina, Borrisokane, Borrisoleigh, Carrig, Cloughjordan, Holycross, Kilcommon, Lorrha, Moyne, Nenagh, Roscrea, Templemore, Terryglass, Templetouhy, Thurles, Toomyvara and Two-Mile-Borris.

A volume of maps to accompany *The Urban Archaeological Survey, Co Tipperary, South Riding* by J. Farrelly & L. Fitzpatrick (OPW, 1993) – includes Ardfinnan, Bansha, Cahir, Carrick-on-Suir, Cashel, Clonmel, Emly, Fethard, Golden, Killenaule, Kilsheelan, Mullinahone and Tipperary.

11   Urban Inventory of Architectural Heritage
Database and maps. Available for Clonmel (1997) and Roscrea (2000)

12   Heritage Atlas of the Civil Parish of Roscrea
Compiled as a FAS project under the direction of W.J. Hayes (n.d.)

13   Historic Towns Atlas, 13: Fethard
Published by the RIA in 2003 and edited by Tadhg O'Keeffe, this is the first in the *Irish Historic Towns Atlas* series dealing with a settlement centre in Tipperary.

Dúrlas Éile (Ó Gliasáin)

14   Cashel & Emly Diocesan Atlas
Published in 1970 under the direction of the late Archbishop Thomas Morris.
Maps one inch to one mile.

15   Discovery Series
This is the most popular commercially available series of maps, covering the entire country. Tipperary County is covered in maps 53, 54, 58, 59, 60, 65, 66, 67, 73, 74, 75.
Townlands but not townland boundaries are shown.

16   Special Areas of Conservation Maps
Designated under 1997 legislation by the Dept of the Environment.
In County Tipperary the areas are:

Liskeenan Fen	Silvermines Mountains West
Philipstown Marsh	Rivers Barrow and Nore
Lower River Suir	Lower River Shannon
Blackwater River.	

17   Tipperary Town Military Barracks
A number of late 19th century maps and ground plans.

18   Thurles Mid-19th Century
Recreation of Thurles housing mid-19th century based on Griffith's Valuation and Rating Records. (Jim Condon.)

19   Bogs North Tipperary
A map compiled in 1811 in association with a government commission on bogs.

20   Railway Maps
Part of the work of the 1836 government commission on railways.

21   Encumbered Estates Court Maps
For details of these see Part Three of *Finding Tipperary*.

22   Bagwell Estate Maps
Ten maps, 20th century. **See Part Three**, (TL/F/20/9).

23   Cole-Bowen Estate Map
Large volume of maps for Tipperary portion of estate, 1863. See Part Three, (TL/F/6/1).

24   Taylor & Skinner 18th century Road Maps
G. Taylor & Andrew Skinner, *Maps of the Roads of Ireland*. This was first published in 1778.

25   Large scale town maps
Ordnance survey maps of Carrick-on-Suir (1886,16 sheets), Clonmel (1874, 24 sheets), Nenagh (1879, 16 sheets) and Tipperary town (1880, 14 sheets) on a scale of 10.56 feet to the statute mile. The Clonmel maps are shown in colour.

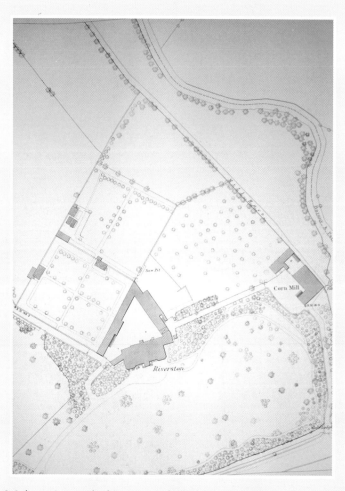

© Ordnance Survey Ireland/Government of Ireland Copyright Permit No. MP 005206

PART SIX

Photographs

Tipperary Studies has a large collection of commercially produced postcards from well known studios such as Lawrence and Valentine, as well as scenes produced by local businesses such as Carey in Clonmel, Cleary in Carrick and Carrigan in Tipperary. Postcards for the Irish market also came from Britain. The period covered is the first half of the 20th century.

Place	Number of Postcards
Aherlow	9
Cahir	9
Carrick-on-Suir	16 (Also a series produced locally showing Carrick and places in the South-East of the county and Co Waterford.)
Cashel	110 (Also: 7 "Mason & Dunraven" studies of the Rock; a 1933 housing scheme).
Clonmel	53
Nenagh	28
Roscrea	23
Templemore	19
Thurles	11
Tipperary	58

There are twenty-five other postcards: Kilbarron, Killenaule, Dundrum, Rockwell, Kiltinan, Cloughjordan (5), Fethard (2), Dromineer (2), Limerick Junction (2), Lough Derg (2), Marlfield (3), Holycross, Ballina, Athassel, Kilcooly.

Killenaule
(Joe Kenny, April 2001)

Tipperary Studies has a number of other small collections:
William Lawrence prints.
King Edward's 1904 visit to Clogheen.
Muintir na Tire Rural Weeks.
New Tipperary.
Brittas Castle (copies).
Barnane House (copies).
Woodrooffe House.
"Our Own Place Photographic Project", Oct 1993, 24 views of the county.
Irish Tourist Association folders, 1940s, misc. photographs.
Scully Family photographs (TL/F/1/3).
Holy Cross photographs (TL/F/2/5).
Crannagh Castle, Templetuohy.
Knockane Castle, Templedowney.
Archbishop Croke Centenary Exhibition Silver.
Funerals of IRA members Russell, Burke & Shea, executed Nenagh 1923.
Thurles Camera Club Thurles collection 1980s and 2000.
Also the well-known sketches of 1848 and 1867 from the Illustrated *London News*.

Tipperary Studies has two collections of slides. 'Treasures of Ireland' shows Irish portraits and landscapes from the National Gallery Collection and includes examples of the works of James Barry, Nathaniel Hone and Sir William Orpen, among others. It also shows documents from the National Library of Ireland dating from the Norman invasion to the twentieth century covering topics such as agriculture and industry, architecture, battles, eminent Irishmen landlords, sports, transport and travel. The slides from the National Museum depict various antiquities of Ireland, including the Glankeen Bell Shrine.

The 'Our County' series is a collection of views of the whole country's heritage sites.

INDEX

IRISH INDEX